POLICY FOR
The Social Work Practitioner

DEAN PIERCE

Mercy College—Bronx Center, and the
Westchester Social Work Education Consortium

Longman
New York & London

Policy for the Social Work Practitioner

Longman Inc., 1560 Broadway, New York, N.Y. 10036
Associated companies, branches, and representatives throughout the world.

Copyright © 1984 by Longman Inc.

Developmental Editor: Nicole Benevento
Editorial and Design Supervisor: Russell Till
Production/Manufacturing: Ferne Y. Kawahara
Composition: Centennial Graphics, Inc.
Printing and Binding: Alpine Press

Library of Congress Cataloging in Publication Data

Pierce, Dean, 1943–
　　Policy for the social work practitioner.

　　Bibliography: p.
　　Includes index.
　　1. Social work administration—United States.
2. United States—Social policy.　3. Social workers—
Training of—United States. I. Title.
HV95.P53　1984　　　　361.3′068　　　　83-22179
ISBN 0–582–28403-1 (pbk.)

MANUFACTURED IN THE UNITED STATES OF AMERICA
Printing: 9　8　7　6　5　4　3　2　1　　Year: 91　90　89　88　87　86　85　84

POLICY FOR
The Social Work Practitioner

TO

CHARLETTA PIERCE

and

CLETUS A. PIERCE

My mother and father,
with whom I had my first discussions
about social justice and the responsibility
of each person in working toward its realization

AND TO

CAROL ANN PIERCE

My sister,
whose creativity and inspiration led me
to write this book.

Contents

Preface

SOCIAL WORK AND SOCIAL WORKERS have relied too long on people outside the profession to make the policy that guides practice. For example, the profession has become overly dependent on political liberals for the development of social policy. These politicians have less respect for the needs of social work, and the profession now finds that it has lost its protected status. Instead, it is treated like a rejected outsider, without favor in the social policy-making arena. Hopefully, the lesson to be learned from this situation will be to find ways of liberating the profession from policy dependency. We must learn to speak for ourselves and to make as powerful an input as possible in policy formulation.

The dependence of the profession on others to create policy stems in part from the educational preparation of many social workers; their training does not prepare them to bring about the enactment of policies that are important to their practice. Only a select few seek out policymaking opportunities. The rest rely on the professional association's lobbyists and its few active members, on those engaged in social welfare planning, and on the few line practitioners who use policy and who attempt to make changes in it.

In this book, I propose that the profession recognize how policy activities constitute a critical part of direct service work. In acknowledging policy as part of direct practice, social work can and should turn to its professional membership to be active in the creation of policy according to its own needs. As you will discover, this is a large task, and one that cannot be undertaken lightly.

Many have contributed to the development of ideas in this book. Thanks to all of you for listening when I wanted to talk, for discussing ideas that needed development, for leaving me alone when I needed to work, and for being supportive all of the time.

The input of Betty L. Baer has been especially important to me. I am immeasurably indebted to her, as my mentor and colleague, for the value of her assistance and support. Ron C. Federico encouraged me to write this book and offered many suggestions for its improvement. Thanks to my students in my policy classes during 1982 and 1983 for providing feedback on earlier drafts of the manuscript. I would like to single out a very helpful member of Longman's editorial staff—Nicole Benevento—for invaluable advice on how to write a textbook. Special support came from many of my colleagues in the Westchester Social Work Education Consortium and Mercy College. I am grateful to Mercy College's Academic Dean, Dr. James F. Melville, Jr. for providing me with a faculty development grant. Many thanks to Rosemarie Cornacchia for her support and to Michael Cooper for typing the manuscript.

Dean Pierce
The Bronx

A Policy Model for the Generalist Social Worker

"When we meane to build, We first survey the Plot, then draw the Modell."
—WILLIAM SHAKESPEARE
(The second part of)
King Henry IV, I., iii, 142.

THIS BOOK IS WRITTEN for those who want to learn how to use, analyze, and develop policy at the direct services level of social work practice. The book achieves this goal by developing a model for learning and using policy. It is assumed that students in BSW programs, MSW students who will enter direct services, and practitioners in the field who wish to enhance their skills in policy analysis and policy-related interventions will be the major users of this book. The book focuses throughout on defining policy from the perspective of direct services and emphasizes developing the kind of policy skills useful in practice at this level. This book is about policy and how practitioners can use it.

Policy is an exciting part of professional social work practice. It determines who social work clients are and what resources they will receive. Understood in this way, policy undergirds all of social work, since without it there would be no services. Policy serves to translate a society's sense of responsibility to its citizens into specific services. It is in the policy arena that issues are debated and decided on regarding *who* ought to get *what* and in which format. Naturally, questions of *funding* must be addressed as part of the debate about the allocation of social resources. And, as this book will emphasize, struggling with society's conception of social responsibility takes place on several levels: the governmental level, in communities, in social agencies, in families, and by individuals. It is clear then that social work practice cannot be fully effective without policy.

Consider the following situations:

☐ In an agency where a social worker is employed, the worker discovers that a colleague routinely refuses to refer clients to the social work department.

☐ The local chapter of the National Association of Social Workers is approached by a group supporting the establishment of a women's shelter, but the association takes no action.

☐ The Reagan Administration attacked social welfare programs by reducing federal outlays for Medicaid, restricting Aid to Families with Dependent Children (AFDC) eligibility and reducing benefits, cutting back Social Se-

curity disability benefits, and changing Food Stamp eligibility requirements to reduce costs.

☐ An application for a new program to develop a shelter for runaway youths
is turned down by the local United Way, although its allocation for scout-
ing is increased.

☐ An elderly client states that she will not live with her son because she
wants to remain independent. She also feels that her son's children are
ashamed of her appearance following her recent stroke.

☐ Your supervisor informs you that the prison where you work has adopted
a new policy of not hiring women, a policy you have strongly opposed in
the past.

☐ The state regulatory agency responsible for hospital programs proposes a
regulation to remove BSWs from its list of specially recognized service
providers.

Each of these situations involves policy and the need for policy analysis and
action on the part of social workers. Certain of these situations contain policy
of large systems, others focus on policy made by organizations. This text
helps students understand how each is a policy of concern to line workers,
how these various policies are made, and how to use or change them.

The excitement of learning how to make policy part of professional practice requires a model that helps practitioners adopt a frame of reference and
strengthen their policy consciousness. This enables them to identify policy in
their practice world and develop the ability to move from knowledge of
policymaking and policymakers to carrying out policy. The model suggested
in this book helps workers develop such a frame of reference. It helps make
real assertions that policy should be a part of social work practice, that policy
knowledge and skills are basic to professional practice, and that policy should
be part of every practitioner's intervention efforts. Generalist social workers
need to be prepared through their education to deliver on the profession's
policy commitment. This book will help in that preparation by using a model
that enables them to value integrating policy with their practice activities.

Social workers also need to be able to identify policies that actually constitute a part of their practice world. If policy is to be used in generalist
practice, its definition must come from the practice parameters and perspective of line social workers. This text's policy model includes a way to define
and identify policies of concern to practitioners within the resource systems
that comprise the generalist practice world. By basing the definition and
identification of policy in practice, the integration of the two is achieved
more easily.

Generalist practitioners need a means to bring policy alive, to help focus
on those aspects of policy that lead to making it a practice activity. Policy's
"life" is to be found through exploration and utilization of the persons and
processes through which policy is made.

Finally, social work practitioners must be equipped with a framework for policy analysis that helps them to analyze and understand the details of policy and planning and to carry out appropriate practice actions based on this analysis. This book will help practitioners attain this ability by linking knowledge of policymaking procedures to policy analysis and interventions (see Table 1 for a summary of the four parts).

Using the needs of the practitioner as the starting point for developing an approach to policy serves to integrate practice and policy. Since policy is derived from the needs of practitioners, it is shown to be a natural and important part of practice at all levels. It focuses on the daily practice realities encountered by social workers, and suggests ways to address them.

This occurs by defining eight resource systems in which social workers practice. These systems represent the specific areas in which policies and policymaking have to be understood. Each is analyzed for kinds of policies used, how they are produced, and how practice can influence them. Then the opportunities are examined for social workers to analyze these policies, and modify them or create new ones. As a result, the day-to-day practice of social work is totally integrated with the policies which influence practice, as well as the procedures which create policy. This is a new approach to policy in that it takes as its major goal the integration of policy and practice.

To understand and address a situation, I believe that one should turn to the people most involved. In social work practice, the profession's people are its line workers, those who provide direct services to and maintain active contact with client systems. In my judgment, the profession must turn to these workers to achieve a needed reorientation toward the definition, use, and formulation of policy.

In defining policy, I have chosen to develop a model that builds on the findings of the West Virginia Curriculum Development Project. Incorporated in this text is much of that material and a belief in the widespread acceptance by social work educators that its statement of generalist competencies is a valid one. Important points of departure for this book, drawn from the Project, include a conception of holistic practice, the idea of resources, the use of policy in practice, and the central role assumed by practice content in curriculum development.

Belief in the importance and power of the line worker in social work led to several emphases in this book, chiefly those about developing a policy frame of reference, defining policies of concern from a practice perspective, and developing a framework for policy analysis and development that incorporates action. These themes follow the thinking of many social workers and educators, although they have not been developed to any great extent in the literature. Basically, the book addresses the issues that have traditionally concerned social work, but moves them into a relationship with daily practice that is both conceptually and pragmatically new and useful. Emphasis is on solving problems between practice and policy in ways that will enrich both.

The basic parts of the policy model will be explored. Part One contributes to an understanding of the relationship between policy and direct services. Chapter one will discuss how a policy frame of reference that heightens policy consciousness and leads to the valuing of policy in practice can be identified and developed. Chapters two and three define and develop an approach to identifying policies of concern to social workers. Part Two addresses how policy is made in the various systems used by generalist social workers. Part Three addresses the analysis and development of policy as part of practitioner assessment and interventions. A framework for policy analysis and action, policy-related role expectations, and illustrations showing the use of policy are offered. The final chapter explores the opportunities and challenges of those who use this model.

Learning from this text will be enhanced by the following strategies:

☐ Read the overview and objectives that follow the title page of each chapter. They contain each chapter's major points and identify several important learning objectives. The objectives correspond to the major sections and subsections of each chapter. The learning objectives mainly apply to understanding the basic concepts covered in each section. The reader is asked to discuss, describe, comment on, or explain chapter content. Read the chapter with the learning objectives in mind, return to them as necessary, and use them after reading the chapter to review its content.

☐ Read the chapter, underlining or outlining as necessary. Concentrate on main points and concepts. Relate these to the learning objectives. After completing the entire chapter review it until the major ideas are completely understood.

☐ Refer to the tables and figures while reading the chapter. In the body of the appropriate section reference is made to a particular chart. The reference indicates its purpose. Some tables summarize a particular section of a chapter. Others expand upon or illustrate what has been read and add to its meaning. All of the tables and figures may be reviewed after completing each chapter, serving to reinforce the reader's understanding.

☐ Use the "For Further Study" section of each chapter. It contains three parts: questions, glossary, and bibliography. The questions are based on the material developed in each chapter, suggesting interviews, self-examination, research, or learning exercises. Unlike the learning objectives, which focus on grasping actual content, the study questions emphasize the application of content. The glossary contains major terms and concepts. Use the glossary to clarify as well as to test out understanding of the terms used in the chapter. The bibliography cites the works used in each chapter.

TABLE 1

Basic Parts of a Policy Model for the Generalist Social Work Practitioner

A. Building *a policy frame of reference* that will support and lead to the integration of policy and practice by raising the worker's level of policy consciousness

B. Utilizing an approach to define and identify *policies of concern to social workers* that is grounded in social work practice

C. Understanding the *policy formulation processes and the policymakers* in the systems used by the generalist practitioner

D. Developing a *framework for policy analysis and development* that uses policy analysis and action guides to develop a policy of concern and carry out policy related interventions

PART ONE

POLICY AND
THE LINE WORKER

Each of the three chapters in this part contributes to building a policy frame of reference and to defining policies from the perspective of line workers. They focus on policy in eight resource systems used by social workers in their practice and relate the definition of policy to the attainment of professional purposes. This section offers one perspective on linking policy to the direct services practice world. Dolgoff and Gordon (1981) discuss three perspectives on the relationship of policy and direct practice. They point out that some scholars suggest that policy and practice play a supportive role for each other. The authors observe that a second group finds that policy is enacted in practice and that policy controls the way practice is implemented. The third perspective, which they favor and propose be further developed, believes that direct practitioners make policy, that they are not merely controlled by it. The discussion in this book represents the third perspective.

The first chapter in this part deals with the important place of policy in the practice of all social workers. It discusses several reasons why line workers can value the use of policy in their practice. This exploration supports the development of a policy frame of reference by line workers. Such a frame of reference leads workers to value policy, incorporate it in their practice, keep informed about policy, and to think of the use of policy as critical to their clients' interests. The second chapter examines ways to define policy. It does so by developing a policy definition that will be more relevant to the direct services practitioner. This does not mean that the policy definitions currently utilized by social workers are not valuable. These definitions, along with ways to connect policy and practice, are examined to pinpoint ideas that define policies of concern to social work practitioners. The last chapter in this part discusses and exemplifies the kinds of policies used by line social workers in their practice. Policies of concern are identified in the resource systems used in practice. The resources contained in each system and the policies each develops for the allocation of its resources are covered. How the resource system's policies relate to professional purposes are also examined.

CHAPTER ONE

A Policy Frame of Reference: Raising the Social Worker's Policy Consciousness

"Although I enjoyed this policy course, I'm more interested in learning how to practice. I still don't know if I'll be able to use policy at all."

—concluding comment made
by a student on a policy
course final examination

"In my practice I quickly discovered that I had to deal with policy or I could not help my clients very effectively."

—BILL AUSTIN
BSW student

OVERVIEW

This chapter will present ideas that support a policy frame of reference. Policy consciousness can be developed in practitioners by learning about and acknowledging the important place policy has in direct services. Support for a policy frame of reference can be located in definitions of the profession, statements of its purposes and values, and conceptions of social work practice. This chapter will build the knowledge foundation for developing a policy frame of reference and lay the basis for the development of the remainder of the policy model.

OBJECTIVES

- ☐ Discuss why a policy frame of reference is important to the generalist line worker.
- ☐ State four ideas that support a policy frame of reference and discuss how one of these is supportive of using policy in practice.
- ☐ Briefly describe a common definition of policy.

GENERALIST SOCIAL WORKERS are busy people, confronted with the opportunities and pressures of the direct service practice world. As the quotations that open this chapter indicate, students may or may not believe that policy will be central to their practice. Some fear that in the rush of their daily work, they will have little time or need for policy. This, of course, is an unfortunate misperception. The best practitioners make policy part of their practice world. They bring to their practice a policy frame of reference, as is reflected in the second quotation, which leads them to use policy; it keeps the importance and value of policy constantly in their minds. Such a frame of reference also supports them in their efforts to make policy. Consistent support for policy intervention is critical in direct service work, from which policy sometimes seems quite distant. The art of policy orientation is not the gift of a blessed few; it can be developed by all entry level practitioners.

Understanding how policy and practice are integrated leads to the adoption of a frame of reference that treats policy analysis and knowledge of policies as a basic part of generalist practice. Integrating the two can stem from exploring ideas about:

☐ the purposes of social work
☐ a generalist conception of professional practice
☐ the utilization of a competency approach to curriculum development
☐ professional social work values as reflected in the National Association of Social Workers' Code of Ethics

PROFESSIONAL PURPOSES

The profession of social work has long been preoccupied with presenting a clear definition of itself and an adequate statement of its professional purpose.

In a special issue of *Social Work* for January 1981, the following statement on the purpose of social work was published:

> The purpose of social work is to promote or restore a mutually beneficial interaction between individuals and society in order to improve the quality of life for everyone. Social workers hold the following beliefs:
>
> — The environment (social, physical, organizational) should provide the opportunity and resources for the maximum realization of the potential and aspirations of all individuals, and should provide for their common human needs and for the alleviation of distress and suffering.
> — Individuals should contribute as effectively as they can to their own well-being and to the social welfare of others in their immediate environment as well as to the collective society.
> — Transactions between individuals and others in their environment should enhance the dignity, individuality, and self-determination of everyone. People should be treated humanely and with justice.
>
> Clients of social workers may be an individual, a family, a group, a community, or an organization.
>
> OBJECTIVES
> Social workers focus on person-and-environment in interaction. To carry out their purpose, they work with people to achieve the following objectives:
>
> — Help people enlarge their competence and increase their problem-solving and coping capacities.
> — Help people obtain resources.
> — Make organizations responsive to people.
> — Facilitate interaction between individuals and others in their environment.
> — Influence interactions between organizations and institutions.
> — Influence social and environmental policy.
>
> To achieve these objectives, social workers work with other people. At different times, the target of change varies: it may be the client, others in the environment, or both.

This working statement would establish policy activities as a social work objective to help achieve the purpose of the profession. It identifies the environment's responsibilities for enabling people to lead healthy, satisfying lives. This is a policy statement in that it takes a position about what *ought* to occur. Similarly, it addresses *how* the environment should act to achieve the stated goal, for instance, making organizations responsive to people. Embodied in this statement of professional purposes, then, are a number of policy concerns beyond its support for influencing policy.

For entry-level practitioners, a presentation of professional purpose and its importance in professional education and practice was spelled out by Baer and Federico (1978, 1979) who point out that professional purposes provide the context within which all practice activities take place and against which they are ultimately assessed. Moreover, these purposes guide the selection of and lend direction to carrying out specific interventions, moving the worker beyond the use of helping techniques in a mechanical fashion to the professional application of skills and knowledge.

In reaching a definition of social work and of its professional purposes, Baer and Federico utilized the earlier work of Pincus and Minahan (1973). Baer and Federico (1978) state that:

> Social work is concerned and involved with the interactions between people and the institutions of society that affect the ability of people to accomplish life tasks, realize aspirations and values, and alleviate distress. These interactions between people and the social institutions in which people function occur within the context of the larger societal good. Therefore, three major purposes of social work may be identified: (1) to enhance the problem-solving, coping and developmental capacities of people; (2) to promote the effective and humane operation of the systems that provide people with resources and services; and (3) to link people with systems that provide them with resources, services, and opportunities.

Professional purpose, thus stated, calls for the integration of knowledge, values, and policy to achieve a holistic focus in practice. It is the basis for a conceptualization of practice and for a holistic approach to the education of the generalist practitioner. Such a statement of professional purpose, moreover, points to three foci in determining which policies are of concern to a social worker: those concerned with enhancing individual development, the allocation or provision of resources and rights to people, and the promotion of effective and humane resource systems.

ENTRY-LEVEL COMPETENCIES

Baer and Federico derived 10 major practice competencies from the three purposes. Entry level practitioners should be able to perform these competencies which, when aggregated, make possible the attainment of purposes.

Baer and Federico propose the following 10 competencies:

1. Identify and assess situations where the relationship between people and social institutions needs to be initiated, enhanced, restored, protected, or terminated.
2. Develop and implement a plan for improving the well-being of people based on problem assessment and the exploration of obtainable goals and available options.

3. Enhance the problem-solving, coping, and developmental capacities of people.
4. Link people with systems that provide them with resources, services, and opportunities.
5. Intervene effectively on behalf of populations most vulnerable and discriminated against.
6. Promote the effective and humane operation of the systems that provide people with services, resources, and opportunities.
7. Actively participate with others in creating new, modified, or improved service, resource, and opportunity systems that are more equitable, just, and responsive to consumers of services, and work with others to eliminate those systems that are unjust.
8. Evaluate the extent to which the objectives of the intervention plan were achieved.
9. Continually evaluate one's own professional growth and development through assessment of practice behavior and skills.
10. Contribute to the improvement of service delivery by adding to the knowledge base of the profession as appropriate and by supporting and upholding the standards and ethics of the profession.

Although each competency has a policy element, as will be further explored in Part Two, for some of them this connection is more explicit. Promoting the functioning of effective systems; creating, modifying, or improving systems; and working on behalf of vulnerable populations or eliminating unjust systems, are the competency statements that appear to be most linked to a general understanding of policy. Baer and Federico, in their outline of the knowledge, skills, and values needed for the attainment of each of the competencies, further emphasize the policy overtones of these and of other competency statements. For example, knowledge of policy analysis skills and policy formation is basic for the attainment of the fourth competency, and knowledge of organizational policy and how it is developed underlies the seventh.

PRACTICE CONCEPTUALIZATION

Professional purpose also provides a point of departure for Baer's (1979) conceptualization of social work practice. According to her definition, social workers attain their primary professional purpose of enhancing human well-being by monitoring, reestablishing, or improving the interactions between people and social institutions. This is achieved by identifying, developing, or linking client systems with resources. Resources are the key factor in Baer's conception of practice, and represent an important reemphasis for professional social work practice. Although referred to by others (Pincus and Minahan, 1973), Baer links resources to categories (or systems) of resources employed by workers in their practice. As in the practice formulations of others, a systems perspective, the processes of the problem solving approach, and the conception of tasks and roles also play an important part in her statement of practice.

The utilization of a systems perspective is intended to assure that a holistic view of practice is achieved. The holistic view stems from the emphasis on professional purpose on people and their needs in relation to social institutions. This broad focus in generalist practice requires that workers incorporate more than the individual client in their understanding of the situation. Briefly stated, a systems perspective is one that views human behavior and needs in terms of the interrelatedness of the parts that comprise a given system. The systems perspective thereby provides a holistic viewpoint for the generalist conceptualization of practice, leading to the consideration of a range of factors. It aids in problem identification and description and in the selection and development of interventions that recognize and deal with the greatest range of factors. It will be covered more fully in Chapter 4.

Similarly, the problem solving approach is associated with many generalist practice formulations. According to Baer, problem solving guides the worker's movement in selecting and developing a plan to address the problem as identified by the worker and client. Problem solving steps include:

☐ initial engagement and problem exploration
☐ data collection and data assessment
☐ establishing goals
☐ discussion and selection of intervention
☐ carrying out and evaluating the intervention plan
☐ conclusion or termination of the worker-client helping relationship

Problem solving, when placed in the context of professional purpose, provides the means to focus helping activities such that they become professional, not merely technical, in their implementation.

Another element in Baer's conception, one also grounded in previous work, is her emphasis on the importance of tasks and roles in explaining professional practice. Tasks and roles relate to the doing (guided, of course, by a systems perspective and the problem-solving process). Baer suggests two general types of tasks: analytical and interactional. Analytical tasks refer to the thinking, cognitive aspects of a helping intervention. Interactional tasks are the procedural or relationship actions carried out by the worker in any problem-solving effort. Roles help organize interventions to carry out the tasks. Chapter nine will assess the utility of this conception in identifying policy-related practice activities.

Finally, as already pointed out resources are especially noteworthy in Baer's conception of practice. They provide a link to the conception of social work developed by its founders, as well as offer us an especially useful way of understanding the exchange that takes place between the person and social institutions. As will be discussed in chapter three, focusing on resources is one way to identify which policies are of concern to the entry-level social worker.

Borrowing from Siporin (1975), resources are held by Baer to be "any valuable thing . . . [of a tangible or intangible nature used] to function, meet a need, or resolve a problem." The "valuable thing" could be a material resource such as food or an intangible one such as an opportunity or service. In Baer's scheme, resources become the worker's major focus in restoring or establishing interactions between people and societal institutions. The range and variety of resources available for utilization by the worker include not only those that help people develop problem-solving skills or those that stem from interpersonal helping skills, but also extend to all resources useful for meeting the range of needs of diverse client systems.

Baer groups these into eight resource systems:

☐ the society at large
☐ the local community
☐ the social welfare institution
☐ the profession of social work
☐ the social worker(s)
☐ the organization or agency setting
☐ colleagues and other helping persons and disciplines
☐ the client

It is sufficient at this point to note that her categorization covers the range of resources available to the worker. These categories or systems of resources provide further direction in identifying the location of policies of concern to the practitioner. Definitions of each and its contribution to a redefinition of policy will be offered in chapter three.

Baer's conception contains several implications for the integration of policy and practice. Holistic practice, or a holistic perspective applied in practice, is one in which action and analysis come together. A holistic approach implies that policy and practice activities should be connected, since the holistic perspective is incomplete without the inclusion of policy. Baer's conceptualization also has other important elements for the integration of policy and practice. The systems perspective and the problem-solving approach have direct bearing on redefining policy and on determining important policy formation processes. In addition, the utilization of analytical and interactional tasks in problem solving lay the groundwork for the development of policy analysis skills, as well as point out practice actions that are related to policy.

PROFESSIONAL VALUES

The social work literature contains innumerable references to the importance of values in practice. Although the primacy of values is often noted, specifics are seldom offered regarding how values might actually guide practice activities or how values relate to policy. As will be seen in chapter four, values play a leading role in policy decision-making. The practitioner therefore needs a set of value guides that supports professional purposes and can be used in monitoring practice and following policy issues.

The National Association of Social Workers' (NASW) professional Code of Ethics provides one source for such values. Certain sections of the code are especially applicable to policy concerns.

Section IV—The social worker's ethical responsibility to employees and employing organizations
  L. Commitments to employing organization—the social worker should adhere to commitments made to the employing organization.
     1. The social worker should work to improve the employing agency's policies and procedures, and the efficiency and effectiveness of the services.
     3. The social worker should act to prevent and eliminate discrimination in the employing organization's work assignments and its employment policies and practices.
Section V—The social worker's ethical responsibility to the social work profession
  N. Community service—the social worker should assist the profession in making social services available to the general public.
     2. The social worker should support the formulation, development, enactment and implementation of social policies of concern to the profession.
Section VI—The social worker's ethical responsibility to society
  P. Promoting the general welfare—the social worker should promote the general welfare of society.
     6. The social worker should advocate changes in policy and legislation to improve social conditions and to promote social justice.
     7. The social worker should encourage informal participation by the public in shaping social policies and institutions.

Social workers, according to the code, should be involved in policy activities in a variety of places and ways. The agency, the community, and society are all arenas for policy activity. Moreover, it suggests that workers should be engaged in supporting, enacting, and developing policy themselves as well as in encouraging the participation of others in policymaking.

Much of the preceding discussion assumes an understanding of a policy definition. A commonly accepted definition refers to the *decisions and resulting guidelines made in a society or one of its systems that control decision making in the allocation of resources and rights to its members.* Such allocative guidelines usually identify the recipients who are eligible to receive some valuable resource and describe the means by which they will receive it. Decision-making approaches, decision makers, the resources or rights allocated and those who receive them become key elements in defining policy and in formulating guides to analyze and understand the policymaking process and its products.

Determining which of these societal policymaking processes and their policies are of concern to entry-level social workers is one of the objectives of this text. A related objective is to offer an elaboration on each and to derive guides for the integration of policy and practice.

Meeting these objectives is served in part by Baer's concept of eight resource systems. In her practice definition, resources cement holistic practice together in service to professional purpose. The policies about resource and rights allocation in each resource system constitute policies of concern to social work practitioners. The policy formulation processes used in each form the basis for the development of policy-related practice skills and activities needed by generalist social workers.

In each of the eight systems, workers seek "policies of concern" that will have an effect on the needs of their clientele. Policy boundaries for social workers are thereby not restricted to legislation, court decisions, or policies of the social welfare institution and its agencies. Those systems that focus on individual workers, their colleagues, local communities, and professional organizations also generate policies that influence users of social work services. So, policies within these systems are of concern to social workers. The direction provided by professional purpose, when linked to the needs of a particular clientele and to the concept of eight resource systems, permits social workers to pinpoint policies and policy activities that are important in their practice.

INTEGRATING POLICY AND PRACTICE

Professional purpose, social work practice competencies, social work practice, and professional values all lend support to an integration of policy and practice and to the development of a policy frame of reference that values using policy in practice. Obvious linkages occur through the problem-solving process (see Figure 1 for an overview of these connections). That process is a part of the practice conception and is found among the elements identified as being important to understanding how policy is defined. Policy foci derived

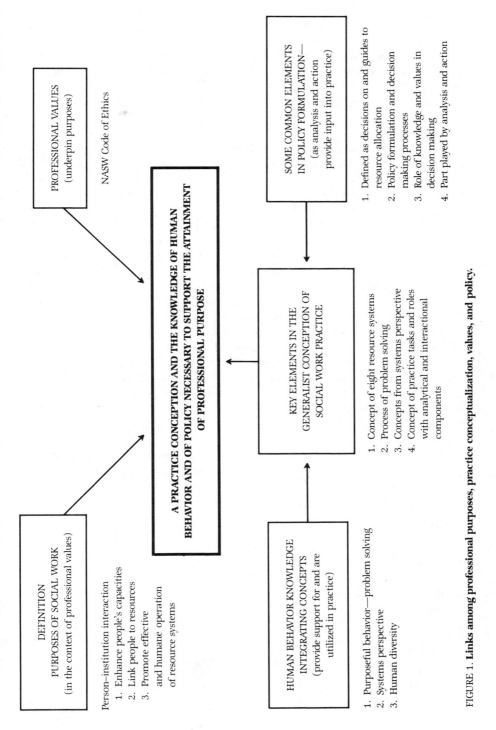

FIGURE 1. **Links among professional purposes, practice conceptualization, values, and policy.**

PROFESSIONAL VALUES
(underpin purposes)

NASW Code of Ethics

SOME COMMON ELEMENTS
IN POLICY FORMULATION—
(as analysis and action
provide input into practice)

1. Defined as decisions on and guides to resource allocation
2. Policy formulation and decision making processes
3. Role of knowledge and values in decision making
4. Part played by analysis and action

A PRACTICE CONCEPTION AND THE KNOWLEDGE OF HUMAN
BEHAVIOR AND OF POLICY NECESSARY TO SUPPORT THE ATTAINMENT
OF PROFESSIONAL PURPOSE

KEY ELEMENTS IN THE
GENERALIST CONCEPTION OF
SOCIAL WORK PRACTICE

1. Concept of eight resource systems
2. Process of problem solving
3. Concepts from systems perspective
4. Concept of practice tasks and roles with analytical and interactional components

DEFINITION
PURPOSES OF SOCIAL WORK
(in the context of professional values)

Person–institution interaction
1. Enhance people's capacities
2. Link people to resources
3. Promote effective and humane operation of resource systems

HUMAN BEHAVIOR KNOWLEDGE
INTEGRATING CONCEPTS
(provide support for and are
utilized in practice)

1. Purposeful behavior—problem solving
2. Systems perspective
3. Human diversity

from professional purpose match up with several policy-related issues and topics contained in the NASW's Code of Ethics. Another connection exists in the reoccurrence of the idea of resources among the various conceptions. Resources are emphasized in the practice conception and play a critical role in the definition of policy.

Policy can be an active part of all professional social work practice. In their education, professional social workers must be aided in developing a heightened policy consciousness that values using policy in practice. If we are serious about professional purpose and professional values, then the policy aspect of practice cannot be ignored. If we are serious about the survival of the profession, the integration of policy and practice must become a highly supported priority of the profession. It is too critical an issue, too fundamental a part of social work, for the profession to assign policy-related practice to a minority of its members. Direct service practitioners skilled in policy use and sensitive to its importance for their clients can make real the promises of professional purpose.

The approach proposed by this text is challenging in several ways: in its expectation that line workers use policy in daily practice, in its contention that policy stems from individuals as well as from institutions and society, and in its hopefulness that the profession is better able to live up to its stated purposes. A policy frame of reference for use in practice will help meet the challenges proposed by this approach and help the profession meet policy crises posed by hostile federal or state administrations. The impact of these crises, such as those of the Nixon or Reagan administrations, can be lessened for social work if policy is better integrated with practice. All members of the profession, in line with professional purposes and values, must keep in mind a policy frame of reference that lends support to their integration of policy and practice. Only in this way will the profession be able to resist efforts by those in any of the resource systems who would use policy to deny people the life-sustaining and enriching resources that they need and want.

FOR FURTHER STUDY

1. Explain what the author means by a policy frame of reference for use in practice.

2. Interview a social worker to determine if and/or how policy is used by that person in practice.

3. What are your thoughts about using policy in your future practice? Had you considered using it? If so, how and why? If you had not thought about policy in practice, why not?

4. Label and describe some of the ideas about professional social work that were used in this chapter to support the position that policy and practice should be integrated. Explain how the ideas you selected are related and how they support the development of a policy frame of reference.

GLOSSARY

Policy frame of reference   The level of policy consciousness of workers leading them to value policy, to incorporate it in their practice, to keep abreast of policy developments, and to consider the policy aspects of the systems in which they function.

Purposes of social work   In line with a professional definition focused on people in their environment, social workers: (1) enhance people's problem solving capacities, (2) link them with resources, and (3) work to create humane and effective service delivery systems.

Competencies   Developed in relation to professional purposes, the competencies define areas of minimum social work expertness and outline what workers should be able to do in practice.

Practice conception elements   Several elements within the context of professional values may be utilized to conceptualize social work practice: (1) resources, (2) a systems perspective, (3) processes of problem solving, and (4) a conception of practice tasks and roles.

Resources   Anything of value such as material or tangible goods, an opportunity or service, or relationship needed by people to meet needs or resolve concerns in their environment.

Eight resource systems   These are categories or locations of resources that define the practice arenas of the social worker. They include (1) the social worker, (2) professional colleagues, (3) client systems, (4) agency settings, (5) the profession of social work, (6) local communities, (7) society at large, and (8) the institution of social welfare.

Professional social work values   The values outlined in the National Association of Social Workers' Code of Ethics. These values are based in the historical and professional development of social work.

Working definition of policy   Decisions and guidelines about the allocation of resources and rights in society and its resource allocating systems that constitute a general framework to direct our future decisions and actions in a given area of policy concern.

BIBLIOGRAPHY

Baer, Betty L. "A Conceptual Model for the Organization of Content for the Educational Preparation for the Entry-Level Social Worker." Unpublished Doctoral Dissertation: University of Pittsburgh, 1979.

Baer, Betty L. and Ronald Federico. *Educating the Baccalaureate Social Worker: Report of the Undergraduate Social Work Curriculum Development Project.* Cambridge, Massachusetts: Ballinger, 1978.

Baer, Betty L. and Ronald Federico (Eds.). *Educating the Baccalaureate Social Worker: A Curriculum Development Resource Guide.* Cambridge, Massachusetts: Ballinger, 1979.

Berger, Robert and Ronald C. Federico. *Human Behavior: A Social Work Perspective.* New York: Longman, 1982.

Dean, Walter R., Jr. Back to activism. *Social Work,* 22(5):369–373, 1977.

Dolgoff, Ralph and Malvina Gordon. Educating for policy making at the direct and local levels. *Journal of Education for Social Work,* 17(2):98–105, 1981.

Dinerman, Miriam. *Social Work Curriculum at the Baccalaureate and Masters Levels.* New York: The Lois and Samuel Silberman Fund, 1981.

Minahan, Anne and Allen Pincus. Conceptual framework for social work practice. *Social Work,* 22(5):347–352, 1977.

National Association of Social Workers. *Code of Ethics.* Washington, D.C., 1980.

Pincus, Allen and Anne Minahan. *Social Work Practice: Model and Method.* Itasca, Illinois: F. E. Peacock Publishers, 1973.

Siporin, Max. *Introduction to Social Work Practice.* New York: Macmillan, 1975.

"Working Statement on the Purpose of Social Work." *Social Work,* 26(1):6, 1981.

CHAPTER TWO

Defining Policy for Practice

"*Social policy theory is stalemated. . . .
The problem lies in part in the . . . reified
nature of recent social policy thinking.*"
—**LARRY HIRSCHHORN (1977)**

"*At the daycare center I used policy
almost from the day I was hired. I've
always thought of policy as being based in
the agency where I practice and in its
collateral systems.*"
—**BERNICE LIDDIE, ACSW**
(personal communication)

OVERVIEW

One conclusion to be drawn from Hirschhorn's suggestion that social policy thinkers have reified their subject matter is that notions about policy need a better foundation in the realities of social work practice. Such a connection to the world of social work should begin with a practice based definition of policy. This chapter will utilize eight resource systems used in social work practice as arenas in which to seek out policies of concern to practitioners. It will also use professional purposes to locate the kinds of policies within these arenas that should concern social workers. Before elaborating on these in this chapter, a search for so-called commonsense elements in policy will be made. Commonsense illustrations and the definitional elements they produce will be used as background for the presentation of two general ways scholars identify policies of interest to social workers. Finally, a third approach to define policy from the perspective of practice will be introduced.

OBJECTIVES

☐ List major definitional elements for the word "policy."
☐ Compare the two major ways that have been used to designate policy for professional social workers.
☐ Discuss two ways in which the definition of policies of concern links policy to practice.

THE WORD "POLICY" EXEMPLIFIES a difficulty frequently encountered in social science literature: defining a word or phrase that already has a commonsense meaning, one that people believe requires little or no further explanation. Social scientists and other scholars, in pursuing the meaning of a word such as policy, explore its definition to its fullest extent. No shading or nuance escapes scrutiny. They clarify the meaning by providing precision in its definition. An examination of policy from a more commonsense perspective will help pinpoint basic themes or elements that are used in defining policy.

People learn about this country's foreign policy, domestic policy, educational policy, agricultural policy, health policy, and about corporate or business policy through the daily newspapers, the radio, or television. Children learn policies that are set by their parents which they are expected to follow. Parental child-rearing policy sets the times to eat, go to bed, and get up. As children get older, new parental policies are instituted. Schools set policy on attendance, a curriculum of study, or in what area we should attend school. Later, people discover company policy regarding work rights and responsibilities. The government, too, has set policies about paying taxes, voting rights, or who should go to war. Movies, restaurants, buses, and other public areas post policies about what people should wear or whether or not they can smoke while on the premises.

People set their own policies. Teenagers may set a policy to disregard their parents' advice. Some people decide to oppose policy established by government. Still others decide on a policy geared to the status quo. Those who question the existence of a foreign policy provide insight into the definition of the word policy. They assume that the nation's leaders should have an agreed-upon framework to guide them in foreign affairs. They do not question that our leaders take actions. They do not question that the policy is set down somewhere. What they do question is the lack of relationship among the actions taken by our leaders, the lack of a sense of coherence that would be provided by a preconceived and agreed-upon policy to guide all actions.

In this sense, some families or individuals also lack policy. They seem not to have an overall reference that guides their actions. Most people assume that for families or individuals such a set of guidelines comes from moral and ethical codes or from the value base they follow. The creation of a family's policy, however, includes more than morals or values. A family's knowledge and experience contribute to its overall approach in making decisions and taking action. For example, though some parents may be aware that it is not just to strike children, the fact that they themselves were punished as children may lead to a child-rearing policy that permits parents to spank their children. Other families' value base and personal experience may lead to a more permissive child-rearing policy.

This sense of how a family should rear its children constitutes its policy. It is a similar set of "what to do's" that guides an administration's approach to foreign relations. The policy of both the family and the government, whether unwritten or somewhat more codified, is used to justify a decision or to explain an action once it has been carried out. Just as a family's child-rearing policy allows parents to punish children, so does a nation's foreign policy permit actions against other nations.

All of which raises the need to distinguish among values, knowledge, and policy and to outline the role of each in providing direction to the actions of an individual or an institution. Values, knowledge, and policy either are or contribute to the "shoulds" and "how to acts" that guide human behavior. Individually and collectively, people create policy. The policies in turn order and guide their functioning and decision-making. As will be developed in greater detail later in this chapter and in chapter five, the decision-making and the behavior of individuals are guided by policy as well as by values. The role of an individual's policy in guiding his or her decision-making and behavior has been overlooked or downplayed in the policy literature. Values and, to a lesser extent, knowledge have been held to constitute the major input for decision-making or choice-taking by individuals. Sometimes the role of values for the individual is defined and treated in such a way that it subsumes the role of policy as it is discussed here.

Levy (1973) points out that some scholars see values as patterns, which, when institutionalized, determine choices and commit people to certain actions. To other scholars, values are rules that prescribe "ought to's" and evaluate actual behavior. In this sense, they serve to guide behavior, a function this text assigns to personal policy.

Values more generally are *ideals about what people think the world should be, the things upon which they place worth.* Values designate those things on which people place more merit than on other things that either are not part of, or would not contribute to, the world as they wish to see it. *Knowledge,* on the other hand, *is our understanding of the world as it is*. Knowledge in this sense comes from empirical, scientifically based investigations of the world. Such formal knowledge contributes to perceptions of how people are, how they behave, and how they decide. In addition to values and knowledge, everyone has experiences. Experience stems from interaction with the world. *Experience* is comprised of *exchanges and interactions with people and with social groupings and social institutions.*

For the individual, as for an agency, social institution, and for society itself, policy emerges from the interplay among knowledge, values, and experience. An individual is guided in decision-making and behavior by this interaction of values (ideals about the way things ought to be), knowledge (formal understanding of the world), and experience (interaction with the world). All this, when taken together, becomes the basis for an individual's policy (guides for acting and deciding). This policy, in turn, reinforces and interacts with values and knowledge, incorporating or rejecting them in behavior and decisions. Similarly, in agencies, institutions, and society, decision-makers create policy from values, knowledge, and experience. Policy is used to control behavior and to guide the allocation of resources, and, as it reflects values and knowledge or experience, it interacts with and is reinforced by them.

In summary, policy is a guide to achieve what people value, given the input of their own knowledge and experience. Policy is derived from formal knowledge or understanding of, and experience or interaction with, the world. Although all these inputs to deciding and behaving interact, policy serves as the general framework for guiding people in the decisions they make and the actions they take. Policy often is a less obvious, less articulated part of behaving and acting than are values, knowledge, or experience.

A policy may be thought of as a more or less formalized, internal set of guides, sometimes subject to change, that directs a person's actions in relating to others, in meeting needs, or in explaining and justifying actions. Such guides do not merely prescribe courses of action; they also place restraints on what people are permitted to do. As a policy leads in one direction and thereby prevents people from pursuing another, it serves to restrict their range of decision-making as well as course of action. A family, an individual, or a nation can become locked into a course of action by its policy in a particular area. Given the value and experiential components of policy, specific policies are frequently difficult to alter. This difficulty, in relation to the decision-making and behavioral limitations placed on people by some policy, can lead to rigid, inflexible approaches.

Further meanings of policy are reflected in these commonsense illustrations. Policies are specific guides or plans, which in their formulation set general parameters on the behavior or expectations of specified people. These people are subject to such policies because they are considered to be members of the grouping or unit that is interested in controlling those who use group resources and power to meet their individual needs. The grouping may be quite small in number, cover all members of a society, or include sizeable subgroupings. Membership may be temporary, as among theatergoers, or more permanent, as with members of a family.

As members of these units attempt to meet their needs, policies are established to regulate how they should behave and to determine what they should expect to receive. The policy also serves as a rationale to account for any differences that are allowed to exist among its members. Parents, for example, may go to bed later than children, presumably because the adults require less sleep. Wide differences exist among groupings about who gets what and why. Moreover, a grouping's policy may be perceived as active and subject to change in light of internal or external circumstances. On the other hand, policy may be seen as rigid and unchanging, regardless of how the members or their needs may differ or change.

There is also wide variance over the means for formulating policy in any given grouping or unit. Policies are formulated and developed in different ways. All or only a few group members may participate in setting them. Such policies, however, frequently reflect the norms, knowledge assumptions, or values of larger social units. The societal context could be national (including all groups in a society) or subcultural (including only members of a particular subculture) in its scope. It could reflect both, as in the case of many minority families. The needs that are to be covered, situations for which the policies serve as rationales, and the structures that are used to establish policies also reflect this larger context. These concerns reflect issues of power, a basic policy ingredient.

In summary, there are several basic elements that characterize the word policy:

☐ Policy provides guidelines that enable decisions to be made just as it restricts the scope and nature of decisions.
☐ Policy serves to justify the actions of people, because policy reflects commonly accepted assumptions, knowledge, and values.
☐ Policy causes people to act in certain ways or sets limits to their actions.
☐ Policy is made by a wide range of groups or units in society, and members of these groupings are expected to follow it.
☐ Policy is not necessarily made by all members of a group.
☐ Policy is made for and by individuals.
☐ Policy is praised and followed or is critiqued and ignored.
☐ Policy is a process and its product.
☐ Policy covers many, many aspects of everyone's life.

Among this welter of policies, policy formulation processes, and policy makers, what should gain the interest of social workers? In trying to narrow down this range of policies and setting up boundaries around areas of scholarly interest, social policy analysts have developed at least two major approaches which have been adopted by social workers to identify policies of interest to the profession. Both focus on policies made in very large social groupings. Inherent in both approaches is the assumption that policies at that level are of greatest concern to the profession. One effort aims at sorting out which among a society's policies are important to the social worker's undertaking. This attempt looks at so-called social policies. Its concern is with policies and policy-setting mechanisms of the largest unit of a society. The second approach also considers the policies of a large unit of society, the social welfare institution. The second has become the chief way of designating policy of particular interest to social workers. In exploring these two approaches the extent to which they could aid in integrating policy and practice will be assessed.

PLACING BOUNDARIES ON POLICY

The first of these approaches focuses on policies at the societal level. In defining areas of policy at this level, policies are sorted into categories and the one that most closely approximates the interests of social work is selected for attention and understanding. In other words, parameters or boundaries are placed around segments of societal policy. Keep in mind that much overlapping exists and that the margins of these policy categories constitute arenas for debate among researchers and scholars. Some policy areas at the societal level include social, domestic, foreign relations, economic, health, educational, social welfare, public, or business. Social policy, public policy, economic policy, and social welfare policy are frequently used labels in the social work literature.

Policies at the societal level that attempt to guide behavior and decision-making can roughly be divided into domestic and international. Domestic (or national policy) covers societal policies within a nation's borders, international (or foreign policy) those that deal with relations among nations. In selecting policies for social work or social welfare, it is the usual practice to focus on domestic policies, although international social welfare concerns certainly exist.

Domestic policies may further be broken down into those of the public and private sectors. The former are policies that more or less stem from the government, the latter from the private sector. The term "social policy" is sometimes used interchangeably with domestic or with public domestic policy. The public domestic policy arena has been more thoroughly analyzed than that of the private sector. To most analysts, social work policies lie in the public domestic arena. However, of increasing interest to social workers are private sector policies, notably industrial developments.

The arena of public domestic policy is further subdivided along the lines of broad issues or interest areas. Educational, health, agricultural, economic, and social welfare policies emerge from the overall grouping. Others would have us make the distinction between economic and a broader, loose grouping of "social" policies. Such a distinction illustrates the narrowing down of public domestic policy into distinctive professional or scholarly areas.

Whether social policy is used synonymously with public domestic policy or is considered to be a narrower subset of it, social policy is frequently further refined or reduced to its social welfare policy aspects. In this process of narrowing the scope of policies by grouping them around a few common areas of human needs or problem areas, authors have not been especially consistent in their efforts to develop such distinctions. Writers offer broad or narrow conceptions of societal policy, supplying specific variables to encompass the scope of policy they propose. They engage in a definitional game of sorts. The game identifies policies by defining, redefining, and refining the territory it should cover (see Figure 2 for examples of policy boundaries).

	DOMESTIC POLICY						FOREIGN POLICY			
	INDUSTRIAL	AGRICULTURAL	HEALTH	EDUCATION	ECONOMIC	SOCIAL WELFARE	IMMIGRATION AND REFUGEES	INTERNATIONAL HUNGER	DISARMAMENT	INTERNATIONAL FINANCE
PRIVATE										
PUBLIC										

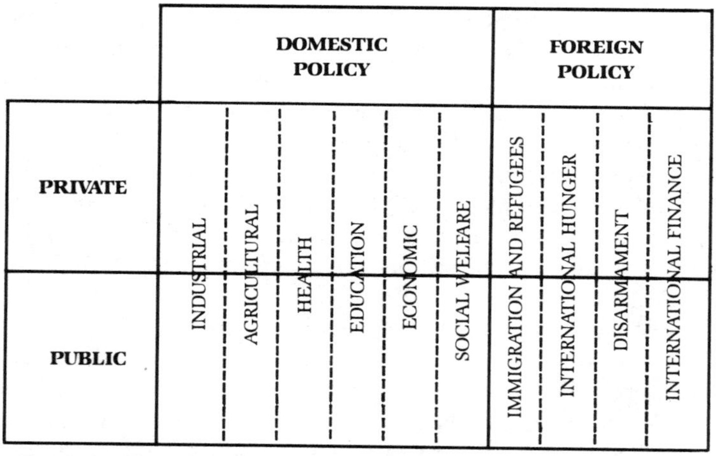

- Domestic policy is emphasized, although there are foreign policy areas of concern.
- The boundaries are frequently overlapping and not precise.
- Public domestic often is held to equal social policies, which ignores the private area.
- Social welfare sometimes only seen as part of public domestic policy, again excluding the private area.
- Public and private social welfare policy thought of as synonymous with policies of the institution of social welfare, although it may be broader and overlap with those of the economic institution.

FIGURE 2. **Examples of Policy Boundaries**

A few examples illustrate this approach, specifically the work of Boulding (1967), Titmuss (1974), Rein (1977), Gil (1976), and Huttman (1981). Several years ago, Kenneth Boulding separated public policy concerns into two broad areas: economic and social. In the British tradition, Richard Titmuss pinpointed social policy by noting the interdependency between certain economic and social policies. More recently, Martin Rein has argued for the joining of economic and social policy. David Gil's formulation would turn to an all-encompassing conception of social policy.

Boulding identified several different processes involved in economic development and in social integration. The differences in human behavior and social relationships that emerged from his analysis of these processes led him to separate economic from social policy. He highlighted the importance of social policy as an emerging field, which in its own realm should attain the level of knowledge development and political application of economic policy. Titmuss, by including fiscal and occupational welfare as well as social welfare, incorporated some areas of economic policy (tax exemptions) and some benefits (pensions or fringe benefits) in his definition of policy. Rein labeled as incorrect the contention that policy can be separated into economic and social aspects. According to him, the two must be considered together in order to move toward social equality. Gil attempted to provide a means of assessing alternatives among social policies and defined policy as decisions and actions related to resource development, status allocation, and rights distribution. Huttman defined social policy as plans to alleviate a social problem or meet a social need. In her definition, the strategy, action, or plan to deal with the problem or need is arrived at after an analysis of choices.

These illustrations are certainly not exhaustive of scholarly attempts to define social policy. They do, however, represent the range of parameters for societal policy used by different theorists, with consequent differences in the scope of the policy. Examples of further restricting policy according to the need or problem addressed include Dempsey's *The Family and Public Policy* (1981), Mechanic's *Mental Health and Social Policy* (1969), and Prigmore and Atherton's *Social Welfare Policy* (1979). In addition, one could consider the perspectives of social policy books such as Rein (1970), Kahn (1973), or Kammerman and Kahn (1976). The first views policy in relation to social services and social welfare and the latter two focus on social services. Rein provides a thorough coverage of the process and pitfalls in using the boundary-setting approach to distinguish among types of policy.

An attempt to sort out various policies at the societal level using the above approach may in the final analysis prove to be of limited pragmatic value to the social worker engaged in direct services. At a general level of social or welfare policy, resources could be identified by the worker, but guides to the selection of specific policy areas are lacking. Moreover, it could be questioned whether all policies within a particular segment of social policy or social welfare policy are those a social worker needs to know and use. Conversely, it might be questioned if it is necessary for a line worker to know every policy in the public domestic area. Also, how much should social workers know about the various policy areas from the perspective of private domestic policy? Even if social workers know how to identify policy from the widest possible vantage point—that of domestic and international policies—how is such knowledge related to their practice? The answer to these questions seems to be that the approach better serves the purposes of people other than line workers. Thus, although it may be a fine and useful introduction to defining policy, it is not entirely helpful in pinpointing policies for use in practice.

THE INSTITUTIONAL APPROACH TO IDENTIFYING POLICY

A second major approach to policy identification limits policies of professional interest to those associated with the programs and agencies of the institution of social welfare. In this approach, distinctions are not made among levels and categories of societal policies, but rather among definitions and functions of societal institutions. What is of interest to scholars is the institution of social welfare, its boundaries and functions. This institution and its policies become the basis of professional concern. The assumption is made that an understanding of its policies fulfills the major policy needs of professional social workers.

In this approach, the institution of social welfare is first defined. Then, its major functional areas are specified. Finally, the policies that are established to aid in carrying out these major functions are identified as those that social workers should understand. It is not the concern of such an approach to link policy and professional practice.

It assumes that the actual planning and development of social welfare policy will be carried out by specialized social workers who "practice" policy from planning positions within social welfare agencies.

Originally, the concept of social welfare as a social institution helped to delineate the arena within which the several social welfare professions (including social work) practice. Within any of the several social welfare professions so identified, none called for a generic practice orientation or one that incorporated policy. The approach proved to be useful in differentiating among the areas of major responsibility for social workers and allied professionals. Since the social welfare institution is not the exclusive domain of social workers, neither are its policies. Its scope is quite broad. Its policies cover several of the resource systems that will be used in this text to identify policies of concern to social workers.

Policies of concern to social workers, of course, do not have to exist exclusively for the benefit or use of social work clients. In this respect, the fact that the policies of the social welfare institution apply to professions other than social work poses no real conceptual difficulty. As in the case of the approach that separates social policy from other societal policies, its utility is limited in that it does not necessarily permit workers to focus on all policies pertinent to a given practice situation. For example, a social welfare policy like Medicaid may be an important part of a practice situation, and a social welfare approach to policy would focus on it. However, a given hospital may have an organizational policy that restricts the number of Medicaid patients it accepts, and a particular client may refuse to go into the hospital—a personal policy—even though he or she may be covered by Medicaid. In other words, knowing the social welfare policy is only part of the policy information needed in this particular practice situation. Furthermore, effective intervention might require efforts to change any of these three types of policies.

Social welfare, of course, is the core of concern to social workers and a major source of policies of concern to the profession. No one would seriously question such an assertion. What can be questioned is whether or not its policies are the only ones of interest to the social worker and whether or not it is the best approach to take in identifying policy for practice. What is required is a balance between comprehensiveness and specificity as demanded by the practice situation. In this sense, the institutional approach may not be entirely useful.

The 1974 undergraduate accreditation standards of the Council on Social Work Education, for example, clearly reflect the social welfare policy approach. In describing content on policy, it called attention to social welfare policy and services (CSWE Standards). The 1983 standards are not as prescriptive regarding any content area, including policy. The accompanying Curriculum Policy Statement uses the terms "social policies and programs," "social and economic policies," and "legislation policies" (CSWE Curriculum Policy Statement Draft). These terms, of course, reflect a broader policy definition and specify that policy content include societal policies, social welfare policies, and a number of other levels of policy which influence practice situations.

REFORMULATING POLICIES CONCERNING SOCIAL WORKERS

Neither of the approaches discussed in the preceding two sections attempts to integrate policy and social work practice. Typically, these approaches have been used to identify policies that are of general interest to the social worker. Without the direction provided by a practice focus, however, their utility is more in line with scholarly interests than with worker needs. This text promised to focus on integrating policy and practice, on exploring approaches and definitions that further the use of policy by the direct service worker. One way to achieve this end is to derive social worker policy definitions from professional purpose and a generalist conception of social work practice.

In this approach, policies of concern become somewhat broader than and even different from those contained in the institution of social welfare. They are, however, much more specific than policies contained in an all-encompassing definition of social policy. As we have discovered, the number of social entities or units that could potentially serve as sources of policies for social workers is quite extensive. In any given practice situation, professional purpose, the resource system or systems being used, and the nature of the client can be used to pinpoint policies of concern. This approach identifies potentially important policy areas for the worker's attention, provides a way to focus them in a given practice situation, and establishes an attitude for the worker to use in practice.

The threefold professional purpose, as set out in the first chapter, includes enhancing the problem-solving, coping, and development capacities of people; linking people with systems that provide them with resources, services, and opportunities; and promoting the effective and humane operation of the systems that provide people with resources and services. Each has relevance to particular aspects of policy as used in practice. Focusing on the enhancement of people's capacities includes policies that do the following:

☐ Recognize and support cultural and lifestyle differences
☐ Promote natural helping and support networks
☐ Provide support to persons who find themselves in transitional situations
☐ Teach or inform others about new information and skills
☐ Further people's involvement in decision-making and developmental opportunities
☐ Encourage self-help activities

Policies that oppose such enhancement should also be of concern, since they make it more difficult for social workers to help people attain their life goals.

Policies covering a system's available resources, services, and opportunities have received much more attention than those concerned with the enhancement of people. This second area involves many of the policies of the social welfare institution. However, policy also governs opportunities and access to resources, and this must also be a concern of social workers in each of the eight resource systems. Services that are inaccessible, or that promote dependency rather than enable growth and decision-making, are not fully supportive of the purposes of social work. Therefore, social workers need to understand policies in the third area of professional purpose which affect access to and guide procedures for obtaining information about a system's operation; describe an agency's or organization's procedures, communication channels, professional roles, and operating rules; and determine fund raising and expenditures. Being concerned with what services are available as well as how they are made available to people flows from the second and third part of the threefold professional purpose mentioned above.

Many would define policy as those abstract guidelines made at the highest level of society and would dismiss other policy as being insignificant. Such abstractions are the policy concerns of scholars. For the practitioner, policies of more immediate concern cover a wider range and deal with policy or procedures that implement policy made at the highest level of society. For line workers, the implementation role is critical to practice as is the use of policy made in smaller units of society. With the broadening perspective of professional purposes in mind, an examination of the eight resource systems provides the range of places in which policies of interest must be sought out and understood by the worker. These resource systems are those that the line worker should routinely draw upon in meeting client need. Some systems may lack specific policies dealing with one of the three parts of professional purpose. In others, policies of one type may be less clearly developed than those of other types. For some systems, policies have been worked out and analyzed in great detail. For others, however, the place of policy *per se* has not been conceptualized as an important part of their operation. Using professional purpose and the resource systems as the basis of a policy definition helps redirect the nature of policy concerns from those of scholars to those of workers.

FOR FURTHER STUDY

1. List synonyms for the word "policy." Would rules, guidelines, frameworks, or overview be on your list? Why? Why not? Support your choices.
2. Compare the definitions of social policy and social welfare policy with policy definitions of the eight resource systems. How are they similar or dissimilar? How would these various definitions fit together?
3. First define and then provide illustrations of policies from your practice setting that would most likely be associated with each purpose of social work. Which was least and which most difficult for you to locate in your setting?

GLOSSARY

Values Our ideals about what we think the world should be like and those things upon which we place worth or that are desirable to us.

Knowledge Our understanding of the world as it is, derived from scientific investigations.

Experience   Our exchanges and interactions with people and social groupings and social institutions.

The policy definitional boundaries game   Scholarly efforts to put boundaries around the realms of public policy, social policy, and social welfare policy and to demonstrate how these policy realms are interrelated.

Institution of social welfare   In defining policy for social workers, this idea limits attention to policies of the agencies and programs in the institution of social welfare, the social institution with a mutual support function.

Policies of concern to social workers   Such policies are found in guidelines made to allocate resources of the eight resource systems that encompass a social worker's practice arena. They are the policies in these systems that would enhance people's coping and problem-solving abilities, would provide resources, or direct a system's functioning in a more humane or effective manner.

BIBLIOGRAPHY

Boulding, Kenneth. The boundaries between social policy and economic policy. *Social Work*, *12*(1):3–9, 1967.

Council on Social Work Education. *Curriculum Policy Statement*. (Draft) New York, 1981.

Council on Social Work Education. *Standards for the Accreditation of Baccalaureate Degree Programs in Social Work*. Effective July 1, 1974, and July 1, 1982. New York.

Dempsey, John J. *The Family and Public Policy: The Issue of the 1980s*. Baltimore: Paul H. Brooks Publishing Co., 1981.

Federico, Ronald C. *The Social Welfare Institution: An Introduction*. 3rd ed. Lexington, Mass.: D. C. Heath, 1980.

Gil, David. *Unravelling Social Policy*. Revised and enlarged edition. Cambridge, Mass.: Schenkman, 1976.

Hirschhorn, Larry. Social policy and the life cycle. *Social Service Review, 51*(3): 434, 1977.

Huttman, Elizabeth. *Introduction to Social Policy*. New York: McGraw-Hill, 1981.

Kahn, Alfred J. *Social Policy and Social Services*. New York: Random House, 1973.

Kammerman, Sheila and Alfred J. Kahn. *Social Services in the United States*. Philadelphia: Temple University Press, 1976.

Levy, Charles S. The value base of social work. *Journal of Education for Social Work, 9*(1):34–42, 1973.

Mechanic, David. *Mental Health and Social Policy*. Englewood Cliffs, NJ: Prentice-Hall, 1969.

Prigmore, Charles S. and Charles R. Atherton. *Social Welfare Policy: Analysis and Formulation*. Lexington, Mass.: D. C. Heath, 1979.

Rein, Martin. Equality and social policy. *Social Service Review, 51*(4):565–587, 1977.

Rein, Martin. *Social Policy: Issues of Choice and Change*. New York: Random House, 1970.

Romanyshyn, John. *Social Welfare: Charity to Justice*. New York: Random House, 1971.

Titmuss, Richard. *Social Policy: An Introduction*. Edited by Brian Abel-Smith and Kay Titmuss. New York: Pantheon, 1974.

CHAPTER THREE

Policies of Concern to Social Workers

"The social worker should support the formulation, development, enactment and implementation of social policies of concern to the profession."
—NASW *Code of Ethics*

OVERVIEW

The last chapter introduced a definition of policies of concern to social workers. This chapter will expand upon that discussion by describing the relationship among the resource systems, defining each resource system and the general role of policy in it, and illustrating policies of concern for work with a particular clientele. This chapter's discussion completes understanding how to define and identify policies of concern to social workers. Such an understanding is required prior to identifying policy formulation processes that are related to social work practice.

OBJECTIVES

- [ ] List five types of policy and briefly define each.
- [ ] For one type of policy define the nature of the resources it includes and state examples of policies that allocate its resources.
- [ ] Comment on one way in which the five types of policy are interrelated.

RESOURCES, ACCORDING TO BAER (1979, 1981), facilitate interactions between people and social institutions. They support people who need help in utilizing societal institutions. They include the family, religion, politics, the economy and market, or even social welfare. Resources that are basic to human life, those that help people develop problem-solving skills, and those that enhance human dignity are but a few of many types of resources to meet human need. Social workers are specialized helpers who identify resources and link people to them, as well as monitor and modify the procedures for allocating resources. *Resources*, then, are *the many kinds of assets or other strengths that are or should be available to people to help them negotiate their social environment.*

Baer identifies the following as systems of resources:

- ☐ the social worker
- ☐ colleagues and other helping professionals
- ☐ the client system
- ☐ the profession of social work
- ☐ the organization or agency setting
- ☐ the local community
- ☐ society at large
- ☐ the social welfare institution

Our discussion will begin with systems focusing on individual characteristics as the basis of that system's resources and policies, and proceed to an examination of larger units. In grouping the eight systems according to size and the nature of policy formulation process, five clusters emerge:

1. personal policies
2. policies of small groups
3. organizational policies

4. social policies
5. policies of the institution of social welfare

(see Table 2 for the distribution of the resource systems within these clusters).

Systems, system theories, or systems perspective are widely used in social work literature. A frequently encountered definition of system includes parts, boundaries, exchange, interdependence, feedback, change, or connections. Baer uses the word resource system in a somewhat different fashion. She refers to categories of resources that are similar in nature and cluster around an identifiable person, group, organization, community, or institution which the social worker would routinely contact to meet client need. In this book, resource system and resource category will be used interchangeably.

Another departure by Baer from the conventional usage of the concept of systems is in labeling some of the eight categories as a system when they could as readily be considered a subsystem of one of the other eight resource systems. Though Baer includes society and the institution of social welfare as resource systems, she breaks the social welfare system into some of its component subsystems and includes these as well. These include social workers, their colleagues, clients, and practice agencies on her list of critical resource systems. Outside the social welfare system, but usually considered as related to it, are other "systems"—society at large and the local community. The profession of social work may be seen as a subsystem either of society or of social welfare.

Baer's approach in sorting out these subsystems as entities unto themselves helps focus attention on the details of their policies and policy formu-

---

TABLE 2

Types of Policies Grouped According to Size of Resource System and Nature of Policy Formulation Process

---

  I. Personal Policies
        social worker
        colleagues
        (individual) client systems
 II. Policies of Small Groups
        (family or small formed groups as) client systems
        (small formed groups as part of a) local community
III. Organizational Policies
        professional associations
        social service agencies
 IV. Social Policies
        (government of) local community
        society at large
  V. Policies of the Institution of Social Welfare

---

lation processes. It calls for a different point of departure in defining the social welfare institution. She would grant a status to some of its constituent elements that makes them independent of and somewhat equal to social welfare itself. By breaking down the larger system into its major social work-related parts, and in identifying policy within the smaller units, Baer's approach becomes helpful in managing the scope, specificity, and complexity of the entire range of policies of concern to social workers.

This text proposes that individuals, whether they are social workers, their colleagues, or their clients, possess policy that directs their actions and affects the utilization of resources in the systems of which they are a part or with which they work. As was noted in the preceding chapter, an individual's policy results from the interaction among that person's values, experiences, and knowledge, and that policy is part of the individual's guide to deciding and acting. However, it is usually thought that knowledge is less used than values and personal experiences in the formulation of personal policies. Keep in mind that values and personal policies, as defined in this text, are very close in meaning.

On the other hand, for decision makers in agencies and institutions, the role of values and knowledge in setting policy is frequently discussed in the social work literature. In other words, it is commonly believed that individuals in agency settings use values and knowledge to set policies for agencies, but that they are less likely to set personal policy this way. This book does not agree with this dichotomy, however. What is being suggested here is that a similar, somewhat less formal process is employed by individuals to set their own personal policy. This personal policy in turn affects resource allocation in systems for which an individual and the individual's professional or personal characteristics serve as the primary base of resources: the resource categories of social worker, colleague, and (individual) client systems.

The following discussion illustrates how the various resource systems develop policies to aid in allocating their own resources. Each system also proposes policy for other systems (to be discussed in Part Two). For now the focus is on policymaking regarding the use of a system's internally controlled resources. (Table 3 provides an overview of system resources, policies, and policy effects.)

PERSONAL POLICIES

The *social worker* is one primary resource available to the client. The resources that workers can provide are based in the professional knowledge, values, and skills they possess. Some of the available resources include support for self-determination by and social justice for all clients; problem solving skills, including communication, problem identification, involving and

TABLE 3
Illustrations of the Impact of Policy within the Eight Resource Systems

Resources, policy examples, and impact of policies	Personal Policies		Policies of Small Groups	Organizational Policies		Social Policy		Policies of the Institution of Social Welfare
	Social worker	Colleagues	(Individual) client systems	(Family or small formed groups as) client	Social service agency	Professional associations	(Government and funding of) local community	Society at large	
Illustrations of resources	Practice, knowledge, and skills	Characteristics of allied field	Personal characteristics	Support from and structure and processes of family or ethnic, social, cultural, or religious group	Specific agency program	Membership benefits	"Social" policy and the people, mechanisms, and ideas that aim to influence such policies		Welfare resources beyond those of worker's own agency
Examples of Resource System Policies	Only practice family therapy	Will not work with social workers	Will not leave the local community	Insistence that the entire family must provide aid to its members	Agency open nine to five on weekdays only	Admit BSW to membership	Economic policy to support military spending at a greatly increased level		AFDC Program
Effect of System Policy on Allocation of System Resources to Clients	Limits client access to fullest range of professional practice skills	Excludes client access to social workers	Limits access to needed resources	Promotes the ease with which family members seek help to resolve their concerns	Reduces program availability	Rethinking of MSW status and benefits	Reduces available resources and employment in other sectors of the economy, such as social services		Define eligibility and benefits for family with dependent child

planning with others, assessment, carrying out plans, and evaluating results; knowledge of resources, policies, and human behavior; access to other needed resources; and collaboration with members of related helping professional groups.

Ideally, the professional would make all these resources available to clients. The worker's personal policy regarding the allocation of these resources modifies their availability and usefulness to the client. The worker's individual limitations and interests, including level of competency, interact to affect the client's full receipt of resources from social workers. The significance of such worker policy and its impact on professional practice, either as a positive or a negative influence, has received scant attention in the literature. Its influence becomes more readily apparent when examples are considered (see Table 4 for a sample of personal policies).

Whether or not professional values support client involvement and self-determination, and regardless of the existence of funding for abortions, a worker with a personal policy stance that opposes abortion would not make available to clients all the resources they potentially could expect to receive. Also, because the social worker possesses the invaluable resource of access to other resource systems, worker policy not only directly affects the allocation of or linkage to available resources with clients in the worker's own system, but indirectly affects linkage with resources in other systems. Moreover, the purposes of social work activity extend beyond linkage and people enhancement tasks to those that promote system effectiveness. As a result, client

TABLE 4
Examples of Personal Policies

I. Personal policies of social workers:
   a. refusal to share access to certain agency or related system resources
   b. work a "fifty minute hour" in an agency
   c. not involve certain clients, such as unwed fathers, in their practice
   d. use certain theories of human behavior, not others, in their practice
   e. consistent selection of certain kinds of interventions, to the exclusion of others, in their practice
   f. job security above all other considerations, to the point that agency guidelines regarding practice and resources are never questioned
II. Personal policies of social work colleagues:
   a. medical doctors who refuse to refer clients to social workers
   b. administrators who establish new discharge planning units in hospitals to the exclusion of social workers
   c. psychiatrists who assign social workers only certain "therapy" duties
   d. health agency director who includes the BSW practitioner as an acceptable professional
III. Personal policies of individual client systems:
   a. to be free of parental influence
   b. refusal to leave the neighborhood in order to seek needed resources

---

linkage with other resource systems and worker change efforts in them would be affected. Worker policy could thereby either serve to block the availability of resources or lead to the expansion of available resources.

Other types of examples readily come to mind. A worker with a personal policy that would support a feminist orientation would be more likely to enhance the developmental and coping skills of women clients. Or, if the worker's policy supports her or his job security above all other concerns, he or she will probably never oppose agency policy or procedures. As a result, client concerns about the effective and humane operation of related resource systems would be unattended. On the other hand, a worker with a commitment to social change would be sensitive to issues in the functioning of self, colleagues, agency, and social welfare systems and would act to alter and improve the functioning of all these resource categories. A worker who uses only certain stock interventions or one without a policy of professional development would deny their clients the fullest range of social work practice knowledge and skills, one of the critical resources of workers. Indeed, of primary importance would be the establishment of a worker's personal policy that calls for lifelong self-development as a professional. This would assure clients access to the best available resources.

Similar in effect is the role of personal policy held by a social worker's *colleagues and other helping professionals.* Although overlooked by scholars, such policy directly affects the availability of resources to social work clients and is thereby of primary concern to the social work practitioner (see Table 4 for examples). The personal policy of these professionals affects the resources available in this resource system. As a system it offers resources to clients that are similar in nature to those found in the social worker resource category. These include the expertness, knowledge, and ethical standards of allied professionals such as physicians, nurses, rehabilitation workers, mental health workers, childcare personnel, ministers, social agency administrators, and lawyers.

For example, the policy of social work colleagues concerning access to and the status of related professionals is crucial to resource allocation. Physicians or other professionals who have a personal policy against including social workers in the health arena effectively block the access of social work clients to resources contained therein. The client of a social worker gains access to resources in a colleague's system through the intervention and connections of the social worker. The crucial role of the social worker in client access to resources, of course, is evident for many of the eight resource systems. When the social worker's access is blocked by the personal policy of another helping professional, social work clientele lose access and resources as well.

With colleagues, the impact of personal policy plays out in terms of teamwork. The primary resources available in the social worker and colleague resource systems are those to be derived from the professional personnel themselves and from their interaction. This interaction is carried out according to some conception of teamwork, whether of a formal or informal nature. The social worker serves both as a bridge between professionals on the team and also as the team's connection to the client's environment. The social worker has responsibility to provide other team members with information about clients for their professional uses. If the personal policy of a colleague excludes or diminishes social work access and expertness in the team, then clients receive considerably reduced professional resources.

In addition to nonsocial work colleagues, other social workers have personal policies that affect the availability of resources to one's own clients. The personal policy of other social workers in such areas as enabling clients to solve their own problems, making service delivery structures more accessible and effective, and cooperating with other social workers will affect not only their own clients, but also those of other social workers with whom they interact. Because service delivery structures operate as systems, one part—including individual people—affects other parts. For this reason, social workers need to analyze and influence the personal policies of colleagues within and outside of social work, a point to be further developed in later chapters.

For the *individual client* as a resource system, the role of personal policy has been even less explored than the personal policies of social workers and social work colleagues. This is so partly because many workers seldom consider the client system as a place to find resources. This shortcoming, when connected with the belief that individuals are not a source of policy, makes it quite unlikely that the policy of individual clients will be considered. When groups or organizations are client systems, policy has more frequently been taken into account. However, the line social worker usually deals with individual clients or with small groups: the family, small formed groups, or segments of community groups. Direct service professionals are less likely to work with organizations. As a result, line workers have not been encouraged to see the people and small groups with whom they work as having their own policy.

Regardless of the size of a client system, it should be considered as a resource and, as such, examined for its policy implications. If the client is an individual, personal policy would determine how the resources under their control are allocated, or how other actors in the client's resource system influence the available resources. An individual client's resources are the personal characteristics, external connections, and access to formal or informal help in their environment that enable clients to meet their need for help. The worker, in the assessment process, must focus on client resources, including coping skills, motivations, support systems, cultural and social factors, and family or friend relationships. For example, the parents of a newly married person may be a resource to help the client deal with marital and financial problems. The client, however, could have a personal policy dictating total independence, especially from parental interference. This personal policy effectively blocks the potential resource contribution from one part of the client's own resource system.

POLICIES OF SMALL GROUPS

Small groups differ somewhat from individuals in their policy setting mechanisms, but are similar in the kind of resources they control and in the implications for social work practice. Small groups as a *client system* may include families, specially formed groups such as therapy groups or self-help groups, and certain elements of the *local community*. If the local community is defined as a social, cultural, ethnic, religious, or neighborhood community, the interaction among its membership regarding policy formulation is somewhat akin to that which takes place in a family or other small group. Details of such a policy formulation process will be covered later. Suffice it to say at this point that participation, power, and authority, and a more formalized decision-making process, are significant issues in groups. In addition to the support and strengths of individual members of the group, the process or interaction of the group itself is a resource to the worker.

The worker would view the characteristics of group members, as for any individual, as a resource for use in meeting needs. Moreover, characteristics of the group itself are also important, such as group support, communication patterns, problem-solving approaches, and access to other resources. Group policy related to the allocation of such resources must also be considered when working with its membership. A worker, for example, might assess family resources and how the family allocates them, or the strengths of a youth "gang" and the rules it expects members to follow in using gang resources, or a kinship network and its ways of helping its members.

ORGANIZATIONAL POLICIES

The resources available to clients from within the resource system of the *profession of social work* are those available to the social worker as a member of the profession, especially as a member of professional associations or organizations. Professional organizations provide the professional with access to specialized knowledge and skills through publications, journals, workshops, meetings, and educational travel. Formal and informal contact with or access to other members of the profession is facilitated during meetings, through committee work, and in the form of professional directories. Professional organizations not only supply workers with a code of ethics, but also with legal and other support structures to assure its application in practice.

A variety of job-related services are provided to members, such as life, disability, and malpractice insurance. Most importantly, the professional organization promotes the interests of its members and of the entire profession in a variety of ways: finding, developing, and protecting professional employment; licensing and other standard-setting measures; lobbying and policy-influencing activities in other resource systems; and the setting of organizational policy designed to support the interests of social work clients.

The resources available to the client from this system are provided somewhat indirectly. They basically serve to protect, enhance, or make more effective the work of social work professionals themselves. Nonetheless, a worker's understanding and use of these resources is critical to the client's best interests. Utilization of and involvement in the policy-setting processes that guide the allocation of the organization's resources are likewise crucial to the line worker's clientele. Questions of how one professional organization functions and sets policy at its divisional, chapter, and national level and the impact of these activities on services available to people will be detailed later. These policies will determine how different categories of professionals (BSW or MSW or other) are supported and protected by the organization. The lobbying and licensing stances of professional associations similarly have impact on what resources, transmitted through which workers, are available to clients. The nature of policy-affecting opportunities for professional development and related programs also ultimately affects clients.

For example, if a division of the NASW, a major professional association, establishes a policy to use part of its annual resources to upgrade worker salaries, how does this policy translate as a resource to clients? If a national social work organization sets a policy to support the civil rights of lesbians and gay men, what impact might this policy have on the profession in terms of support from allied groups? If the policy at the chapter level of the NASW is to lobby against budget cuts rather than lobby in support of the so-called New Federalism, what does this allocation of organizational resources mean for clients?

Similar in policy-setting mechanisms, but dissimilar in the nature of available resources, is the *agency* where the social worker practices. Such agencies are similar to other organizations in their use of policy-setting mechanisms, both formal and informal. However, they are dissimilar in that they make a range of resources directly available to social work clients. What they offer are tangible resources for the client, such as services and programs to meet financial, emotional, health, or other needs. They also provide intangible resources to help clients, such as access to other agencies and other professionals, the stability and sanction of a position in an accepted community agency that is accorded the social worker employed there, and a structure for social workers to use in developing resources that the client may need.

Social workers need to be thoroughly familiar with how their agencies set policy to allocate resources directly to clients and how they establish guidelines and procedures that affect the worker's practice. The first deals with tangible resources, services, and opportunities made available to the client by the agency. The second addresses the way the agency manages worker access to clients and the kinds of practice strategies workers are expected to use. When regulations impede service delivery, the worker may have to develop strategies to try to make the agency's delivery of services more effective and humane.

SOCIAL POLICIES

This grouping of policies and related resource systems focuses on the public (or governmental) development of policy in legislative or other related bodies and in large-scale private welfare funding groups. Aspects of two resource systems—the local community and society-at-large—exemplify such policymaking. The *local community*, as noted above, refers to more than just local government and its legislative processes. Communities also have geographical, cultural, social, and religious boundaries. If the boundaries are formal geographical ones, such as a town or city or neighborhood, a formal or legal policymaking process may exist. If the community is a cultural, social, ethnic, or religious one, the policy-setting mechanism may be more informal. In this case, the nature of its policy is likely to be similar to that of the small group, such as a family or a specially formed group or organization.

The geographic boundaries of the local community often encompass another policymaking body, such as a United Way. This entity is responsible for allocating the private funding resources of the community. The local government deals with the area's policy for its economic and social resources and opportunities.

These governmental units of the local community share with *society-at-large* a legal, political, and economic policy-setting mechanism and related funding structure. Social policies, as discussed above, are the broad social guidelines that determine who qualifies for society's allocation of benefits. For the social worker, the basic resource in society-at-large, as in the local community, is the "social" policies they develop.

Resources utilized in society-at-large include elements of the legislative process: elected bodies, political parties, lobbying or interest groups; a range of professional, educational, and other informational groups that aim to influence social policy; and printed sources of information that influence policy. In the sense used here, social policies that deal broadly with the allocation of an extensive range of resources occur at several levels, ranging from the local community to the largest national grouping (see Table 5 for a comparison of public and private social policies). Resources are available to

TABLE 5
Public and Private Social Policies Produced at Different Levels

	Public	Private
National	Federal statutes court decisions	National organizational policies and rules
State or regional	regulations Statutes court decisions	State or regional agency policies and rules
Local	regulations Local ordinances regulations	Local community funding and service agency policies

workers, directly or indirectly, which enable them to influence societal policy. These range from members of the decision-making bodies to the factors used by others to understand and influence the decision makers.

Generally speaking, this is the policymaking realm of the so-called informed citizen, of political careerists, and of political activists. It is more removed from the direct service worker than policymaking in the other resource systems. Although societal policies are more distant from the line worker's world than are other of the resource systems, they nonetheless have an enormous impact on line workers and on their clients. Consider the federal legislature's cutting of the social service budget, or a local united funding group's allocation of money to a new service. Workers must constantly view the resources of these systems as a critical element in policy-related practice activities.

POLICIES OF THE SOCIAL WELFARE INSTITUTION

Volumes have been written about the general nature and the details of the policies and resources of the *social welfare* system. Preceding sections of this chapter, in dealing with a definition of policy, covered social welfare as a social institution and sketched out the resources it controls. The resources available to the line worker from social welfare are all of those beyond the worker's own professional expertness, agency, and collegial and professional network. The remaining resources of the social welfare system, of course, are quite extensive in scope. Some examples would include major medical programs such as Medicaid and Medicare, retirement benefits such as social security, unemployment funds, job training and development programs, and housing subsidies and programs.

The broad objective of social welfare is to provide resources and mutual support to help people with needs they have not met in other social institutions, such as the family or the economy. The range of services, programs, and opportunities provided by social welfare covers financial, social, health, or emotional needs. Programs, opportunities, and services may focus on individuals, groups, or communities. The structural characteristics and administrative sources of the programs in the welfare system are also resources. The policies of the social welfare institution emerge from statutes and court decisions as applied by private and public bureaucracies implementing regulations and programs.

It should not be overlooked that these various systems are interdependent. They form a network or overarching system of resources, with gaps and overlaps. They have been considered separately to facilitate understanding their details, and to help highlight differences in the nature of their policies and their policy-formulating processes. In the broadest sense, however, the social worker is part of a vast resource network including clients, local communities, as well as formal programs. It is composed of allied helping professionals, all of whom work in agency structures of some sort, most of whom relate to one another through professional associations, and for whom there exists the institution of public social and social welfare policymaking bodies (see Figure 3 for an overview of potential connections among the various resource systems and their policies; double arrows indicate interaction).

POLICIES CONCERNING SOCIAL WORK
WITH WOMEN: AN EXAMPLE

Examples will be drawn from each of the eight resource systems to illustrate policies a line worker might identify as potentially useful for practice with women. In an actual practice situation, the worker might be dealing with an individual woman or with a client group focused on women's issues. In such a case, the need or problem would point the search for policies of concern in one or more specific directions. For purposes of the following illustration, think about a worker who, upon discovering a lack of resources for abused women in the family service agency where the worker is employed, has decided to make an assessment of policies that control resources related to the needs of abused women.

Such a person would consider her or his own personal policies as a worker that relate to enhancing the problem-solving and coping capacities of abused women, that would deal with the kinds of resources such women need and should receive, and that govern their stance on making service delivery systems more effective and humane. The worker would also examine the personal client system itself, evaluate existing agency policy, and determine what policy their own professional association has in the area of spouse abuse.

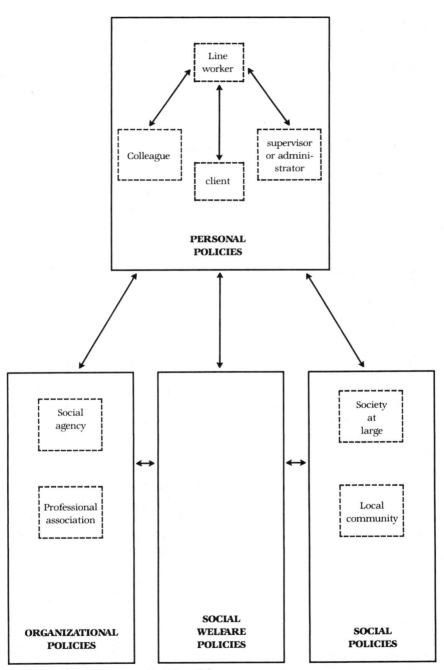

FIGURE 3. **Interaction among policies of the resource systems.**

Then she or he would analyze policy outside the agency that controls social welfare resources for abused women. In each of eight resource systems the worker would focus on identifying policies that deal with the rights of women to develop more fully and to participate more readily in all areas relating to their lives. He or she would also explore policies that allocate specific resources needed by women to meet their needs and that guide the structures that deliver needed resources to women.

Any such listing of policies will not exhaust the possibilities. To compile such a list suggests the need to know where to locate details of policies of concern. Sources of knowledge about policies of concern exist in a variety of forms. These knowledge sources, developed in chapter four, are often related to a system's policy output or policy product. In discussing the policy-formulation processes in the next section, these knowledge sources will be further identified and described. A worker's self-assessment, feedback from colleagues, and data collection with clients would give information on personal policies. Written policy priorities and program plans of professional associations, and material on policy and procedures and annual plans from an agency offer insight into existing organizational policy. Proposed and existing ordinances and legislation, funding plans, and interest-group written documents provide leads for social policy. For the social welfare institution, bureaucratic regulations, published program guides, and service directories yield policy detail.

One example of such a policy inventory by a social worker might look like the following, in which potential policies are identified in all resource systems (see Table 6 for an overview). First, the worker might have a policy that views individual development and change as stemming from client self-motivation. In the case of some abused women, such a personal worker policy would slow or cancel the allocation of worker resources until the client either actively sought help or showed initiative by leaving the abusive environment. Our hypothetical worker might have a policy that married women should rely on family resources. This personal policy, of course, conflicts with the needs of many abused women and would profoundly affect working with them. Couple those two personal policies with our imaginary worker's other policy orientation that supports the agency status quo. An abused woman coming to the supposed agency would undoubtedly fail to receive needed access to additional resources from the social worker.

The potential personal policies of colleagues would be those of all workers in health, mental health, spouse-abuse shelters, employment programs, public social services, and supportive services. Our worker might have discovered personal policies of workers in the area of employment opportunities that support the development of careers for single women outside the home, or those of an emergency shelter program director who gives higher priority to abused women than to runaway adolescents.

TABLE 6

Policies of Concern for Social Work with Women

Policy Range Derived from Professional Purposes	Eight Resource Systems							
	Social Worker	Colleagues	Client	Profession of Social Work	Agency	Local Community	Society at Large	Social Welfare Institution
Enhance People's Capacities	Policy that all clients, including abused women, need to demonstrate self-motivation toward change	Policies of colleagues that educate or train women for careers outside the home	Intent to join feminist support group	Policy to invite consumer participation in program design	Eligibility guidelines exclude abused women from family therapy program	Ordinance prohibiting discrimination in employment opportunities	Equal Rights Amendment	Job training, therapy and treatment programs, self-defense
Link People to Systems That Allocate or Provide Resources	Married women should rely on family-based resources	Policy of director of local emergency shelter program to place high priority on needs of abused women	Policy to seek only temporary short-term help and shelter from family	Policy priority to lobby for development of local spouse-abuse program			Economic policy to support job location for female-headed families	Federal cutback of shelter funding
Promote Effective and Humane Operation of Resource Systems	Status quo policy orientation regarding agency change	Members of local health alliance to establish spouse-abuse services		Policy priority to establish spouse-abuse education program for police force	Proposal before board to replace homemaker service with spouse-abuse education program	Local funding agency proposal to move funds from spouse-abuse program to daycare center	Model legislation to restructure criminal justice system to arrest and detain abusers	HHS Guidelines on spouse-abuse reporting and service programs

In investigating a professional association in which the worker is involved, the local branch may have a policy supporting consumer participation in program development. This provides the opportunity for abused women to develop and grow by planning with others. Similar policies in the professional association may include lobbying for spouse-abuse programs or improving service delivery by working with the local police in their handling of abuse complaints from women.

Social policies in the local community (as government) and of society-at-large might include one that broadens the developmental opportunities for women in employment, as proposed by the overarching Equal Rights Amendment. Policy on available resources could include a national economic policy to find and develop jobs (and child care) for newly independent women (and their children). Model ordinances or regulations aimed at modifying the treatment of abused women in the justice system could emerge from an investigation of policies of the social welfare institution (beyond those of the worker's agency). This is crucial for the worker in this example, because the worker's own agency lacked policy in this area. Social welfare resources could range from developmental opportunities such as training, treatment, and self-defense, through a policy to cut back on federal support for shelters and spouse-abuse services, to Department of Health and Human Services regulations on abuse reporting and program funding.

The preceding discussion lends direction to the remainder of the text. Application of the policy foci derived from professional purpose was illustrated within the eight resource categories. This helped make real the earlier assertion that the approach proposed in this text would provide a means to identify policies of concern to social workers that are based in their practice world. The approach also helps provide workers with knowledge about specific policies of concern.

Each of the resource systems has a means of formulating policy, its own method of deciding what course to pursue in allocating rights and resources, and its own way of structuring resource delivery in its own system as well as affecting the resource allocation of other systems. An understanding of these different policy-formulation processes and decision makers, coupled with knowledge about the policy-related needs of a given clientele, leads to a policy-practice merger by indicating points of intervention for line workers. Interventions must be based in knowledge about policies in all resource systems, knowledge of how decisions are made in each system, and knowledge about strategies to improve resource delivery. The remainder of the text will be devoted to the objective of making policy an activity, both in analysis (knowledge about) and in action (policy-related practice activities).

FOR FURTHER STUDY

1. Construct a blank "policies of concern" chart, modeled after the one on page 55. Select a client and identify as many relevant policies as possible. What do any blanks represent about our response to the needs of the client you selected?

2. Interview a social worker to determine the range of systems in which the worker believes that policy has an important effect on the worker's practice. Try to obtain specific examples of policies and how they are differentiated by the worker.

3. Examine a situation in your practice setting. To what extent did personal policies play a role? For that same practice situation can you pinpoint how social and social welfare policy affected its outcome? Which held greater weight—agency or personal policy? Why do you think this is so?

GLOSSARY

Personal policies   Policies set by individuals to allocate resources controlled by them as social workers, individual client systems, and social work colleagues. They may be called personal "resources" policies. Personal policy also covers policies made regarding resource allocations in other systems. These deal with personal policies for external resources.

Policies of small groups   These policies guide the resource allocation of families, small formed groups, or small groups of a local community. They may focus on the system's internal resources or those external to it.

Organizational policies   Policies found in professional associations and social service agencies that allocate resources they control or seek to control.

Social policies   Policies that allocate resources in society-at-large and in local communities. They are a major source of social work policy and are made by elected public officials and their staffs and by members of local groups charged with the collection and allocation of private welfare funds.

Policies of the institution of social welfare   Policies derived from federal, state, and local bureaucracies charged with implementing social welfare services. These policies have been the major area of scholarly research and study and contribute a large proportion of the resources used by social workers in their practice.

BIBLIOGRAPHY

Baer, Betty L. "A Conceptual Model for the Organization of Content for the Educational Preparation for the Entry Level Social Worker." Unpublished doctoral dissertation, University of Pittsburgh, 1979.

Baer, Betty L. "A Conceptualization of Generalist Practice." Westchester Social Work Education
Consortium, 1981.

Baer, Betty L., and Ronald C. Federico (eds.). *Educating the Baccalaureate Social Worker: A
Curriculum Development Resource Guide.* Cambridge, Mass.: Ballinger, 1979.

Dolgoff, Ralph, and Malvina Gordon. Educating for policy making at the direct and local levels.
Journal of Education for Social Work, 17(2):98–105, 1981.

Federico, Ronald C. *The Social Welfare Institution: An Introduction.* 3rd ed. Lexington, Mass.:
D. C. Heath, 1980.

PART TWO

HOW POLICIES OF CONCERN ARE CREATED

Policies of the eight resource systems were clustered into five types: personal policy, policies of small groups, organizational policies, social policy, and policies of the institution of social welfare. Each cluster is composed of resource systems that have similar procedures and people that guide their policymaking. The purpose of this section is to provide a basic understanding of the major processes used to formulate policy in these five clusters of policymaking. Systems ideas will be used to discuss each process. Each will be examined also for points of practitioner input into its policy formulation and feedback about the policies produced by the process. Understanding where input can be made is critical for moving into policy-related practice activities.

Major components in the creation of policy include:

☐ *Policy analysis and development by a range of concerned people, those who directly or indirectly contribute to the development of policy*
☐ *Policy-formulation processes used to produce policy*
☐ *Policy-implementation activities that modify policy or provide feedback about it*

The first component is often characterized as a process used by professional planners. Policy analysis and development, however, are based also in the personal policymaking and policy-related problem solving of all people. Understanding the connection between personal policymaking and professional problem solving can translate into policy analysis and developmental skills for all workers. The same basic process and its related skills are used by all persons, whether specialized experts or an individual client system, to analyze and develop policy. How individuals make policy and the role of values in that process will be introduced in the first two chapters of this section.

As will be developed in chapter four systems ideas can be used to explain common themes in the five policymaking processes. The bulk of the chapters in this section will use these ideas to explore the details of policy formulation. Chapter five will discuss two policy-formulation processes: personal policy-making and small group policymaking. Separate chapters will be devoted to formulating policy in organizations, setting social policy, and making policy in the institution of social welfare.

Implementation of policy is critical in policy creation and will be addressed throughout this section. An entire system may be charged with creating guidelines to implement policy formulated in another system, and individual workers might also be charged with interpreting and implementing these policies. In many systems, line worker implementation is a major means of feedback in these systems' policymaking.

In addition to covering knowledge of how policy is formulated, this section will introduce how and where practitioners might locate a more detailed knowledge of the policies made in each system. A knowledge of policy products and an understanding of formulation processes play a key part in analysis and action. The products are sources of knowledge and as such become ingredients in the analysis and assessment phases of practice. Knowing about and using policy-formulation processes help workers plan and carry out interventions that utilize, alter, or develop policy.

CHAPTER FOUR

Policy-Formulation Processes and the Makers of Policy

"The body is a system or constitution: so is a tree: so is every machine."
—**BISHOP JOSEPH BUTLER**
Sermons, 1729

"Justice is a machine that, when someone has once given it the starting push, rolls on of itself."
—**JOHN GALSWORTHY**
Justice, 1910

OVERVIEW

Keeping in mind the policy frame of reference, policies of concern, and the overview of policy in each of the resource systems, the discussion in this chapter uses systems ideas to understand the people and processes that give life to each system's policymaking. This chapter will introduce how knowledge about policy formulation will be covered in the remainder of the text, explore the role of values in policymaking, and examine sources where a more detailed knowledge of policies may be found.

OBJECTIVES

- ☐ Label and define the major parts of each system's policymaking.
- ☐ Comment on the importance of values as an input in policy formulation.
- ☐ Describe where to find detailed knowledge about three types of policies of concern.
- ☐ State the parts that make up the format to describe a policy product.

POLICYMAKING IN SYSTEMS

So far in the text, attention has been given to a resource system's policy product, to what has been called "policies of concern." Their importance, development, and identification have been covered already. In those discussions, it was concluded that policy is a guideline to provide direction for the decisions made or actions taken regarding needed client resources. They cover the allocation of a system's own resources, its internal policies. They also include policies each system makes to affect the determination of resource allocation in other systems.

One way to understand how policy is made is to use "system" terminology to analyze it. Hence, for each system the identification of policy-related inputs, the policymaking process along with the policymakers who use it, the outputs or policy sources that describe the system's product, and feedback mechanisms that modify the policy product are important pieces of knowledge for a social worker to learn.

The makers of policy, the policy-formulation process, and the policies or products of these procedures are obvious parts of a system's policymaking. These basic elements can be further understood by knowing about the input of values and knowledge used by policymakers and others in setting policy, about the point in time or the stage in the process when policy-related decisions are made, and about the sources where a worker might look for details or fuller descriptions of a system's policy.

The first of these basic elements, knowledge and values, are critical policy inputs. Values as an input into a system's policymaking have tremendous impact on the formulation process that develops a policy. The decision-making point is critical to the timing of interventions. Without a sound knowledge of where to find each system's sources or descriptions of its policy, a worker is ignorant of critical details for use in assessment and intervention (see Figure 4 for an overview).

POLICY-RELATED INPUT
Experience
Knowledge
Values
Assumptions
Existing policy
Policy from other systems

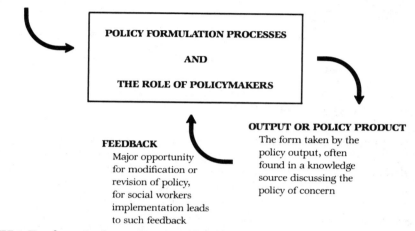

POLICY FORMULATION PROCESSES

AND

THE ROLE OF POLICYMAKERS

OUTPUT OR POLICY PRODUCT
The form taken by the
policy output, often
found in a knowledge
source discussing the
policy of concern

FEEDBACK
Major opportunity
for modification or
revision of policy,
for social workers
implementation leads
to such feedback

FIGURE 4. **Key elements of a resource system's policymaking.**

For example, when individuals make their personal policy they use values, knowledge, and experience as inputs. For groups, the input is similar. Both individuals and groups utilize problem solving to make their policy. For the individual social worker, as well as the National Association of Social Workers, the profession's Code of Ethics supplies the value base for such policy development. The individual professional and the professional association's membership also rely on their experiences in appropriate policymaking arenas. The NASW uses prioritizing and special groups to make its policy. For agencies, value positions are contained in mission statements, but also emerge from board or staff member positions as policy is made. Local communities use local laws, traditions, and history as value positions. In making policy, a local United Way also uses its experience with existing agencies. In legislative bodies, the setting of social policy uses party platforms and legislators' perspectives on social responsibility as some of its value input. In the development of social welfare regulations, the values and goals in social legislation, the regulatory agency's traditions and experiences, and the values and goals of the current administration serve as input (see Table 7 for additional examples of input, process, and output).

VALUES AS INPUT INTO A SYSTEM

Many scholarly discussions of policy emphasize the importance of the knowledge and values people use to develop policy and to influence the decisions of policymakers. Such discussions usually assign non-decision-making roles to line workers; for example, the collection and presentation of data to decision makers for use in policy development. Direct service workers are typically held to be the (unquestioning) implementors of policy.

The approach developed in this book challenges the belief that line workers are only gatherers and presenters of data, or are those who unwittingly enforce a system's policy. As data collectors, they too can apply the information they obtain to the policy-formulation process. This could be especially true if they possess a policy frame of reference and if they understand how to intervene within the processes and with the persons through which a system's policy is made. As makers, or as part of a system's input, their values also have tremendous impact on policy.

The first step in understanding how to intervene necessitates knowing who policymakers are and developing a general idea of the part played by the policymaker's values. Conventional definitions of social policy and of social welfare policy maintain that the role of policymaker belongs to legislators and lobbyists, judges, decision makers in funding bodies, grant writers and social welfare planners, and to social welfare bureaucrats and administrators. The focus on these two resource systems has precluded an examination of the role of policymakers in other systems.

In the approach developed in this text, additional policymakers drawn from other systems include:

☐ social workers
☐ social work-related professionals
☐ clients (individuals, families, and small formed groups)
☐ members and leaders of professional associations
☐ supervisors in agencies
☐ social work agency colleagues
☐ agency executives and staff members
☐ members of small community groups
☐ special-interest group members
☐ staff of social welfare-related research organizations

In their role as policymakers, these actors attempt to exercise control over decisions that lead to the development of policy within their own systems as well as within other resource systems. Values and knowledge contribute to the policy stances that are supported by the various actors and as such are

TABLE 7
Examples of Policy Inputs, Processes, and Output

| | Policy Formulation Clusters Derived from the Eight Resource Systems | | | | | | | |
| | Personal Policy | | Small Group Policy | Organizational Policy | | Social Policy | | |
System Elements	Social Worker Colleagues	Individual Client		Profession Social Work	Agency	Local Community	Society at Large	Social Welfare
Input: Values Used By Decision Makers And Others	NASW and other professional codes, cultural values	Cultural values	Group values	NASW Code of Ethics	Mission statements	Community standards and values	Orientation toward social responsibility	Conception of social justice
Elements of Policy Formulation: Policymakers	Professional self-assessments	Client and members of client system	Group members	Members, representatives—divisional, chapter, and national	Agency director, supervisor, board members	Local politicians, service planners	President, cabinet, legislators	Bureaucrats, administrators, planners

Policy Process	Problem solving	Problem solving	Group problem solving and decision making	Prioritizing and policy development process	Problem solving, social planning, board work	Political action, local planning process	Cabinet meetings, legislative hearings	Social welfare policy analysis and planning frameworks
Examples of Critical Policy-making Points	Stages where decisions are made	Stages where decisions are made	Member-leader styles and relationships in deciding	Priority balloting	Board meeting, informal decisions	Officials voting, citizen review panel decisions	Cabinet and committee voting	Hearings on regulations
Examples of Output as Source of Knowledge about Policy	Worker and colleague policy orientations from self assessments	Client policy derived from feedback and data collection	Group regulations about use of group resources	NASW policy priorities, lobbying, papers	Agency policy and procedure manuals, board reports, annual plans	Local ordinances, United Way plans and allocations	State and federal laws	Bureaucratic regulations, social service plans

critical inputs whether from a policymaker or from those who try to influence policy. For individual professionals, their value base should derive from the ethical code of their profession. They may possess what Falck (1981) refers to as an ideology of social welfare, believing in fairness, entitlement, and citizen obligation. In addition, strongly held social, cultural, or religious values contribute to their own policy positions as individuals and become part of their input to other systems' policymaking. For individual clients and for members of small formed groups, families, and for local community groups, cultural or religious values frequently are the major ones used in policymaking.

Those policymakers who contribute to organizational policy are significantly influenced by professional codes, personal values, and by the beliefs or objectives outlined in an organization's mission statement or program description. The personal and/or professional value base of a decision maker cannot be discounted within the context of organizational policymaking. At the larger level of community, society, or social welfare institution, the values of individuals are aggregated. Policymakers presumably use such group values when making their decisions. For example, legislators must be sensitive to the values of their constituencies. Nonetheless, the values of the individual legislator interact with the predominant values of the group the legislator represents. Also for decision makers at this level, some sense of social justice is represented in their decisions. Social justice defines for society who deserves to receive an allocation. Social justice identifies whom we value and why they deserve to be valued. Social justice is not a single value. There are competing ideas about what social justice should be. The input of ideas about social justice into a system clearly has impact on that system's policy for allocating the resources over which it has control. Examples of ideas or thoughts about social justice include a sense of fair treatment, equality, social welfare as residual or institutional, the "American way" or "dream," individualism vs. collectivism, the Puritan work ethic, entitlement, social Darwinism, and affirmative action.

The impact of values on a policy depends on those who provide input to a system about a given policy issue. In the case of an individual client, an adolescent pregnant unwed woman for example, the value input could be as divergent as a parent's opposition to teenage abortion and a social worker's support of client self-determination. For an agency board trying to decide about employee job rights, value input could range from ideas about union organizing to concepts extolling the worth of voluntary service. For the institution of social welfare, value input regarding food stamp regulations might range from the notion of pulling oneself up by one's bootstraps to the support of societal responsibility for those most oppressed and discriminated against.

CRITICAL STAGES IN POLICY-FORMULATION PROCESSES

Just as an overall understanding of policymaking is heightened by an appreciation of the impact that values have as an input to decision making, so will our sense of policy formulation be strengthened by insight into critical stages in the processes by which a system's decisions are made. An understanding of the input of knowledge and values into a given system points to strategies through which workers could influence how such knowledge and values affect policy. Potential points for implementing or carrying out policy-related interventions are indicated by those stages in a system's policy-formulation process when decisions are made.

As a system's process moves toward producing a policy, a series of decisions are often made, usually at a specific stage in the process. Intervention is possible at any of these points, although reshaping of the product is naturally more difficult as more and more decisions are made and as the product nears completion. Specific interventive activities associated with such points will be developed in the final section of the book. In the remaining chapters of this section, each of the policy-formulation categories will be examined in light of such stages or points for input (see Table 8 for lists of the stages in policy formulation for the five types of policy).

For example, the policy-formulation process that produces the personal policies of social workers, their colleagues, or their clients is problem solving. It is composed of several steps including information gathering, problem or policy identification and analysis, resource identification, and plan or policy development. Families, small formed groups, and local community groups use a somewhat similar problem-solving process in their development of policy. Each stage in this process involves deciding, and, as such, is open to the influence of other persons, including the social worker.

Organizational policymaking within professional associations or within the agency setting is carried out by individuals or group decision makers who follow established procedures. For example, the NASW's policy is developed through its policy-prioritizing process. From the point when the leadership publishes policy proposals, through membership discussion and decisions, to delegate decision making, there are clearly demarcated places for input and influence.

Like any organization, including the agency where the social worker is employed, the NASW also follows a modified social-planning process to set additional policy, especially policy that relates to organizational functioning. Social planning and the NASW's prioritizing process are variations of the problem-solving model. This problem-solving approach also incorporates the knowledge and values of the chief policy makers. An agency also sets policy

TABLE 8
System Stages in Policy Formulation

Problem Solving and Self-Assessment (for personal resources policy making)	Group Decision Making	Organizational Policy Planning	Legislative and Judicial Processes	Development of Bureaucratic Regulations
Data collection Identification of concern Development of statement of concern, issue, or problem Reflection on possible policies Selection of a policy to allocate resources Evaluation of policy as necessary	Problem solving in the context of a variety of modes of group interaction	Board member actions Issue identification Data collection by committee or staff Placement on agenda Board discussion and hearings Board vote or decision The NASW policy prioritizing process: Issue identification Leadership presentation of policies Staff reports Member decisions	Legislative Bill drafted Committee hearing and testimony Bill revisions Legislative debates Membership vote Judicial Challenge to law Case development Hearing set Hearing held Decision	Review of issue or law by staff Interpretation by legal counsel Publication of proposed regulation Hearings (public input) Final draft of regulations Regulation publication Implementation and evaluation

through the formal actions of its board of directors. In its deliberations, recognizable points of worker intervention include agenda setting, public debate and information collection by the board, formal votes, staff reports, and research.

For social policy the legislative process, with proposals for new statutes, hearings, debates, and votes, and the judicial process with hearings, witnesses, and judicial response, both consist of regular, ongoing steps through which the worker can intervene. Both of these processes are made accountable to the public due to the openness of their decision-making. This public forum is a useful one for social workers in their assessment and intervention.

The policy-formulation process of the social welfare institution, as carried out by bureaucrats and social welfare planners, is based in more or less consistently applied frameworks for policy analysis and planning. These frameworks guide problem identification, plan development, and plan implementation. In many ways, such frameworks are also special adaptations of the more general problem-solving approach. Within these approaches are points where public or line worker input is sought as well as other points for such input, even if it is not solicited.

Each step or decision-making point in any system provides a place where the worker could possibly have input. Such input, of course, is critical, because from it emerges the system's policy product.

SOURCES OF KNOWLEDGE ABOUT POLICY PRODUCTS

One basic factor in a social worker's policy activities is knowledge of each system's policies or products. Knowing sources where one may learn about policy will flesh out a worker's understanding of a given system's policies. Knowledge from these sources enriches the worker's assessment of the situation by providing significant analytical detail. The form taken by a system's policy output or the place where workers can find out about such products helps relate policy to practice activities. Meenaghan and Washington (1980) refer to such outputs and imply that the sort of policy a system produces is of little value if a worker does not know where to locate an adequate description of it. Such sources of knowledge about policies were briefly introduced

TABLE 9
Sources of Knowledge about Policies Developed in a System

Policy	Knowledge Sources about the Policy of Concern or the Form Taken by a System's Policy Output
Personal Policy	Self-assessments Personal codes
Small Group Policy	Family rules Small group rules Community charters Interest group position papers
Organizational Policy	Board decisions Manuals of policy and procedures Annual plans Professional priorities Program guides
Social Policy	Laws Statutes Court decisions Local ordinances
Social Welfare Policy	Bureaucratic regulations Planning reports

along with the illustration of policies of concern with women (see Table 9 for examples of sources of knowledge).

The personal policies of social workers, their colleagues, and of individual clients usually are not written down for public examination. The source of knowledge about personal policy may only be found in a worker's self-examination or from similar reflection about colleagues. The written sources, if any, are the worker's own recording of such self-assessments. Worker policy on resource allocations in other systems, of course, may be available in the more public, formal stances they take.

The public sources for locating and studying organizational policy are twofold: the official policy stances of the NASW, and the policies and procedures produced by an agency for its staff to follow. The NASW records its policy stances in newsletters, professional journals, lists of proposed policy priorities, lobbying papers, and published statements of support for political candidates or social issues. Most agencies produce and distribute manuals covering procedures and policies. These manuals contain guidelines on agency operation and worker roles, that is, on policies governing agency functioning. They often include charts or tables listing decision makers. Minutes of board meetings, annual reports, executive directives, supervisory statements, program guides, and workers' organization material all provide insight into official policy. Case records, interaction at staffings, and informal directives give insight into agency policy as well as an understanding of the interaction of agency and personal policies.

As is readily apparent when comparing the sources of knowledge about organizational policy with those of personal policy, organizational policy is more codified, more formal. The more formal, recorded sources of organizational policy reflect the process by which it is developed. Social policy is even more codified, more likely to be recorded or published. Major sources of local community or society-at-large policy are published judicial decisions, statutes and legislative records, local ordinances, and funding-agency guidelines. Similarly, the policies of the institution of social welfare are published in bureaucratic regulations. Laws, decisions, and regulations are not only readily available sources of policy, but they are also quite extensive in volume.

Regardless of the formality of its recording, a source or place to learn about details of a system's policies is important to the worker. The above should provide some introduction to the types of sources of policy knowledge available in each system. The worker must be creative in identifying and using these sources and others as guides to learning about a particular system's policies.

FORMAT OF A POLICY PRODUCT

In examining the description of a policy of concern, a common format emerges. A policy usually states *who the recipient* will be. This might be stated in terms of potential beneficiary, client, or recipient. Also included in the policy will be a description of *what resource* the recipient is entitled to receive. The resource, of course, is what is being allocated by that system and is something that would be of value to the recipient. Finally, *how the resource will be delivered* to the recipient will also be spelled out.

Depending on the resource system that makes the allocative policy, one or more aspects of the format sre stressed. Social policy, for example, usually outlines the three aspects of allocation in broad terms. Social policy is more precise about who gets what, often less detailed about how the recipient will be connected to the allocated resource. Other systems, such as social welfare or social agencies, are much more concerned about the third allocative area— how the resource will be delivered to the recipient—because these systems are charged with implementing policy.

The first area, that of the recipient, focuses on issues and descriptions of eligibility. The second encompasses all the types of resources we have discussed so far, including material things as well as services and opportunities. The area of resource delivery could involve arrangements that vary from a government check or voucher for material resource allocation to access to a professional for services or to a specific institution to take advantage of a special opportunity.

The above format takes on various appearances within different systems. A bureaucratic regulation or legislative bill may be quite clear and formal in appearance. An agency or organization's policy will be formally written also. The personal policy of a worker, colleague, or individual client system implicitly states the recipient and may or may not clarify how the potential benefit will be delivered. Internal policy of a system, that which deals with resources over which the system already has control, focuses on the third area, that of service delivery. Policies to implement resources granted from another system often spell out the third area in detail. Much of the effort made in one system to influence another focuses on increasing the beneficiaries or the resources they receive. This format will be one of the ideas used in chapter ten to develop a practitioner's framework for policy analysis and development.

IMPLEMENTING POLICY: SYSTEM AND WORKER FEEDBACK

In many instances the policy of concern to a social worker in a given system does not overlap with the policies of concern in another. The internal policy of one system might have little connection to that of another. Policies are linked, of course, as systems try to influence one another and as policy is modified as it moves from system to system. In other cases the development of policy in one system is affected by resource-allocation guidelines developed in another. This is clearly demonstrated if one analyzes the policy-related input of various systems on a given issue (see Table 10 for an overview of the relationship among system inputs and products). For example, a state law is

TABLE 10

Relationship among System Inputs and System Products

System	Policy-Related Input	Formulation Process	Policy Output
Society at Large	Societal values and policies	Legislation or judicial decision	Social policy
Social Welfare Institution	Social policy	Bureaucratic regulation (federal, state, or local) about implementing social policy	Social welfare policy
Agency	Social welfare policy	Agency policy guidelines about service delivery	Organizational policy
Social Worker	Organizational policy	Social worker policy about use of resources in implementing agency policy	Personal resources policy

enacted to fund methadone drug-treatment programs to reduce addiction in neighborhoods. This new social policy falls under the auspices of a state regulatory agency. That agency not only designates the neighborhoods, but also sets up one implementation guideline prohibiting the congregation of addicts in or near any single treatment facility in a targeted neighborhood. A large metropolitan agency that has been funded to set up a methadone program decides on a service-delivery scheme of locating treatment facilities on different floors of several neighborhood buildings. This approach would permit the reduction of addiction and avoid addict congregation. The social workers and their colleagues in the metropolitan agency, however, decide that the treatment program is too fragmented for the delivery of effective services and instigate a work slowdown.

The above example of the interaction among policies and the feedback from system to system explains what many see as differences between a social policy's initial purpose and some of its outcomes for clients. The original intention of the policy was to reduce drug addiction in given neighborhoods. Resources were so allocated. The intention of the personal policy of the workers was to reduce service-delivery fragmentation as a response to the implementing policy of the social welfare agency. The outcome at the level of worker implementation was not the same as that intended by either of the other systems.

This example, in pointing up the interrelatedness of policy among systems, also highlights the potential significance of personal policy and worker implementation as a feedback mechanism. A focus on social or social welfare policy to the exclusion of the effect of personal policy overlooks key policy elements. Policy analysts, social workers, professional colleagues, and client systems may overlook personal worker policy and fail to deal with its impact on overall policy. The net result for all would be ineffective efforts to influence the course of policy. The example also illustrates how worker implementation constitutes feedback, or modification of a policy.

POLICYMAKERS, POLICY-FORMULATION PROCESSES, AND POLICIES OF CONCERN

As was noted earlier makers of policy play an important part in policy creation through their decision-making activities, through greater control of a given system's policy-formulation process, and through the input of their knowledge and values. We also noted that the policy-formulation process of each system can be conceived of as a series of stages, each of which involves decision making or other points where the process can be shaped or influenced through the worker's input. Moreover, we identified another major part of policy formulation as the product or output of each system. This output constitutes the policies of concern for social workers. These policies are the ones we defined and identified in chapters two and three.

For the practitioner, each of these parts has a significance for and utility in practice (Figure 5). Viewed as a system, inputs to the policy-formulation process are the values and knowledge bases of policymakers and of those who influence policymaking. These serve as the basis for the process that policymakers use to develop or produce a policy. The policy product is recorded in or made available to others by means of some more or less public source of knowledge about the details of the policy. Such sources, of course, usually are the very policy product itself—a published regulation, a legislative bill, an agency manual, or an organization's listing of policy priorities. Finally, for line practitioners, their role as implementors is an important part of feedback.

Knowledge and use in practice of each of these parts of a system's policymaking process lead to the integration of policy and practice through assessment and intervention. Knowing the values and knowledge base of policymakers is useful for developing strategies and planning interventions regarding policy aspects of a specific practice situation. Knowledge of general policy-formulation processes and the stages they follow enables the worker

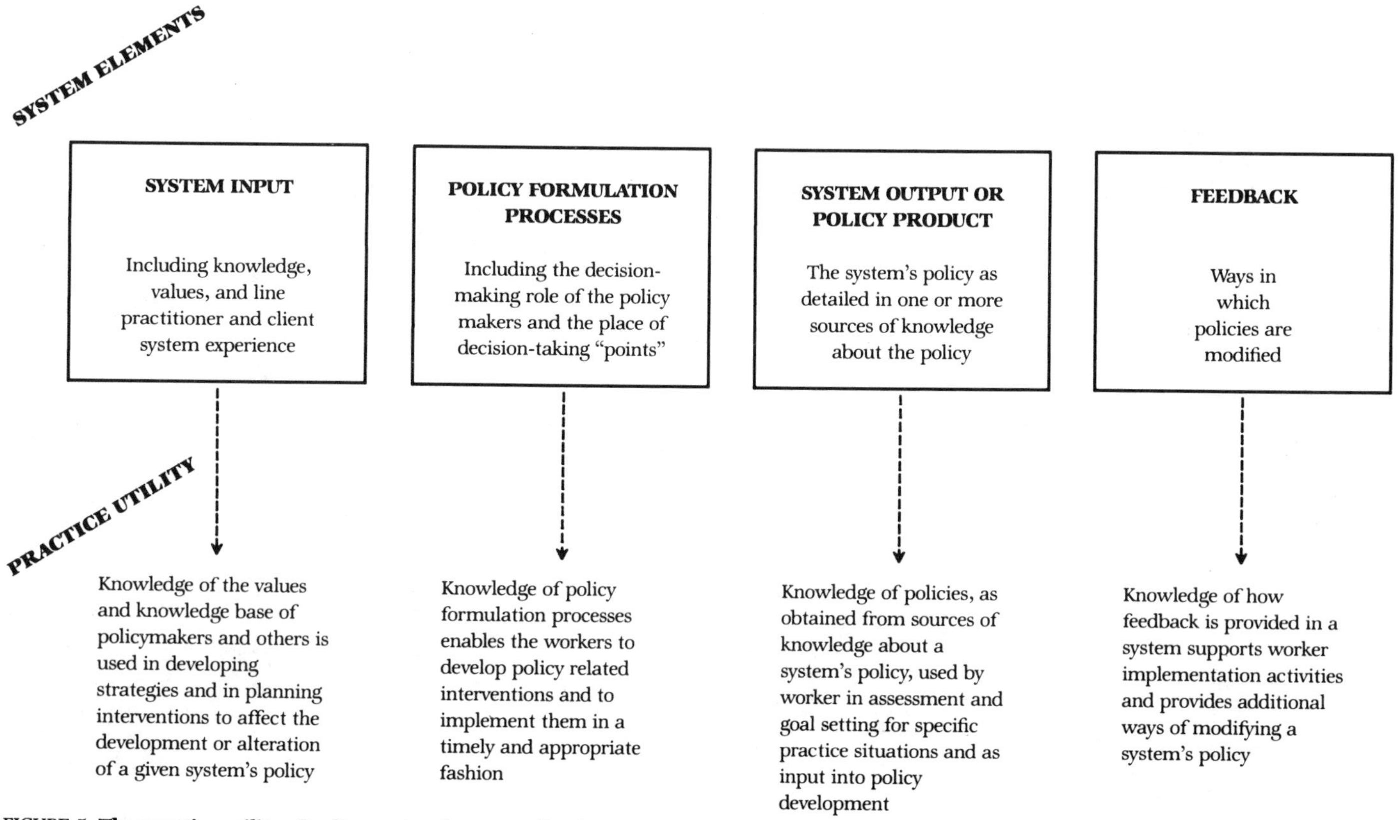

FIGURE 5. **The practice utility of policy system inputs, policy-formulation processes, and sources of knowledge about policies.**

SYSTEM ELEMENTS

PRACTICE UTILITY

SYSTEM INPUT

Including knowledge, values, and line practitioner and client system experience

Knowledge of the values and knowledge base of policymakers and others is used in developing strategies and in planning interventions in the development or alteration of a given system's policy

POLICY FORMULATION PROCESSES

Including the decision-making role of the policy makers and the place of decision-taking "points"

Knowledge of policy formulation processes enables the workers to develop policy related interventions and to implement them in a timely and appropriate fashion

SYSTEM OUTPUT OR POLICY PRODUCT

The system's policy as detailed in one or more sources of knowledge about the policy

Knowledge of policies, as obtained from sources of knowledge about a system's policy, used by worker in assessment and goal setting for specific practice situations and as input into policy development

FEEDBACK

Ways in which policies are modified

Knowledge of how feedback is provided in a system supports worker implementation activities and provides additional ways of modifying a system's policy

TABLE 11

Overall Nature of Worker Policy-Related Practice Activities

	Personal and Small Group Policies	Organizational Policies		Social Policy		Policies of the Institution of Social Welfare
		Professional Associations	Agency	Local Community	Society at Large	
Policy Formulation Process	Problem solving	Policy prioritizing	Agency planning, board decisions	Political action, local funding agency planning	Legislative process, judicial interpretations and decisions, executive actions	Social welfare policy analysis and planning frameworks
Overall Nature of Policy-Related Practice Activities	Self-assessment, evaluation of colleague's practice, assessment of client situation, persuasion and influencing, teamwork	Participation as member in professional organization, committee work, holding elective office	Skills in organizational "shaping" and policy implementation	Political participation	Legislative lobbying, committee testimony, judicial testimony, political involvement, coalition building	Social planning and policy analysis skills, monitoring

77

to develop policy-related interventions and to implement these in a timely and appropriate fashion.

Generally speaking, a worker needs self-assessment and evaluative and influencing skills to intervene in the personal policy arena. Skills in organizational analysis and shaping and in professional participation lead to policy competency in organizational policies. Political participation, legislative lobbying, political advocacy, and legislative testimony are abilities needed to be effective in dealing with social policymaking. For social welfare policy, social-planning and policy-analysis skills are useful to the worker (see Table 11 for an overview of policy related activities). Knowledge of the products, the policies of concern to the social worker, is used by the worker in assessment and in goal setting. Such knowledge also serves the worker as input into the policy-formulation process of a given system.

The third area in the creation of policy, implementation, is a major component of feedback—how policy is modified. Policy that comes from analysis and development by individuals, either for use as a system input or as a personal policy, and from the policy-formulation process of each system, can be critically modified or adjusted during implementation. Such activities, as they guide a system's policy formulation or a worker's policy-related practice activities, will be detailed in the upcoming chapters.

FOR FURTHER STUDY

1. Consider a personal policy you have made about allocating a resource over which you have direct control. What part did your values, beliefs, ideologies, or assumptions play in your policymaking?
2. Identify a controversial area of human rights, such as those of lesbians and gay men, or a controversial social issue, such as abortion. What social policy would you favor in these areas, and what values and knowledge did you use in reaching this policy position? Use the policy format to organize your policy statement.
3. Contact an appropriate member of the staff of a social service agency or social welfare bureaucracy to locate sources of knowledge about policy output. What form does it take, and how available, understandable, and usable is it?

GLOSSARY

Policy-related input   Using system terminology, input would be the ideas and material used in each system's policy-formulation process to produce its policy. Knowledge, values, assumptions, experiences, ideologies, and the output of another system are all examples of such input.

Policy-formulation process   The procedures or mechanisms used in a given resource system to develop policies regarding the acquisition or allocation of its resources and the stances it takes to influence another system's policies. These range from problem solving to board meetings and legislative and regulatory procedures.

Policy output or product   The actual policy produced by a given system's policy-formulation process. These may be self-assessments, manuals, laws, executive orders, or bureaucratic regulations.

Policy knowledge sources   Sources of knowledge about policies that are sometimes contained in whatever form a system's policy output takes. They range from personal self-assessments through highly formal laws and bureaucratic regulations. Knowledge sources about policy are critical in developing understanding of policies in all systems and in obtaining a knowledge base of policies of concern for utilization in problem identification and assessment. Use of these sources enables workers to keep abreast of policymaking in all systems.

Format of policy statements   Policies designate who will be a beneficiary, indicate what the resource will be for those who are eligible, and propose how the resource will be delivered to or connected with the beneficiary. In their policy products, systems emphasize different parts of this format.

Problem solving   The policy-formulation process used in developing an individual's personal policy. In modified form, small groups also use problem solving to develop policy.

NASW prioritizing   One policy-formulation process used by the National Association of Social Workers to produce policy.

Social planning   Used in organizational and social welfare-policy formulation. Planning represents an adaptation and formalization of the problem-solving process.

Legislative, judicial, and executive budgeting approaches   The processes most often used in setting social policy.

BIBLIOGRAPHY

Burns, Eveline M. *Social Security and Public Policy.* New York: McGraw-Hill, 1956.

Falck, Hans S. Now what? *Journal of Education for Social Work,* 17(1):3–4, 1981.

Gilbert, Neil and Harry Specht. *Dimensions of Social Welfare Policy.* Englewood Cliffs, N.J.: Prentice-Hall, 1974.

Levy, Charles S. *Social Work Ethics.* New York: Human Service Press, 1976.

Meenaghan, Thomas M. and Robert O. Washington. *Social Policy and Social Welfare.* New York: The Free Press, 1980.

Prigmore, Charles S. and Charles R. Atherton. *Social Welfare Policy: Analysis and Formulation.* Lexington, Mass.: D. C. Heath, 1979.

Rein, Martin. *Social Policy.* New York: Random House, 1970.

Romanyshyn, John. *Social Welfare: Charity to Justice.* New York: Random House, 1971.

Ryan, William. *Equality.* New York: Pantheon, 1982.

CHAPTER FIVE

Personal Policymaking and Small Group Policymaking

"I have a dream that one day this nation will rise up and live out the true meaning of its creed: 'We hold these truths to be self-evident; that all . . . are created equal.' "

—DR. MARTIN LUTHER KING, JR.
"I Have a Dream." Speech delivered during the March on Washington, August 28, 1963.

"It is expected that all those accepted as members of the committee would contribute their time [and that each] assessor accept three new cases every two months."

—Procedures and Standards of the Assessors' Committee of S.A.G.E. (A volunteer organization to provide services for the elderly lesbian and gay population in New York City)

OVERVIEW

This chapter will explore two policy formulation processes: how individuals and small groups use variations of the problem-solving approach to analyze and develop their policies. Keep in mind, however, that the two are quite different in their application of problem-solving and should be thought of as separate policy formulation processes. The approach used by each in setting internal and external policy will be detailed. Individual problem-solving approaches and decision-making styles will be presented. Group problem-solving will also be examined, including the part leaders, members, and group norms play in group policymaking. Conclusions will be offered about how knowledge of these two processes can be utilized in assessment and intervention planning. The chapter will discuss how knowledge of individual and group policymaking helps the practitioner understand policymaking in other systems. How the processes used by individuals and small groups in their policymaking relate to the policy analysis and development skills of professionals will also be explored.

OBJECTIVES

- ☐ Use goal directed behavior and the steps in problem-solving to define how individuals make personal policy.
- ☐ Describe three decision-making styles of individuals.
- ☐ Comment on differences among the personal policymaking of individual social workers, their colleagues, and individual client systems.
- ☐ Use group norms, goal setting, and membership roles to define how groups make policy.
- ☐ Describe three types of group decision making and their significance for policy interventions.
- ☐ Discuss how knowledge of individual and group policymaking contributes to social work practice in the policy arena.

WE HAVE EXPLORED THE IDEA that for social workers policy formulation deals with the people, processes, and products that establish a system's guidelines for allocating the resources people need in negotiating their environments. Such policies are made through several processes in the eight resource systems used by social workers in their practice. Policy is made in all resource systems, including those of social workers, their colleagues, and individual and groups of clients.

Policy is made to allocate the resources controlled within each system. Moreover, each system either makes policy in relation to, or attempts to affect the resource-allocation policies of other systems. This is so not only because some systems grant resources to each other, but because systems do not always grant those resources needed or expected from them by another system. This latter development leads to a situation in which the policy-makers of one system try to influence the policymaking process of another. Each system's policy-formulation process involves both kinds of policymaking: those dealing with internal and external resources. Each system sets policy to allocate its own resources, as well as proposing policies for adoption in other systems.

PROBLEM-SOLVING PROCESSES AND PERSONAL POLICYMAKING

Individuals, whether they are social workers, other professionals, or individual clients, set policy to allocate the resources over which they have direct control, to which they have access, or which they would like to make part of their system of resources. How an individual makes policy grows out of how that person sets goals, solves problems, and makes decisions. Knowledge of the general steps used in problem solving and an understanding of the concept of goal-directed behavior help inform the line worker about how an individual makes personal policy.

In the last decade or so professional helpers and educators have (re)discovered the value of the notion of problem solving. Professionals employ it in their work, and social work authors utilize it in their conceptions of practice. For example, one professional purpose calls for enhancing the problem solving, coping, and developmental capacities of people. Educators stress helping people become problem solvers, with the ability to apply a systematic thought process and to utilize a formal body of knowledge in solving life's problems.

In Western civilizations, problem solving is valued and is related to rational frameworks to understand behavior. The so-called scientific methods of the Western world's academic disciplines, as well as the problem-solving approaches used in related helping professions, exemplify the application of this idea. Although such a scientific problem-solving approach is not uniformly valued, with some denying the utility of rational approaches in the resolution of issues or in understanding our world, it has nonetheless become a major part of the functioning of our basic institutions. It, of course, stems from and reflects the problem-solving or coping approaches of individual members of our society. The belief that human behavior in its social context is goal directed supports the notion that most people are rational in their problem resolution. Indeed, contemporary definitions of mental illness include an irrational approach to situations and excessive rigidity, in other words, with poorly developed problem-solving skills.

According to this definition of problem solving, many individuals appear not to be particularly rational in their behavior. Such appearances stem from too limited a definition of what constitutes problem solving. For many people, environmental factors frequently preclude applying and ordering the steps of problem solving as they are defined academically. The discovery that the coping behaviors of individuals is a legitimate way of dealing with concerns, and that it constitutes a meaningful problem-solving approach, coincides with the recent emphasis in social work on the value of human diversity. Diversity in group and individual behavior, derived from cultural, ethnic, biological, or societal factors, is reflected in subtle variations in how people reach decisions or solve their problems. The concept of human diversity suggests that the rich differences among people's behavior extend also to their mechanisms for problem resolution. To value human diversity and to look for strengths and resources in the behavioral differences among groups and individuals supports the conclusion that while a general framework for problem solving can be identified, individual approaches to problem solving differ. These differences do not necessarily mean that other persons are not employing a problem-solving approach in dealing with their world. It does mean, however, that the social worker's understanding of the formulation of personal policies must include an appreciation for differences in individual problem-solving and decision-making styles.

Goal-Directed Behavior

Berger and Federico (1982) summarize the assumptions and evidence in support of their viewpoint that human behavior is rational or logical in its underpinnings and that such purposive behavior leads humans to employ a systematic problem-solving approach in dealing with their environment. The authors focus their comments on the topics of motivation and meeting needs, goal setting, purposive behavior, and problem solving.

In identifying human behavior as purposive, they locate motivation in those factors that stimulate behavior, especially to meet biological and social needs. Needs, of course, vary greatly by individual, group, and social or cultural structure. As people strive to meet their needs, they set goals. The authors point out that purposive behavior derives from the goal setting people engage in around meeting their needs.

When needs meeting is blocked, adaptive or coping behavior develops. The former entails a restructuring of one's goals, to suit what is available in the environment for needs meeting. The latter is defined as the development of a plan, based in rationality and the necessity to be flexible, in a situation in which goal attainment has been frustrated.

How people determine their needs, how they set goals to attain their needs, and how they respond when goal attainment is blocked are all applications of the problem-solving process. Purposive behavior, as dictated by needs meeting and directed by problem solving, revolves around an individual's goals and that person's plans to reach them. Berger and Federico stress how important it is for social workers to place value on the idea that people behave in a purposive way. They conclude that most people use some type of problem-solving process, although people's use of such a process may be more informal, more limited in scope, and less systematic in application than their use of formal or scientific problem solving. The authors' conclusion that people use problem solving in setting goals to meet their needs points in the direction of how people develop personal policy.

The other side of needs meeting and the setting of goals to meet these needs occurs after people settle on the resources they need. They may have secured the resources they were seeking, they may simply realize they already possess the needed resources, or they may decide they must make do with what resources they have on hand. With the resources determined, additional goals or behavioral guidelines must be set to allocate and to use such resources in order to ensure an ongoing ability to meet their needs. This type of purposive behavior, an extension and modification of needs-related goal setting, is the application of problem-solving processes to the setting of personal resource-allocation policy. In other words, an additional way to understand goal-directed or purposive behavior is in relation to people's personal policies, the setting of goals and rules to guide resource allocation.

How the Problem-Solving Process Enables People to Achieve Their Goals

As summarized in chapter one, the formal steps in the helper's problem-solving process are discussed in the social work practice literature by such authors as Compton and Galaway (1975), Pincus and Minahan (1973), Siporin (1975), and Baer (1979) with worker-client interaction in mind. Some of the steps described by these authors require modification if they are to apply to the more informal approach to problem solving and to the different nature of its application in personal policymaking. They need to be modified in the direction of the issues, evidence, planning, and evaluation of personal-resource allocation. The steps listed in chapter one can be modified to include:

☐ Identifying and defining a resource-allocation issue, problem, or concern
☐ Collecting and analyzing evidence or data
☐ Thinking about policy goals and options
☐ Using knowledge, assumptions, and values to decide on a policy course
☐ Applying and testing the policy over time
☐ Evaluating the effects of the policy (see Figure 6 for an overview of the policymaking of social worker, colleague, and client).

The first step in problem solving covers the identification of a problem or concern. The issue could involve resources controlled by the worker or re-

POLICY-RELATED INPUT
Personal experience with issue
Knowledge base
Value or belief system or ideologies
Assumptions
Existing policy of the individual

PROBLEM SOLVING APPROACHES (AS MODIFIED BY HUMAN DIVERSITY VARIABLES):
Identification of concern
Data collection about concern
Identification of policy options
Selection of policy implementation strategies
Application of policy over time
Evaluation

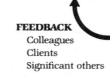

OUTPUT OR POLICY PRODUCT
Self-assessments
Policy stances

FEEDBACK
Colleagues
Clients
Significant others

FIGURE 6. **Personal policymaking of social worker, colleagues, and individual client systems.**

sources needed from other systems. In the first instance, the issue to be dealt with by the personal policy could arise from concerns or questions about how that person's existing resources or strengths will be allocated. These resources could be professional, as in the case of a social worker, or a professional colleague; or personal, as in the instance of an individual client. Such resources are characteristics or abilities over which the individual, more or less, has direct and personal control. The resource issue could also arise by identifying needed external resources; for the professional from aggregating cases, for the nonprofessional from seeing an external resource needed to meet a need.

One's personal or professional resources or strengths are usually considered to be givens, and it would seem that efforts about extending or (re)allocating them are infrequently given conscious consideration. Issues or concerns about personal resources are usually thought of as being less clearly delineated than other personal issues, but do arise out of problems or crises in the individual's life. Changes in one's resources do create an issue of concern. Similarly, issues about allocation arise when professional or personal resources are overextended, their usefulness is questioned by others, or a different or unexpected demand is made on them.

The identification of a personal policy issue is bounded somewhat by changes in or challenges to a person's resources. The collection of data or information about these personal resources is also restricted by the limited range of what an individual defines as resources and the mechanisms used for feedback and self-assessment. To the professional, data collection involves reflection on or research about professional skills and knowledge or access to needed additional resources. To the individual client, the gathering of evidence would cover thinking about her or his own strengths.

In both cases of personal policy, most evidence usually comes from personal experiences with resources, rather than from data collection done by others or from other sources of knowledge. Less attention is given to a reconceptualization of one's resources by reference to new knowledge. It is this greater emphasis on the collection of data by and about oneself that distinguishes personal-resource policymaking from the formal policymaking deliberations of other systems. By definition, it is also this focus on the introspective nature of the process that separates the steps an individual employs in selecting, implementing, and evaluating policy from the similar, but more interactional steps in a professional helper's problem-solving efforts.

In the problem-solving process for the individual social worker, thinking through a new plan or policy to reallocate or obtain resources, deciding on a policy course, and evaluating outcomes entail the application and analysis of newly collected data. Professionals are much more likely to use data beyond that supplied by personal experiences. This process also applies to an individual professional's policy stances about resources in other systems. On the other hand, in thinking about and deciding on a personal-resources policy or plan, the individual social worker might or might not seek out new information or involve others. Plans may be modeled after the resource-allocation policy of others, or they may simply reflect a modification of the individual's earlier efforts.

Similarly, for personal-resources allocation, implementation focuses less on involving others than on an individual professional's application of the policy over time. In selecting personal-policy stances for other systems, implementation involves others, especially colleagues and clients. In evaluating personal-resources policy, others are also less involved in its monitoring. The individual must develop self-assessment mechanisms to monitor and test the effectiveness of personal-resources policy after it has been implemented. Such actions are not undertaken in any systematic fashion. The need to develop new policy and to reflect on it lead to whatever evaluation is undertaken. Feedback from others is important.

In most instances, an individual's use of problem solving to set either type of personal policy is informal. One or more problem-solving steps might not be employed, and a given step might be utilized in an incomplete fashion. Especially underemphasized are the steps of collecting new and objective evidence and of evaluating outcomes. Frequently, values or assumptions are substituted for knowledge in the analysis and evaluation of issues and plans. The problem solving utilized in personal policymaking falls somewhere between the emphasis on the analytical steps in the scientific method and the blend of analytical and interactional activities found in the professional helper's use of problem solving.

For personal policymaking, the interactional, except in feedback, is deemphasized, although not eliminated, especially as it affects other systems. Due to its emphasis on internal aspects of data collection in the form of personal experience and self-reflection, it does not precisely parallel the scientific approach's emphasis on external and objective evidence and data collection (see Table 12 for a comparison of three uses of problem solving). Nevertheless, the professional person is, as noted above, more attuned to the use of data from external sources than is the nonprofessional when engaging in personal-policy formulation.

Consider social workers faced with changes in policy about unwed fathers and their children. A Supreme Court decision in 1972 stated that such men had a right to be considered as parents. California passed a Uniform Parentage Act to implement the policy change contained in the court decision. That act, as interpreted by the state agency responsible for adoptions, called for the unwed father to be considered as a parent under certain circumstances. Workers were permitted a range of actions from excluding to including the father in five general situations: if the mother couldn't identify the father, if the mother identified more than one man as the father, if the father's identity was known but his whereabouts not, if the father was known and available,

TABLE 12
Problem Solving in Three Contexts

Problem Solving in the Scientific Method	Interactional Steps Involved in Professional Problem Solving	Problem Solving Steps in Personal Resources Policymaking
Conceptualization or formulation of a research question or problem	Initial engagement and problem exploration with client system	Identifying and defining a resource allocation issue, problem, or concern
Development of a study or research design	Data collection and data assessment	Collecting and analyzing evidence or data
	Goal establishment with client	Thinking about policy goals and options
Data collection	Discussion and selection of intervention plan	Using knowledge, assumptions, and values to decide on a policy course
Data analysis and/or hypothesis testing	Carrying out and evaluating the intervention plan	Applying and testing the policy over time
		Evaluating the effects of the policy
—	Conclusion or termination of the worker–client helping relationship	—
Presentation of results, including conclusions and interpretations	—	—

and if the court already had identified the father. These situations range from little likelihood to a high probability of the father getting the child. Hence, the values and experiences of individual workers produced different policies. Workers, for example, might try to include the father in their practice only in the first two situations, ones in which there was a limited chance that the father and his child would be united. Others might work hardest to include the father in the last two practice situations, those with the greatest chance of his getting the child. In other words, given different values and experience inputs, workers developed different personal policies to allocate their professional resources in working with the unwed father (Pierce, 1980).

Individual Decision-Making Styles

As has been pointed out earlier in this chapter, individuals are not expected to follow the processes of problem solving in exactly the same way. Different aspects are emphasized. Some people seem to reach a policy or plan as soon as an issue is raised, seemingly skipping many steps used in the problem-solving approach. Others seem to mull over an issue, collecting information and related solutions in a never-ending process.

Such differences among individuals in problem solving can be described as "styles" of decision making. Exploring a few examples of such styles is useful in helping to analyze differences in people's problem-solving approaches. It also helps develop an understanding of how and where to intervene in an individual's policy-formulation process. Variations in emphasis in the steps of the problem-solving process are what lead to differences among decision-making styles. These different emphases and related styles point to likely interventions for workers contemplating how to provide input in an individual's personal policymaking. Examples of such styles include:

☐ The ideologue
☐ The user of expertise and knowledge
☐ The indecisive
☐ The easily persuaded
☐ The passive, either a fatalist or a "coin flipper"

Those who rely more on values (or assumptions) than on knowledge or data collection can be referred to as *ideologues*. They do not just jump to conclusions; their conclusions are predetermined by an ideology, by a value or belief system that permits them to collect and interpret information in ways consistent with their ideology. In other words, their decisions revolve around their values. Understanding their values emphasis becomes a critical factor in assessing and affecting their policy-formulation process. A strict adherence to their positions naturally makes intervention more difficult if the objective is to change their policy position.

Quite different in style from ideologues are those who stress knowledge in decision making and emphasize the collection and analysis of information in their problem solving. In approach, the *users of expertise and knowledge* resemble the ideal problem solver. They review and read material about an issue. They talk to others, especially those with expert knowledge. To them, deciding is preceded by expanding their knowledge of an issue, including, if necessary, a heightened objectivity in self-assessment. The worker's input in the policy formulation of such persons can be quite rational.

Knowledge users, of course, do reach and stick to decisions. The *indecisive*, however, might rely either on values or on knowledge in their assessment and analysis. They also might not collect evidence at all. Whichever the data-collection procedure, they agonize about issues and about related policies or plans. They usually are not able to decide on issues, to narrow down goals, or to select a policy. Some seem endlessly to collect information. Others formulate intricate policy by modifying it over and over. Though they are easily led to think about other policy courses, it would be difficult for workers to gain a commitment to a single course of action from them.

The *easily persuaded*, on the other hand, decide readily enough. Just as frequently, they are inclined to change their minds when confronted by new evidence, different solutions, or fresh evaluations. The policy or plan they decide on seldom is implemented and almost never reaches the stage where it might be evaluated. They constantly alter their stance on an issue or policy. They change their policy as they come across new evidence or through the introduction of new ideas by someone who has influence over them. Workers could influence them or have difficulties in pinning them down.

A related group of decision makers are the *passive*. In this category, people are characterized by a lack of active participation in decision making, even as it relates to their own lives. The passive range from the "fatalistic" to the "coin flippers." The fatalistic believe that policy outcomes are predetermined, that regardless of their input the policy course is set. Coin flippers are those who, through an attitude of apparent risk taking, also exhibit the belief that they do not control their options, deciding instead by the chance pursuit of one or the other path. As with the indecisive, the passive present workers with difficulties in helping them identify a policy to which they are truly committed.

The Social Worker's Personal Policymaking

As has been stressed, personal policymaking is twofold. One part represents those policies that are made to allocate resources over which the worker has direct control. Here the resources are derived from their professional knowledge, skills, and roles. The other part covers those policy stances developed by the worker to bring about alterations in the resource allocations of other systems. In this second area, workers' personal-policy stances stem from their interest in resource-allocation issues in other systems to whose resources they wish to have access.

The latter area of personal policy employs the more conventional use of policy-related problem solving. Little attention has been paid to the former area, neither to its products nor to its process. This section will suggest ways in which line workers can translate skills in self-assessment, an ability they presumably possess, into personal-policy development and assessment skills.

Increasingly it is being recognized that line workers engage in a variety of policymaking activities. This is reflected in the efforts of those who encourage social workers to be politically active (Mahaffey and Hank, 1982). These efforts, however, need not focus just on linking line workers with the political processes that make social policy. Indeed, the line worker's policymaking role is also being examined in arenas other than the political or legislative. In such examinations, of course, not all of the policy activities described reflect the discussion in this text of a worker's personal policies or how they are formulated. Nonetheless, these represent encouraging efforts to extend what the profession defines as the policy-related practice activities of the line worker.

For example, Dolgoff and Gordon (1981) catalogue how direct service workers make policy. The authors label it "micro policy," policy made at the local or direct service level. They include in their listing of worker-made policy those decisions taken when agency policy is unclear, poorly defined, or designed to permit workers latitude; choices made from a particular social work-theoretical perspective that determines courses of action in practice; the election of strategies that use the degree of play in a system either to support or to alter the policy originating from other levels; and the aggregation of their decisions in order to affect other agencies. As is evident from this listing, Dolgoff and Gordon discuss policymaking by line workers in systems, such as agency or local community, that extend beyond the social worker's own system of resources.

Their conclusion that workers make policy concerning choice of practice strategy, theories of human behavior to be used, worker roles to be performed, and intervention activities to be carried out approximates the idea of a social worker's personal-resources policy as used in this text. Such policy covers the resources over which workers have control. The other part of personal policy, its effect as an input in the policymaking of other systems, coincides with Dolgoff and Gordon's discussion of a worker's aggregation of decisions to create an impact on other levels, including colleagues and agencies.

In making the personal policy that is related to the allocation of their professional assets, social workers might consciously apply the problem-solving aspects of self-assessment. This, however, occurs in the context of making policy rather than of assessing and developing practice skills. Self-assessment usually focuses on an analysis of the worker's practice effectiveness in one or more interventive situations. In such an application of problem solving, a client practice issue would be identified, evidence about it collected and analyzed, and alternative practice approaches considered and compared with those approaches actually undertaken. In this fashion, self-reflection, based on the process of data collection from and about one's own practice, results in a determination of practice effectiveness. A similar process would be carried out in determining and/or altering the worker's personal policy. Self-assessment, then, can be understood as yet another version of the application of problem solving (see Table 13 for a comparison of the steps in problem solving and self-ssessment).

The adaptation of problem solving for the purposes of policy development, as discussed in this chapter's treatment of the general problem-solving process, would be used by workers to develop a policy stance about resource allocations in other systems that are involved in their practice. Procedures of self-assessment and policy-related problem solving are used to guide the development of both types of personal policies: those that allocate the resources over which workers have personal control and those regarding external resources over which they desire greater control.

TABLE 13
Problem Solving and Self-Assessment Steps Compared

Problem Solving	Self-Assessment
Problem exploration and identification	Emergence of a practice related issue
Data collection and assessment	Data collection about and reflection on actions in one or more practice situations
Goal establishment	Development of knowledge-based practice alternatives
Discussion and selection of intervention plan	—
Carrying out and evaluating the intervention plan	Comparison of worker practice actions and alternative approaches
Conclusion or termination of worker-client relationship	Development of new practice approaches and conclusion of self-assessment

At issue, it seems, is less whether or not workers make decisions that could be called personal policy, either by using self-assessment or policy-related problem solving, but how conscious they are that these decisions constitute a policy of sorts. That social work authors have only recently discovered that such decisions might be equated with policy does not necessarily lead to the conclusion that workers were unaware of such decision making. Workers, like other people, vary in their own decision-making styles about policymaking. Some consciously and carefully make them, others decide quickly with little apparent thought. Line workers, however, are not unaware that their decisions related to resource allocation make a significant impact on policy, which has an effect on themselves as well as on other resource systems.

Whether or not workers or social work authors have been aware of the value in line workers' formulation of personal policy, the ability to make and alter their personal policy can easily be developed. Self-assessment skill, applied to personal policy, will enable workers to identify and monitor those policies they use to allocate their professional resources. It will also enable them to understand better their input in the policymaking of other systems.

Personal Policy of Colleagues and Individual Client Systems

The colleagues with whom social workers deal use similar problem-solving, decision-making, and self-assessment processes in formulating their personal resource policy. Social workers and many of their colleagues share a professional socialization process that emphasizes problem solving and self-assessment. The latter procedure is used by many professionals to reach decisions about their practice performance. A similar process of self-reflection could create or make changes in their personal-resources policies. On the other hand, individual clients might not have been socialized in any problem-solving process that parallels the professional's self-assessment.

Everyone, client and professional alike, will have developed a decision-making style. Such styles range from little or no use of knowledge and a complete reliance on values to careful use of objective data. Evidence, from values or knowledge, might be used to decide quickly or to avoid reaching any decision. People may be formal and decisive or informal and indecisive. Some do not change their positions easily; others change with the slightest new input.

The stages used in professional self-assessment or in client decision making become points of intervention. Issues of personal policy arise when individuals must examine their own guidelines for allocating the resources over which they have control. Recognizing when these occur, such as at times of stress, enables the worker to anticipate when intervention will be needed. The kind of input made by the social worker into the policy-formulation process of colleagues or individual client systems is determined by their emphasis on values or knowledge. The worker's input is also affected by the decision-making styles of colleagues and clients. Understanding how decision-making styles and the varying emphases on stages in problem solving individualize the development of personal policy permits the worker to develop appropriate interventions. Workers also will be better able to help colleagues consciously assess their own policymaking regarding their professionally based resources.

GROUP POLICYMAKING

The mechanics of how policies are formulated by small formed groups, interest groups, small community-based groups, informal groups of colleagues, and groupings of family members may also be understood by social workers in relation to problem solving, goal setting, and decision making. The policies of these groups are important resource-allocating guidelines affecting critical systems used by social workers in their practice. In most instances of policymaking, these groups utilize some type of problem-solving or goal-setting format. With groups, the relationship of leaders and members and the norms of the group help explain these goal-setting or problem-solving approaches. For individuals as well as for groups, the general steps in problem solving are similar: problem or issue identification, data collection, data analysis and policy–goal selection, implementation, and evaluation. The interaction among group members, of course, is much more important than in an individual's personal resources-policy formulation. Although a large part of the individual's policy-related problem solving leans in the direction of introspection, group decisions rely much more on interaction. The nature of the interaction itself is modified by the group's leadership and the relative position of each member in the group. Group norms or principles about group functioning are akin to policy in their behavior-guiding aspects and should be recognized as such by the worker.

Norms and Group Process

Basic to an understanding of groups is the concept of group norms. Group norms are rules or codes that members must recognize, learn, and follow. Group norms are a way of defining the group's culture. Norms are a complex set of shared principles or ideas that inform all members of a group about what each member may or may not do during a given group activity or in a particular situation involving the group or its interests. Norms govern the organization and relationships of primary groups, such as families, with their focus on personal feelings and intimate interaction. In secondary or technical groups, group norms tend to emphasize the technical performance of skills and a more limited emotional involvement of their members (Olmstead, 1959; Mills, 1967).

Norms also outline the duties, rights, privileges, power, and obligations of members and leaders. These help to define how groups regulate member–leader relationships and interactions. These concepts are important also in categorizing group decision-making styles. Who has a right to make a demand of the group, who has the power to reject or guide it, or who is obliged to fulfill the demand, outline the normative control of potential group relationships (Mills, 1967).

Norms may be conscious or unconscious, written or unwritten. As in our earlier definition of policy, group norms prescribe behavior and, taken together, constitute group culture. If violated, norms are enforced by sanctions, the means to enforce member compliance (Olmstead, 1959, and Mills, 1967). Norms define the group and identify the status of members and leaders. The age and strength of a group and the members' acceptance of group norms vary. So does the nature of behaviors and beliefs controlled by the group's norms. Such variance affects the ease with which group norms can be identified and understood. These factors lead to different climates or cultures in groups, such as the degree to which they are authoritarian, laissez-faire, democratic, consensual, cooperative, competitive, or focused on primary relationships versus task or technical undertakings.

Norms of groups change and develop in response to changes in group composition and member interaction. Such changes may be subtle or sudden. Some group norms constitute basic group policy about resource allocation. In the sense that group norms allocate group resources and rights, they are somewhat similar to the personal policy of an individual. Such norms point to the internal-resources policies of groups, thereby helping us to understand how a group allocates rights, statuses, privileges, power, and opportunities to its leaders and members.

Group Purpose, Goals, and Problem Solving

Another level of group process involves group goals or tasks and how they are set. As indicated above, groups have two major purposes: task attainment or pleasurable interaction among the members. Task relates to achieving a goal and emphasizes group activities aimed at achieving the goal. Interaction focuses on member relationships or how they get along. Goals, of course, might emerge from either aspect of a group.

Group goals are different from the goals of individual members of the group. A group goal is the conception of a desirable state for the group. It, of course, is generally shared by all group members. The goal does not arise from outside the group, although what the goal seeks to accomplish often involves factors outside the group. In a task group, members assume a so-called instrumental or task role in striving for the achievement of a group goal or in carrying out the tasks assigned to them. They set aside personal goals in trying to achieve the group goal. Members assess one another in terms of their effectiveness in moving the group toward goal attainment. Members contribute what skills or knowledge they possess towards task accomplishment.

In such goal- or task-oriented groups, effectiveness is a critical issue. Effectiveness in member actions is served by providing individual members with incentives. This may be done by making the group goal akin to the personal goals of members. Effectiveness is further served by the degree of member attachment to the group that helps to create a cohesive unit. Members are more likely to contribute their knowledge and skills to group goal attainment if they feel close to one another. Such compatibility is related to cohesiveness. As groups achieve success in meeting goals or in completing tasks, their cooperation is heightened. Conversely, effectiveness is undermined by the dissenting, disinterested, and dissatisfied members of the group (Heap, 1977; Mills, 1967).

Group goals may emerge in either primary (interaction) or secondary (task) groups. They may be conceptualized as an idea about altering some aspect of the group's existing system, about gaining new resources, or about using group resources to obtain a desired change in external relationships. Group goals, by their nature, cover a wide range of group needs and plans. Some of these goals deal with resource allocation and resource attainment. (Marby and Barnes, 1980).

The goal or task to be accomplished corresponds to group policy, and the actions taken to achieve it correspond to the implementation of the policy plan. To the degree that group goals focus on elements external to the group, they are similar to personal policies of individuals regarding access to or greater control of resources in systems other than their own. Group goals, and a division of labor among group members to reach them, can be determined by the leadership or by the entire group. The process for setting goals can either be an informal or a formal one. It is based in problem solving and grows out of those group norms that regulate the allocation of member strengths to ensure the effective establishment and achievement of group goals.

Groups are widely used in our society to solve problems and to facilitate decision making. Business people use a variety of formal and informal groups in this capacity. They rely on the shared creativity or problem-solving ability of a group. Social group work bases its intervention methodology in the use of group dynamics to solve two types of problems: to accomplish a group task or reach a group goal, and to assist members in solving problems of an individual nature.

Many have been in groups that have used brainstorming to enhance problem solving. Most professionals, including educators, use the small work group to discuss and develop new plans or to prepare solutions to problems (Olmstead, 1959). Legislative committees, bureaucratic and social agency staffs, and professional association policy task groups are all formalized versions of problem-solving task groups. Similarly, certain members of a family come together to decide on a plan to deal with a family problem. In all such group activities, the planning revolves around setting and reaching a goal.

How groups set goals and how they work together to reach these goals vary considerably. Group size, age, composition, norms, its nature as a primary or secondary group, and the effectiveness of its task, and its process (interaction) roles all alter how decisions are made and how goals are set and reached. One way of summarizing such variance in group decision-making types is to consider member and leader roles. These are determined by how group norms allocate the power or authority to control and decide, and how group purpose shapes member roles. Such a consideration will help develop a means for classifying groups into decision-making types.

Member and Leader Roles

For both primary and secondary groups, implicit in the discussion of goal setting, task attainment, or problem solving is the importance of member efforts to move the group toward or away from achieving its goal. This part of the goal-related group process is referred to as *locomotion* and is related to instrumental roles. Instrumental or task roles deal with who carries out the tasks identified as necessary for the group's attainment of its goals. Feedback from the environment about goal attainment is important. In this arena, roles such as technician, expert, dissenter, persuader, executive, idea person, problem solver, analyst, clarifier, or mobilizer all emerge. Of equal importance is group cohesion, or those behaviors that help the process of a group operate smoothly and that help to maintain pleasurable relations among group members. Process or expressive roles deal with a group's solidarity, with its network of emotional ties. Some effective roles include style setter, consensus manager, harmonizer, peace maker, stabilizer, cooperator, or tension reducer (Heap, 1977; Olmstead, 1959).

Another way of conceptualizing roles in a group is by looking at how norms align member–leader relationships. A leader could be benevolent, with members who show appreciation for the sensitive and caring way the leader ensures that their needs are met. A different member view of leadership arises when members are rebellious or disinterested and their aggressions and dissatisfaction are held in check by the constant pressure from the more authoritarian and powerful dictatorial leader. Such groups tend to divide into factions with each side viewing the other with distrust. Another common type is the bureaucratic group which operates through elaborate rules and task division. These rules serve to insulate members from one another and from outsiders by a hierarchical organization designed to avoid error. Bureaucratic leaders enforce rules and are accountable for making decisions. Unlike bureaucratic leaders, charismatic or idealistic leaders represent an ideal or principle which group members admire. They follow their leader with utter devotion or with suspended criticism. The opposite of such member roles are groups with a more equal or shared member–leader degree of participation; for example, democratic groups in which leaders and members are seen more as partners and all members may be viewed as potential leaders. The member role is not based on a strictly defined sense of subordination (Marby and Barnes, 1980; McQuail, 1975; Mills, 1967).

Types of Group Decision Making and Points of Intervention

The discussion of member–leader relationships suggests types of decision making that the social worker might encounter among groups. In setting group goals and in working to achieve them, leader–member relationships as well as the emphasis on a task or a process orientation in the group point to such a categorization. A few types of group decision-making cultures will be described briefly and the general implications they raise for intervention will be explored (see Figure 7 for the approach used by groups to make policy). They include:

☐ Democratic or cooperative
☐ Authoritarian or dictatorial leadership (benign or harsh)
☐ Charismatic leader
☐ Competitive membership
☐ Leaderless or consensual

In the democratic or cooperative group, all members work together to define a goal and to decide on how to achieve it. Leaders may serve as representatives and function more as elected chairpersons than as authorities or experts. The atmosphere is highly cooperative and participatory. The outline of and agreement to a plan leaves members highly satisfied by the level of their participation. Informal task groups of colleagues and other professionals often function in a democratic fashion. Interventive input is usually based in rational tactics of persuasion and participation.

POLICY-RELATED INPUT (from individual members and shared by group as a whole)
Experience
Knowledge
Values or ideologies
Existing goals and policies
Member power and skills
Leadership style
Group norms

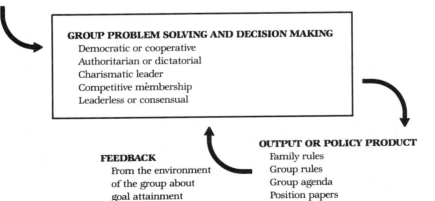

GROUP PROBLEM SOLVING AND DECISION MAKING
Democratic or cooperative
Authoritarian or dictatorial
Charismatic leader
Competitive membership
Leaderless or consensual

OUTPUT OR POLICY PRODUCT
Family rules
Group rules
Group agenda
Position papers

FEEDBACK
From the environment
of the group about
goal attainment

FIGURE 7. **Group policymaking by families, small formed groups, interest groups, and local community groups.**

Opposite to democratic groups are those in which one or more leaders have the power to dictate goals and roles. They may be benign or harsh in this position. The leadership of some gangs as well as that of some families is vested in such an authority figure. Intervention, albeit difficult, often must be based in conflict strategies unless the leader is in total agreement with the worker's policy plan.

In a charismatic group, members adhere to its principle and to the leader who symbolizes the group ideal. Goals, closely related to the group's cherished beliefs, are often set by the leader acting alone or with a trusted and obedient part of the membership. For members, process roles are emphasized over task roles, the latter being left to the leadership. Some local community groups with an ethnic or religious orientation operate like charismatic-headed groups. Some interest groups, in their dedication to a principle, come close to such groups in their operation. Intervention should move through the leader or be aligned with the group ideal and its related policies. Such groups often are amenable to coalition strategies with like-minded groups.

A competitive climate or culture may also be found in groups. A weak, ill-defined, or challenged leadership results in a group without cohesion and one in which interaction is minimal. Decision making itself is difficult, and intervention by the worker in the group is hard to determine. Small community groups being challenged by emerging groups exemplify this type. Some groups of colleagues engage in such competitive behavior, especially in situations of new leadership.

Leaderless or consensual groups are those in which members have the right to equal input into decision making and goal setting. Agreement on goals is reached by consensus, in which thorough discussion results in unanimously supported compromise agreements on policy. Some families function in this way. Intervention must follow the often frustrating and fruitless role of persuasion.

UNDERSTANDING HOW INDIVIDUALS AND SMALL GROUPS MAKE POLICY

The models of individual and group policymaking discussed in this chapter are important in several ways. The first, of course, lies in the enhancement of the social worker's abilities to understand and to assess and intervene effectively in these resource systems. Furthermore, such interventions will be made on behalf of client systems, both individuals and groups. The extent to which personal and group policies either enrich or block a social worker's efforts can be included in the worker's assessment and intervention planning with the client system. Knowledge of personal and group policies and how they are formulated helps the worker to unlock potential strengths of clients and related systems, as well as to direct members of these systems into areas enabling them to change and develop. Moreover, as workers assess their own personal policy they may discover similar avenues for change in their own resource system.

A second contribution lies in how workers use their increased knowledge and understanding of their own policies to enhance their input into other policymaking processes. How one allocates one's own resources offers valuable insight into the use of policy-related knowledge, values, and assumptions in other systems.

A third contribution to be derived from understanding these models of individual and group-made policy is the insight it provides into the actions and behaviors of policymakers in the policy-formulation processes of other resource systems. In other systems, individual input into policy formulation is more highly formalized, as, for example, in the legislative process used in society at large. Many other processes are formalized versions of group problem solving. Although these processes can be understood in their formal sense, additional insight into their policy operations can be gained by viewing how, as individuals and as members of informal small groups, these actors influence policy. The personal policymaking process of an individual and types of member–leader interaction in the policy-formulating process of groups remain useful concepts for the worker to employ in assessing and planning interventions into a system's policymaking.

Fourth, the steps in the problem-solving process serve as the basis for the policy-formulation processes of many other resource systems. Understanding the problem-solving steps utilized by individuals and groups lends insight into their adaptation and utilization in other systems. The nature of the adaptations will be presented in the remaining chapters of this section.

FOR FURTHER STUDY

1. How faithfully do you follow the steps of the problem-solving process? What decision-making style do you usually follow in your problem solving? Do you (or does anyone you know) consciously assess your (their) own personal policy that controls the allocation of your (their) own resources?

2. Do you agree with the belief that human behavior is purposive? Describe someone you know who seems not to have or to set goals. In what ways do they seem to set and follow goals, and in what ways do they not pursue goals? Does any type of behavior or human action seem to lack purpose?

3. Ask a social worker about his or her use of self-assessment. Does any part of the worker's description correspond to its use in the assessment and formulation of personal policy?

4. Consider the clients you have in your practice setting. How do they make ·
and use personal policy in their lives? How many are aware of such policy-
formulation activities?

5. Describe how a group you have been a member of solved problems or set
goals. Relate this process to one of the categories of group decision making
described in this chapter.

GLOSSARY

Problem-solving process   A rational, ordered process composed of identifiable
but related and overlapping steps or stages used to solve problems, identify goals
and decide on a plan to reach them, and assess one's environment and functioning.

Helping profession's problem solving   While interacting with the client system,
the problem is identified, data about the problem and about solutions to it are
collected and analyzed, and interventions explored, agreed to, carried out, and
evaluated.

Human diversity   Differences among individuals and groups, based on social,
cultural, biological, and social variables, which lead to differences in needs identification and problem-solving emphases and approaches.

Goal-directed or purposive behavior   The belief that human behavior is logical
and based on goal setting and problem solving to identify and meet needs.

Coping and adaptation   Problem-solving approaches utilized by people when
needs attainment is blocked. Goals and approaches are altered in flexible, logical
ways.

Decision-making styles   Based on human-diversity variables and different emphases placed on the steps of the problem-solving process, several styles of individual policy-related decision making can be identified. Examples include:
1. Ideologues who emphasize values in their decision making
2. The users of expertness and knowledge in data collection, assessment, and
   planning
3. The indecisive who, regardless of data-collection methods, are unable conclu-
   sively to settle on an issue, policy, plan, or assessment
4. The easily persuaded who alter course when faced with the pressure of influential others or with newly uncovered evidence or policy options.

Self-assessment   An adaptation of the problem-solving process. It is used by
professionals to reflect about, evaluate, and decide on more effective approaches
in their practice.

Group norms   The guiding ideas or principles shared by group members, which
define its emphasis and delineate leader and member rights and roles and which
constitute a group's culture. When norms deal with resource allocation, they
constitute group policy.

Group process and goal setting   The means by which groups decide on shared
objectives. Differing from norms or individual member goals, members utilize

instrumental roles in trying to attain the goal. If resources are covered, such goals correspond to group policy.

Group purposes   Groups may have a task (goal) orientation or a process (relational) orientation.

Group problem solving   An extension of group goal setting by which groups set goals and divide labor to attain these goals. It is widely used in our society.

Member–Leader roles   In task or process groups, group norms determine the leader-member relationships. These relationships provide insight into group decision making. Types of group decision making include:

1. Democratic—All member–leader participation with all eligible to be leaders.
2. Authoritarian or dictatorial leadership—Leader and members are at odds, with member aggression held in check by the leadership's power.
3. Charismatic leader—Leader, as representative of the group ideals, is obediently followed. Member roles emphasize a process orientation.
4. Competitive membership—Little movement toward decisions as members compete for dominance and the acceptance of their ideas by other members.
5. Leaderless or consensual—Decisions reached through unanimously supported compromises.

BIBLIOGRAPHY

Baer, Betty L. "A Conceptual Model for the Organization of Content for the Educational Preparation for the Entry Level Social Worker." Unpublished doctoral dissertation, University of Pittsburgh, 1979.

Berger, Robert and Ronald C. Federico. *Human Behavior: A Social Work Perspective.* New York: Longman, 1982.

Compton, Beulah and Burt Galaway. *Social Work Processes.* Homewood, Ill.: Dorsey Press, 1975.

Dolgoff, Ralph and Malvina Gordon. Education for policy making at the direct and local levels. *Journal of Education for Social Work,* 17(2):98–105, 1981.

Germain, Carol B. and Alex Gitterman. *The Life Model of Social Work Practice.* New York: Columbia University Press, 1980.

Heap, Kenneth. *Group Theory for Social Workers.* New York: Pergamon, 1977.

Mahaffey, Maryann and John W. Hanks (eds.). *Practical Politics: Social Work and Political Responsibility.* Silver Spring, Md.: National Association of Social Workers, 1982.

Marby, Edward and Richard E. Barnes. *The Dynamics of Small Group Communication.* Englewood Cliffs, N.J.: Prentice-Hall, 1980.

McQuail, Dennis. *Communication.* New York: Longman, 1975.

Mills, Theodore M. *The Sociology of Small Groups.* Englewood Cliffs, N.J.: Prentice-Hall, 1967.

Olmstead, Michael S. *The Small Group.* New York: Random House, 1959.

Pierce, Dean. "Adoption Policy and the 'Unwed Father': An Exploratory Study of Social Worker Response to Changing Conceptions of Fatherhood." Unpublished doctoral dissertation: University of California, Berkeley, 1980.

Pincus, Allen and Anne Minahan. *Social Work Practice: Model and Method.* Itasca, Ill.: F. E. Peacock Publishers, 1973.

Siporin, Max. *Introduction to Social Work Practice.* New York: Macmillan, 1975.

CHAPTER SIX

Formulating Policy in Organizations

". . . the Foundation is dedicated to the coordination of educational activities, development of interdisciplinary educational programs, research in the area of lesbian/gay health care issues, solicitation and distribution of funds for these purposes, and the establishment of a central clearinghouse for lesbian/gay health concerns."

—The National Gay
Health Education
Foundation

OVERVIEW

This chapter discusses how the social agency and the professional association utilize a number of distinct methods to allocate their resources and to try to influence the policymaking efforts of systems that hold resources they need. Some private or voluntary social service agencies use a formalized process involving a board of directors. These boards set internal policy, as well as make decisions about external resource issues. Many public social agencies formulate their policy in a different way. In these agencies, designated staff members develop a policy proposal, submit it to interested constituencies and/or the general public for comment, revise their proposal in light of this input and that of legal advisors, and develop and publish a final policy. This type of procedure formulates their internal policy to implement guidelines coming to them from the large public social welfare bureaucracies of which they are a part. In addition, this chapter explores how a major social work professional association makes its policies. For each process, how workers may have input into or modify the policy is covered.

OBJECTIVES

☐ Describe how private social agencies use boards to make policy and discuss three types of boards.
☐ Discuss one way in which public social agencies develop their policy.
☐ Explain three approaches used by the National Association of Social Workers to make its policy.
☐ Outline the various ways line workers could have input into organizational policymaking.

VARIATIONS IN ORGANIZATIONAL POLICY FORMULATION derive from the ways in which agencies receive their resources and how they are made accountable for their use of these resources. The so-called private or voluntary social agency is accountable through its board of directors. It makes policy to handle resources received by the agency from private (voluntary) donations or public funding sources. Often the public agency is held responsible to its public funding sources through legally mandated procedures for developing and reporting their policies. These policies serve to interpret and implement regulations made by public social welfare regulatory bureaucracies.

Agency policymaking procedures and accountability mechanisms are the formal and most visible policy-formulation processes used by social agencies. Agency policy is also affected by the personal and small-group policymaking of its staff. Some personal and group policies are closely linked to agency-made policy and serve to block or facilitate its implementation. The connectedness of these different levels of policymaking should be kept in mind. Although social agencies use formally organized boards and/or legally prescribed policy development and review procedures; informal staff processes also contribute to the development of agency policy.

The professional association is another kind of organization that makes policies of concern to the line worker. The major organization of professional social workers is the NASW which uses its national board of directors to set internal policy. The organization also calls upon its Delegate Assembly to use a special prioritizing procedure to set policy and program goals. This prioritizing process involves goal development by its board, input from members, and debate and approval by the association's elected representatives.

Two specialized NASW groups are charged with influencing the policymaking of other systems and with helping the organization reach some of its policy goals. These two special groups are Education Legislative Action Network (ELAN) and Political Action for Candidate Election (PACE). ELAN and

TABLE 14
Examples of Formal Policy Formulation Methods Used in Organizations

	Social Service Agencies	Professional Association
Formulating Internal Resource Policies	Staff Board of directors Planning and review process Public agency advisory committee with internal policy development	Board of directors Prioritizing program and policy goals
Influencing External System Policies	Board of directors Public social agency liaison with executive or legislative branch	Education Legislative Action Network (ELAN) Political Action for Candidate Election (PACE)

PACE are charged with overseeing the NASW's efforts to influence the formulation of social and social welfare policy in line with goals set during its prioritizing process. Divisions and state chapters, as well as the national organization of the NASW, use boards and special committees to set their own policies and to influence the policymaking of other systems (see Table 14 for an overview of organizational policymaking processes).

PRIVATE SOCIAL SERVICE POLICYMAKING

The processes social agencies use to make policy have formal and informal aspects. The formal side includes the work of official policymaking bodies such as a board of directors; the activities of executives, their staffs, and department heads; and the legally mandated procedures of policy development and review. At the informal level, supervisors and workers contribute input through their personal policies and in their role as implementors of policy set by other systems. This includes the agencies and organizations associated with their practice.

Boards of directors are a basic part of the formal structure of privately funded agencies and of some agencies that receive federal funding. Most public agencies, as will be discussed later in this chapter, do not operate with a board of directors. Boards usually represent the community served by the agency. Agency bylaws define the method of board selection, which could be either by election or appointment. The qualifications of members can include the extent of their community-based power and influence, their place of residence, their professional status, or the degree of interest in the agency's mission.

Boards are the legal entity through which agencies gain the right to develop and carry out their programs and services. Boards establish overall agency policy and are responsible for changes in agency policy and goals. Boards are also charged with gaining funds and resources for the agency. This last task has been an important one for the traditional private social service agency, and has had significant impact on the selection of board members.

Boards are organized with officers such as a chairperson or president, a secretary, and a treasurer. Sometimes they are divided into subcommittees that provide direction for basic agency operations such as staffing, developing programs and policies, and funding. Conventional boards follow parliamentary procedures and operate according to democratic principles with decisions arrived at after debating and voting. The boards sometimes listen to testimony from the agency's administrative staff, board staff, subcommittees, or from agency workers. The agency executive is generally employed by and accountable to the board, and is the most important staff member to whom the board listens and relates. Outside input is infrequent.

Regular meetings are scheduled, and agendas are followed, usually as developed by the agency executive. Minutes are kept and distributed, often to the entire staff of the agency and to interested outsiders. Boards often meet on a monthly basis; those that do not meet as frequently usually have less impact on the development of agency policy (see Figure 8 for an overview of policymaking in private social service agencies). In such a case, and in other instances, the executive effectively controls the agency. The agency executive and staff controls the training and information the board receives. The board and its executive usually cooperate closely, especially when board members view their role as self-aggrandizing. In such cases, members are satisfied with efficiency, completed agendas, and organized preparatory reading and background material that enables them to reach decisions quickly. They are less concerned with self-involvement or independent participation.

As with individual and small group decision making, boards may be characterized according to the nature of their interaction and decision making:

- [ ] the high-powered board
- [ ] one person
- [ ] small cliques or executive committee structure
- [ ] consensual
- [ ] "rubber stamps" (see Weissman, 1973)
- [ ] activist boards

High-powered boards are usually composed of prominent, successful business people who leave decisions to the executive, allowing that person to develop policy. Such boards are interested in efficiency and fund raising. For

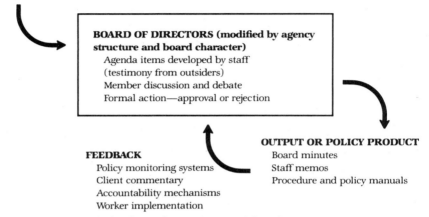

POLICY-RELATED INPUT
Competing client needs
Staff reports
Subcommittee reports
Board member experience and values
Existing policies

BOARD OF DIRECTORS (modified by agency structure and board character)
Agenda items developed by staff
(testimony from outsiders)
Member discussion and debate
Formal action—approval or rejection

OUTPUT OR POLICY PRODUCT
Board minutes
Staff memos
Procedure and policy manuals

FEEDBACK
Policy monitoring systems
Client commentary
Accountability mechanisms
Worker implementation

FIGURE 8. **Organizational policymaking: private social service agency.**

other boards, one person from the board itself serves as the chief decision maker. This single board member, because of the person's fund-raising prowess or other source of power in assisting the agency, controls the board and a great deal of the agency operations. Some boards are dominated by more than one person, such as a small clique or so-called executive committee. Such cliques control other board members and their decision making. Differing from such member-dominated boards are those that operate in a consensual manner. All members contribute to decision-making and agree with the outcome of board deliberations. Other boards, due to agency structure or board member disinterest, become mere "rubber stamps" for their executive. Still others, because of member interest and commitment to an agency, demand and carry out an activist role in policy development and agency operations and management.

For line workers, effort must be expended in opening communication channels to the agency board. Such communication regularly takes place between the agency executive and board members. Any opportunity, be it in response to a memo, a note, or letter channeled to the board, or the chance to testify, must be pursued. Some boards are more open to worker input, some guard against it. Activist and some small clique-dominated boards might be amenable to worker input. The high-powered board and the rubber stamp are less likely to be interested in line worker input.

Once the policy has been developed, how it is modified comes from any means developed in the policy to collect data about its operation, any means to evaluate, and hence modify. Client comments and the mechanism by which the agency is held accountable to its funding sources may lead to modification. A major means of feedback, of course, comes during worker implementation, which was stated in the introduction to this section and which will be emphasized in discussions about other policymaking processes.

PUBLIC AGENCY POLICYMAKING

(The following discussion is derived in part from interviews with members of the Westchester County, New York, Department of Social Services.)

Public social service agencies at the local or direct service level may use advisory committees to help the agency director set policy. These committees, unlike a board of directors, are consultative and advisory in nature. The director or agency executive is the person within the agency structure responsible for making policy. Part of that responsibility involves the implementation and refinement of policy directives made at higher levels in the public social service delivery structure.

In such agencies, policies or procedures that implement guidelines from higher levels are developed through a process of review and feedback. The process is intended to develop program guides for use by line workers in their practice. The guides are designed to promote consistent implementation of the policy by line workers and to heighten the accountability of the agency itself (see Westchester County Department of Social Services, 1980).

The review process may involve designated individuals in the agency or utilize a panel or group of reviewers. Comments are solicited by the person responsible for drafting the policy proposal from these interested, knowledgeable staff members. The author of the draft and those who comment on it are in essence providing feedback and input to the policy decision making of the agency's chief executive or the executive's representatives. Those who comment are already familiar with the area where the policy is to be developed, with the issues involved, and with the existing policy. The actual procedures used for the solicitation, handling, and utilization of comments vary from agency to agency. The degree of staff involvement also differs from agency to agency.

Basic to the process, however, is the development of a program or procedural guide for commentary by the agency's legal counsel and for approval by the agency head. The agency head, in turn, transmits the agency's newly developed program guide to the appropriate office at a higher level for approval. Feedback will come to the agency in this fashion. This step in the process is aimed at keeping the local agency in compliance with all regulations issued by the applicable state and federal social welfare bureaucracies (see Figure 9 for an overview of how policy is made in public social service agencies).

Such review and feedback procedures seem to preclude line worker input or feedback. Although the process appears to be a highly technical one, resulting in a translation of policy made at one level into implementation guidelines at another, in actuality line workers, through their collegial networks, can provide input in such policy development and review processes. Their personal policy about new regulations and guidelines can be provided regularly to supervisor and department heads in supervisory conferences and staff meetings. Line worker policy stances, regardless of the degree of agency flexibility in developing new program guides, can be checked out against the new guides. Moreover, workers can also provide their input in an informal fashion to those persons who are used regularly in the agency's review process. Workers, of course, would consider these points of contact as places for their interventions. Line workers can use this connection between the formal and informal structures in an agency to increase their input into the review process and provide feedback about it. Their own implementation supplies further feedback to the policy.

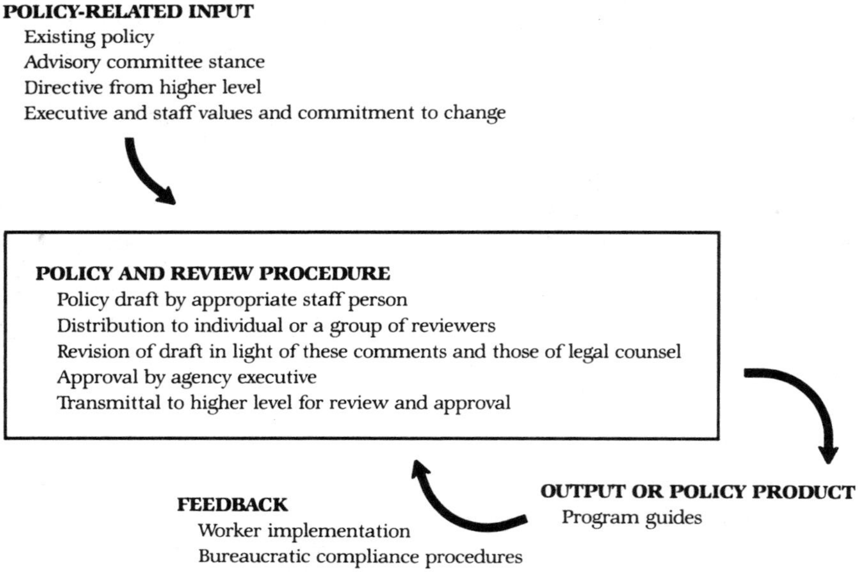

POLICY-RELATED INPUT
Existing policy
Advisory committee stance
Directive from higher level
Executive and staff values and commitment to change

POLICY AND REVIEW PROCEDURE
Policy draft by appropriate staff person
Distribution to individual or a group of reviewers
Revision of draft in light of these comments and those of legal counsel
Approval by agency executive
Transmittal to higher level for review and approval

FEEDBACK
Worker implementation
Bureaucratic compliance procedures

OUTPUT OR POLICY PRODUCT
Program guides

FIGURE 9. **Organizational policymaking: public social service agency.**

FEEDBACK AND ORGANIZATIONAL SHAPING

The input of line workers in making desired policy changes in an agency involves cooperative and noncooperative tactics, and relies heavily on their connections with others, their ability to use these connections, and appropriate agency channels. Workers, as professionals, are somewhat autonomous and can use discretion to decide about policy in their delivery of services to clients. Agencies, on the other hand, write manuals to take care of contingencies and to standardize worker performance. Workers are expected to cooperate, and most do because the agency has sanctions it could use against workers who choose to resist policy too actively. The agency, however, relies on the discretion of workers to make scarce resources go as far as possible and tolerates some changes in policy as workers implement it. In other words, agencies expect some modification in their policy. This amounts to an expected feedback of sorts (Lipsky, 1980).

If workers wish to have real input in policymaking of the agency, especially if they wish to make changes in it, they need to understand the political nature of agency functioning and to appreciate power and its use. Moreover, they must prepare in advance for their use of power to achieve any policy changes they will attempt in an agency. The expected role of organizational change will be connected to policy interventions in chapter eleven.

Workers can use influence to have impact on the policymakers of an agency. In order to do so, workers need to develop power. They must establish contacts and develop a professional presence in their agencies so they will be listened to when they decide to present their policy positions. Connections with constituent groups of an agency are important. Such groups include colleagues, supervisors and administrators, and the staffs of important agencies that have regular contact with the agency and of funding groups (Lee, 1983).

There are other activities the worker can pursue in developing power. Power comes from knowledge or expertise in a given area. Workers can maintain current, accurate information to support arguments and to present a professional image of competence. The worker's credibility can be furthered by being responsive to agency demands and needs, flexible in interaction with staff, and consistent in all situations; providing leadership; maintaining accountability; and showing initiative in needed policy areas. Workers can also reach out to other power structures that interact with the agency that employs them. For example, in schools, boards and parent organizations are important, as well as special interest groups. Workers should reach out to and develop connections with constituencies outside the agency. The same kinds of activities can be followed in other organizations to build power, credibility, and professional image (Brager and Holloway, 1978; Lee, 1983).

PROFESSIONAL ASSOCIATION'S POLICYMAKING

All professional associations make policy for their members to follow. They allocate their organization's resources, and guide their input in the policy-making processes of other systems. One need only reflect on the role of the American Medical Association in influencing resource allocation in the medical field and affecting health-care policy in the federal political arena.

This discussion will focus only on the NASW, although other social work associations also affect policymaking. Founded in 1955, by the early 1980s, the association had over 90,000 members. A national office is maintained in Silver Spring, Maryland, near Washington, D.C. There are 55 chapters—one in each state as well as Washington, D.C., New York City, Puerto Rico, the Virgin Islands, and Europe. Most chapters are broken down into smaller divisions. In addition to providing member services, developing information and communications, and sponsoring conferences, the NASW is involved in policymaking. All segments of the NASW make policy on the local, state, and national levels.

At the national level, policy is created in two broad ways:

1. Setting policy concerning the resources it controls. In part this is done in the policy-prioritizing process at its Delegate Assembly, a national biennial meeting of elected representatives. This process sets directions

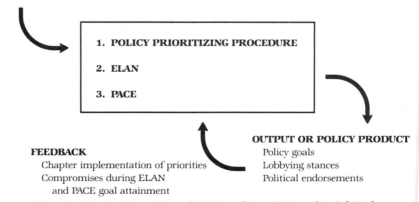

POLICY-RELATED INPUT
Professional knowledge
Values and code of ethics
Existing policies
Member feedback
Client interests

1. **POLICY PRIORITIZING PROCEDURE**

2. **ELAN**

3. **PACE**

OUTPUT OR POLICY PRODUCT
Policy goals
Lobbying stances
Political endorsements

FEEDBACK
Chapter implementation of priorities
Compromises during ELAN
and PACE goal attainment

FIGURE 10. **Organizational policymaking: the National Association of Social Workers.**

for the organization. In addition, other committees and the national board of directors also contribute to the creation of policy.

2. Influencing policy made in other systems concerning resources over which the NASW would like to have greater control.

In the first area, it operates partly like other organizations or agencies in setting policies, whether they are of an internal organizational nature or aimed at another system. The fact that the NASW is a member organization necessitates the modification of its organizational policymaking procedures to ensure the input of membership. The biennial delegate assembly as well as the national board of directors set major policy directions. In the second area of policy creation, the activities of ELAN and PACE are involved. These groups have major responsibility for the NASW's efforts to influence the policy making of other systems (see Figure 10 for the ways in which the NASW makes policy).

PROGRAM AND POLICY PRIORITIZING

In 1975, the NASW's delegate assembly directed the national board of directors to devise a systematic approach to determine its program priorities and major policy initiatives. The system developed was first used at the 1979 assembly and again, in a modified form, at the 1981 assembly. A multitiered approach was created for arriving at major priorities. The first step in the process on both occasions was to form an ad hoc task force to develop proposed priorities for the association. Prior to the convening of the 1981 assembly, for example, priorities were developed in each of the association's four functional areas:

☐ Practice advancement or professional development
☐ Professional standards
☐ Social policy and action
☐ Membership and organization

Practice advancement or professional development covers continuing education, national conferences and symposia, programs, and a range of publications such as journals, encyclopedias, and books. Professional standards deal with licensing, job classification, and legal regulation of the social work profession. The Academy of Certified Social Workers, classification standards, third-party vendor programs, and a register of clinical social workers comprise association efforts in this area. This area focuses on setting goals for the allocation of internal resources. Membership services include a range of benefits enjoyed by those who join the NASW, including life, health, and practice liability insurance. Social policy and action deal with identifying and influencing legislation. The functional area of social policy deals directly with resource issues of external systems.

In developing the proposed 1981 priorities, the task force emphasized the overarching concerns of the NASW with racism, sexism, and poverty. Particular groups and interests or vulnerable populations were not a focus. The intent of this approach was to avoid unnecessary multiplication of goals. After the task force finished its work, the proposed priorities were circulated among chapter presidents and staff as well as members of the national board, the national program committee, and national staff for review, comments, and suggestions. The national program committee incorporated all of these comments into a revision of the proposed priorities and submitted them to the national board of directors. The national board in turn approved them and forwarded them for consideration by the 1981 Delegate Assembly.

The priorities as accepted by the 1981 assembly will guide the NASW from July 1, 1982 through June 30, 1984. The action taken by the Delegate Assembly signifies its position as the designated policymaking body of the NASW. Delegate Assembly action binds other segments of the association to support these priorities for two years.

The actual ranking procedure utilized by the delegates at the 1981 assembly asked them to rank the proposed items within each functional area according to maximum, moderate, or minimum emphasis. Delegates were also asked to vote for five paramount priorities, without regard to functional area. All chapters must work on the five priorities, selecting their own approach in dealing with the others. The development of paramount priorities was a refinement introduced for use at the 1981 assembly.

A modified Delphi Method, with three ranking steps, was employed by the delegates. Prior to the assembly, the delegates individually ranked the proposed priorities. The individual rankings were reranked by small groups at the assembly itself. The last step in the development of association priorities was formal action at the Delegate Assembly. Parliamentary procedure was used that permitted four assembly actions whenever a motion was made to adopt the small group rankings as the association's priorities. These actions were adding priorities, altering the wording of priorities, moving priorities from one another level of emphasis, and redefining what weighting should separate the minimum, moderate, or maximum level of emphasis.

The intent of the prioritizing procedure was to obtain sizable input from members to guarantee member commitment to the Association's priorities. (Table 15 shows some proposed policies and the preliminary agenda. Table 16 outlines some of the policies that were actually adopted by the assembly.)

The policymaking process used by the NASW appears to be more sensitive to member input than does the board policymaking of private agencies. Board members, however, do represent the constituency of the agency, although not as directly as elected delegates. The NASW's policy-prioritizing

TABLE 15

Delegate Assembly Proposed Program and Policy Priorities

Proposed 1982-84 Program Goals for Priority Ranking by 1981 Delegate Assembly

Following are the proposed 1982-84 NASW program goals developed by the association's volunteer National Program Committee. The goals cover the four functional areas of NASW program activity: professional advancement, professional standards, social policy and action, and membership and organization. In June, the NASW National Board of Directors approved the placement of these proposed goals on the 1981 Delegate Assembly agenda. The Assembly may change the proposed goals, and will rank the final goals according to the emphasis (maximum, moderate, or minimum) that each should receive in guiding the association's 1982-84 activities.

Professional Advancement

To advance the quality of social work practice, improve the knowledge base required for such practice, and to promote professional development related to improved practice

P.A. 1 To further the development of a specialization program

P.A. 2 Improve social work practice through direct provision of continuing education programs of assured quality and the development and promulgation of standards for the provision of continuing education.

P.A. 3 Improve practice by developing vehicles for communication for constituencies within various specialty areas.

P.A. 4 To promote social work practitioners' concerns in professional social work education and profesional social work education standard setting bodies.

P.A. 5 Advance social work knowledge by promoting and disseminating research on social work practice and social policy issues.

Professional Standards

To promote the strength, unity, and recognition of the social work profession and the acceptance and utilization of its standards.

P.S. 1 Promote public recognition and sanction of social work.

P.S. 2 Develop and refine practice standards for significant practice areas. Promote the adoption and utilization of NASW standards by human service delivery systems, programs of social work education, and other standard setting bodies.

P.S. 3 To promote the adoption and utilization of NASW standards on personnel practices, salaries and compensation and other standards related to improved working conditions for social workers.

P.S. 4 Empirically establish the validity of social work practice by developing a functional classification system of the social work labor force which is based on validated competencies. Promote the adoption of validated classification systems by human service agencies in the public and private sectors.

P.S. 5 Develop and maintain a comprehensive social work labor force data base.

P.S. 6 Obtain vendorship status for qualified social work practitioners.

P.S. 7 Secure, maintain, improve and evaluate legal regulation of social work practice.

P.S. 8 Develop, maintain and expand the scope and effectiveness of competency certification programs.

P.S. 9 Promote the understanding of and adherence to the NASW Code of Ethics.

P.S. 10 Identify and support emerging areas of practice.

P.S. 11 Develop appropriate programs to improve or refine relationships between social work and other human service professions.

P.S. 12 Promote equal employment opportunities and advancement for women and ethnic/racial minorities at all professional levels of social service delivery systems.

Social Policy and Action

To promote and advance sound public policies and programs aimed at human need and improved quality of life.

S.P. 1 To advocate for adequate allocation of public/private financing for health and human services and income maintenance with recognition of the proper responsibility at every level of government, and to work toward reduction in military expenditures. Work to prevent cutbacks in human service programs in local, state and federal government budgets.

S.P. 2 Work for reduced reliance on military force as an instrument of foreign policy via support of non-violent strategies for resolution of national and international conflicts.

S.P. 3 Promote measures that advance universal, comprehensive, and cost effective health and mental health programs and improve the health care delivery system.

S.P. 4 Promote the development and improvement of public and private social services delivery systems.

S.P. 5 Press for the maintenance and enforcement of Affirmative Action programs to protect the rights of and provide opportunities for women, minority persons of color, and handicapped persons.

S.P. 6 Combat discrimination, and its effects and promote human rights and unimpeded access to services for all residents of the United States.

S.P. 7 Press for Federal/state/local legislation that provides for an adequate standard of income supports.

S.P. 8 Promote programs and economic policies to increase employment for the economically disadvantaged.

S.P. 9 Impact local, state and Federal government policy decisions by the direct involvement of social workers in political (including legislative) processes.

S.P. 10 To promote the development of community based services as an alternative to institutionalization.

S.P. 11 Press for (a) the development of adequate energy resources within necessary ecological concerns; (b) a system of allocation of resources which recognizes energy as a public policy, and (c) programs to address the need of areas and persons impacted by energy development and costs.

S.P. 12 Promote tax policies that reinforce or promote NASW social policy goals.

S.P. 13 Promote, support and protect the civil rights and civil liberties of consumers of services, particularly institutionalized persons.

Membership and Organization

To improve the effective functioning of NASW as a national organization and to improve the way in which it serves its members.

M.O. 1 Maintain current membership services and benefits and explore additional services as resources permit.

M.O. 2 Increase the membership by 15% between 1982-84 through membership recruitment and retention efforts with special attention to students, BSW practitioners and recent graduates.

M.O. 3 To improve the functioning and capacity of Chapters and the National organization.

M.O. 4 Provide employment information and/or assistance to members of the Association.

M.O. 5 To develop a membership and management information system and increase our data processing support to programs, committees and chapter activities, including responses to membership inquiries.

M.O. 6 Account for NASW programs to NASW members by continuing implementation of the Association-wide Program Accountability System.

Reprinted from *NASW News*, 26(7), July, 1981.

TABLE 16
Excerpts from Policies Adopted by the 1981 Delegate Assembly

Priority Goals

The priority goal-setting process began long before the Assembly convened in Philadelphia. Last summer all delegates were asked to rank priorities. The tabulations were presented at regional coalition meetings in the fall, after which time the coalitions had an opportunity to discuss and perhaps resolve any differences they might have had with one another.

At the Assembly, small groups met to make final adjustments to the rankings before they came to the Assembly floor. The goals this year, as in 1979, were arranged in maximum, moderate, and minimum categories.

There was, however, one important difference from past procedure. At the recommendation of the NASW Board of Directors, the delegates agreed to add another category of five priorities which would serve as the association's overarching goals for at least the next three years. These were to be drawn from those goals already voted to be in the maximum category.

The decision to place special emphasis on five maximum categories began to take shape several months ago. The board, at its June 1981 meeting, agreed that in order to effectively cope with the hardships imposed by Reagan Administration policies, NASW would have to sharpen its sense of direction and more carefully target its admittedly limited resources.

The delegates, as if in recognition of this need, adopted the top five priorities unanimously, three of them being special policy goals. They are:

• Improve social work practice through direct provision of continuing education programs of assured quality and support the development and promulgation of standards for the provision of continuing education.

• Promote public recognition and sanction of social work to include securing, maintaining, improving and evaluating legal regulation of social work practice.

• To advocate for adequate allocation of public/private financing for health and human services and income maintenance, with recognition of the proper responsibility at every level of government, and to work toward reduction in military expenditures. Work to prevent cutbacks in human service programs in local, state, and federal government budgets.

• Combat discrimination, and its effects, and promote human rights and unimpeded access to services for all residents of the United States.

• To develop and mobilize the political potential of the membership in order to impact local, state, and federal government policy decisions by the direct involvement of social workers in political (including legislative) processes.

To streamline the priority-setting process even further, the delegates adopted a motion made by Daphne McClellan Rupert of Oklahoma to limit the maximum category in each functional area, i.e., professional advancement, professional standards, social policy, and membership and organization, to twenty-five percent of the total number of goals in that area. Moreover, no less than fifty percent were to be placed in the minimum emphasis category.

Other than the top five mentioned above, three other goals fell into the maximum category:

• To develop and refine practice standards for significant practice areas, and promote the adoption and utilization of NASW standards by human service delivery systems, programs of social work education, and other standard-setting bodies.

• To press for the maintenance and enforcement of affirmative action programs to protect the rights of and provide opportunities for women, minority persons of color, and handicapped persons.

• To improve the functioning and capacity of chapters and the national organization to include an accounting of NASW programs to NASW members by continuing implementation of the association-wide program accountability system.

Some goals relegated to the minimum category looked strangely out of place based on the attention they have been given by the profession in past years. Among them were goals to further the development of a specialization program, to expand the scope of competency certification programs, to identify and support emerging areas of practice, to intensify efforts to initiate "coalition-building relevant to the association's goals,"

TABLE 16
Excerpts from Policies Adopted by the 1981 Delegate Assembly (continued)

and to develop a membership and management information system, with increasing data processing support to programs, committees and chapter activities.

Professional Issues

The professional issues plenary session went more smoothly than any other on the agenda. The delegates adopted policy statements on declassification, industrial social work, the role of social work in health maintenance organizations, relationships with other social work organizations and human services disciplines, and the role of social work in home health care.

Three of the statements, i.e., declassification, health maintenance organizations, and human services disciplines, passed virtually unchanged from the original statements carried in the July NASW NEWS.

Another, the one on industrial social work, was left intact except for changes which reflected the role of the community and the corporation in the prevention and treatment of problems of workers, and which emphasized the need for more research in that field.

The original statement on home health care was substantially edited. Coalitions agreed on a revision designed so that it could easily be subsumed under some future comprehensive NASW policy statement on health. It also delineated more precisely the functions of social workers in home health care.

The revision passed on the Delegate Assembly floor with no opposition.

Social Policy Issues

The coalitions also worked well together in preparation for the plenary session to consider social policy issues. Delegates readily passed eight of ten policy statements and defeated two others.

The two defeated were on personal social services and problem pregnancies.

No one seemed to disagree with the premise of the personal social services statement, i.e., the need for a well-integrated nationwide personal social services delivery system with social work as its cornerstone. But most seemed to think that the proposed statement was inadequate.

The proposal, a revision of the one printed in the NEWS last July, was prepared by the NASW Social Services Task Force. Its critics on the floor of the Assembly said, among other things, that it was incomplete, had not sufficiently addressed Title XX of the Social Security Act, and did not include provisions for client confidentiality.

One supporter said the statement was "admittedly inadequate, but would be better than nothing." Delegate Marsena Buck of California countered with "poor policy is not better than no policy at all," and suggested that a Delegate Assembly resolution on personal social services, rather than the proposed policy, be the means of handling the subject for now.

The issue was, indeed, tabled, and a resolution later passed which urged that "NASW's actions reflect a commitment to new approaches to service development and delivery, and not simply the defense of what now exists."

The debate on the problem pregnancy statement was short but forceful. The proposal was intended to replace the current policy, which explicitly states the client's right to choose abortion. Kathryn Getz of Salt Lake City, Utah, who introduced the proposed policy statement, claimed that the present policy "allows only one option—abortion." She said the proposed statement was more realistic because it included other services social workers provide for a client with a problem pregnancy.

Others, including representatives of the National Committee on Women's Issues, claimed that the proposal backed away from the commitment to "freedom of choice" set forth in the current policy statement and embodied in the NASW Code of Ethics.

The proposal included language which would have required the social worker to "take into account the rights both of the prospective child and the child's father." Delegates voted resoundingly to defeat the problem pregnancy proposal.

Only policies on energy, hospice care, housing, and social work in rural areas were sub-

TABLE 16

Excerpts from Policies Adopted by the 1981 Delegate Assembly (continued)

stantially changed from the version the delegates were originally given to consider last summer. And in these cases, coalitions worked to see that by the time each issue came up on the floor of the Assembly, any major differences of opinion had been resolved.

In short, the revised policy on energy gave more attention to the impact of the energy crisis on urban populations, and called for the determination "of the appropriate roles and responsibilities of governmental units (local, state, national), energy companies, universities, and lay citizens in addressing and resolving the energy crisis.

The revised hospice care policy statement defined hospice care and the social work role in rendering it in a more specific manner than the original one and stressed the need for "new and flexible sources of public and private financing" for the hospice.

The housing statement changes were largely editorial, with some expansion on the phenomenon of "gentrification" of old inner-city neighborhoods and clarification of tax abatement policies.

There were a considerable number of editorial changes in the rural social work policy proposal, but very little substantive change.

None of these four statements drew any heated debate. An overwhelming majority of amendments made were so-called friendly amendments. The statements passed with little or no opposition.

The same was true of the remaining policy statements, those on alternative work patterns, community development, families, and international human rights. (They are not reprinted here because the final versions are not significantly different than those published in the July *NASW NEWS.*)

Reprinted from *NASW News*, 27(1), January, 1982.

process also seems to cover more resource issues than those dealt with by the policy-review process of a public agency, with its emphasis on implementation of and compliance with bureaucratic regulations. Issue selection, however, is limited for the NASW by the ideas and general direction of the group that initiates the priorities and by the major concerns of the association. Line worker input into the NASW's process is more likely than in either of the agency formats.

NASW WORKER INPUT

Input by a line worker into the process, of course, occurs through contact with assembly delegates from a division or chapter. Such input is built into the process, guaranteeing broad participation. For the line worker, procedures for member input and participation become a key point for intervention in the development of association policy; however, they require that the worker be a member of the NASW. Membership is open to all persons with baccalaureate or master's degrees from accredited programs.

Chapters are responsible for encouraging full member participation in the multitiered process that leads to the adoption of the association's policy priorities. Chapters set up meetings with members prior to the assembly.

Members meet with delegates to ensure the widest possible input. Other ways that line workers may be involved is to serve on any task force or committee designated by their chapters to study a proposed policy issue, to meet informally with delegates, or to serve as delegates themselves. Of equal importance is member input during chapter meetings and in the discussions that translate national policy priorities into chapter guidelines and procedures to implement them. Except for the five priorities to be followed by all segments of the NASW, latitude is permitted chapters in implementing the association's policy priorities. This latitude leads to additional worker participation in the policy-implementation procedures followed by the association. This implementation is a major feedback process, leading to policy modifications.

EDUCATION LEGISLATIVE ACTION NETWORK

Differing in emphasis are the policy-creation processes of the NASW's ELAN and PACE organizations. The aim of these two groups is to increase the association's influence over the development of national and state legislative policies. The ELAN was begun in 1970 with the aim of achieving better communication throughout the professional association on legislative matters. In 1979, a newsletter, *The Advocate for Human Services*, was added to the ELAN communication network between the national office and the other parts of the NASW. In order to achieve its goals of advancing human-service programs and policies, better utilize membership expertise, and increase social worker influence over social legislation, a network of members from the local through the national level was developed. Basically, the ELAN is a network for the purpose of lobbying. The structure was created to enable members to contribute in a systematic fashion to the development of policy initiatives and to aid in getting them adopted. For example, a local ELAN member might identify a policy issue and alert a district leader, who in turn would contact the state coordinator of the ELAN. State coordinators contact the national leadership if appropriate. At each level, important legislative contacts are maintained. Moreover, the three levels (district, state, and national) work cooperatively in setting goals, responding to member input, and in coordinating communications.

This illustration clarifies the ELAN's aim to mobilize informed members who will work to influence politicians at all levels of the social policymaking procedure. The mobilization of members grows out of the ability of the ELAN leaders, at each level, to maintain contact with informed, active members. The ELAN uses a telephone network to mobilize interested persons and active members of the entire team. Members are trained in the best approaches to use in trying to influence legislation. Some of these include meeting with elected representatives, contact with key aides, and follow-up letters to representatives. These approaches apply at the community, city, state, and national levels.

The ELAN works with other pressure groups to influence legislation. Furthermore, it develops rating charts of the voting records of legislators. Such ratings permit social workers to assess how responsive each official has been to the social policy interests of the profession.

In addition to pressuring elected officials and rating their voting response to such pressures, the ELAN is concerned with the creation of a system of contacts which includes appropriate local politicians and community-based social policy experts. Members of like-minded pressure groups are also courted as potential allies. The organization also focuses on the development of appropriate publicity campaigns for the advancement of the NASW policy positions. Publicity involves a range of media coverage, press releases, and news conferences.

POLITICAL ACTION FOR CANDIDATE ELECTION

Political Action for Candidate Election was created in 1976 when the national Board was authorized by the delegate assembly to develop an independent organization to support candidates favorable to the association's policy goals. PACE as such, and less so than the ELAN, is not directly part of the policy-formulation process. It attempts to ensure the election of policymakers in the legislative process who will support the policy goals defined by the profession. It functions as a political action committee, trying to influence voters. The national PACE organization has its own board of trustees and staff. All interested members of the NASW constitute the grass-roots network. The PACE activities include:

☐ attempting to elect candidates whose positions are consistent with the NASW goals
☐ working to get social policy adopted that is in the interests of the profession
☐ creating political awareness and action among professional social workers
☐ developing voter registration procedures and developing effective coalitions

Political Action for Candidate Election committees are established at the chapter level as well as at the national level. All of the PACE organizations follow appropriate election laws and regulations. A committee guides the chapter organization in its identification and development of active volunteers; it also guides a viable funding campaign to support the endorsement of candidates. Political Action for Candidate Election determines which candidates to support by surveying their interest in and willingness to support the profession's policy stances, and by examining voting records in relation to the NASW policy priorities. Given this information, chapter members decide which candidates to endorse and/or support as well as recommend to the national PACE for its endorsement.

Critical in deciding to endorse a candidate are the person's policy stances, support for social work political involvement, voting record, chance of success in the campaign, opponent, and degree of potential legislative influence. Endorsement may lead to funding or supplying volunteer workers. Endorsements for local candidates follow consultation with the local division. Congressional endorsements are made by the national PACE after divisional and chapter consultation. During the election campaign, volunteers might be used to conduct door-to-door canvasses or to contact voters by mail or phone to promote the candidates endorsed by the NASW.

In addition to candidate support and endorsement, the PACE committee is often involved in voter registration efforts. Such efforts are also one way of establishing contacts that lead to the development of coalitions. The establishment of coalitions effectively extends its activities and resources. The PACE resources, in active members and financing, have been growing. Fund raising is a vital part of its activities. These funds support candidates, as do the canvassing, voter registration, publicity efforts, and get-out-the-vote drives carried out by the PACE volunteers.

The significance of these activities lies in the influence that active members of the PACE have with an elected official once the election campaign is over. The endorsements of candidates are based mainly on their support for social work policy positions. The chances of the NASW's input into social policy formulation is better assured by backing a legislative policymaker who might support a policy that the profession desires once in office.

In 1978, Florida became the first state chapter of the NASW to organize a PACE committee. The NASW chapter in Florida chose to develop a political action committee to complete their goal of comprehensive policy influence at the state level. The chapter saw development of a PACE organization as a normal extension of the association's involvement in a political system of competing interest groups. Traditional anxiety about violating the Hatch Act and antipathy toward lobbying and political action were addressed directly by the PACE organizing group. They gained executive committee and executive director support. Florida PACE established itself under the state election laws and selected some NASW board members to serve among its trustees. This demonstrated its connection to the NASW goals. After its formation, the PACE committee advertised itself in the state NASW newsletter, highlighting its support within the NASW leadership. In 1978, Florida PACE initially focused on candidate endorsement, granting it only to candidates who, when invited to do so, asked for an endorsement and supplied written material, including answers to a thorough questionnaire on policy issues. Small donations were also given to the endorsed candidates. The gubernatorial candidate supported by the PACE committee and some of the legislative candidates it supported won election. The newly elected governor asked members of the PACE to participate on the inauguration committee. The investment by Florida PACE in candidate endorsement legitimated the group, greatly increased social work visibility in the state, and extended the potential for strong input in social policymaking by Florida social workers (Mahaffey and Hanks, 1982).

LINE WORKER AND ORGANIZATIONAL POLICYMAKING

Line workers can definitely be involved in the policy-influencing activities of the NASW. The effort of organizations like the ELAN and PACE is to support social work backed legislation and candidates at all levels. Line workers know the policy needs of their clientele and the overall policy goals of the profession. As informed professionals, they can play an important role in efforts to influence social legislation.

Active, informed members are necessary to the success of these policy-influencing efforts of the professional organization. In addition to influencing social legislation, activities within the NASW that create its own policy constitute an arena for line worker efforts and input. Social workers, as active members of the professional association, can either serve as policymaking delegates or influence those who are delegates. Implementation assures feedback.

The ability to maintain professional or collegial connections is just as important in the social agency policy-formulation processes. Whether or not the worker is part of the public agency's policy-review process or regardless of how distant the relationship between board member and line worker may seem, someone in the agency has contact with the review process or with the board's decision making. Line workers must have connections directly with the process and policymakers or maintain indirect connections through those who have access to it. In this fashion, workers can ensure that they maintain input in the policymaking process of the social service agency.

FOR FURTHER STUDY

1. Identify the ways in which your practice setting makes policy. Discuss with the social workers who work there how they are involved in formulating policy. In what ways do you think they could be more or better involved?

2. Discuss with a worker in a private agency and one in a public agency the major ways policy is developed in their agency. Assess the role of formal and informal structures in making agency policy.
3. Study several private agencies in your area by analyzing their board structure. How would you characterize the decision making of each board?
4. Discuss with members of the NASW division in your area how they reacted to and implemented the policy priorities adopted at the 1981 Delegate Assembly.
5. Investigate the role of the ELAN and PACE organizations in influencing policy. How effective have they been? What role might you play?

GLOSSARY

Private or "voluntary" agency   An agency where funding comes more from so-called voluntary donations. These agencies are held accountable for use of these funds through the actions of a board of directors.

Public agency   Such agencies rely for their funding on public, government sources. They are accountable to elected officials through bureaucratic procedures.

Board of directors   The directing authority of most private agencies. Such a group of (lay) persons determines the broad policy of the agency.

Policy review process   A procedure used by staff in many public agencies to develop policy drafts, send them to designated persons for review, revise them according to their responses, and transmit them to appropriate higher officials after approval by the agency executive.

Program guide   The outcome of a public agency's policy development and review process. It is designed to bring the agency into compliance with a policy directive or regulation issued at a higher level in the public service delivery structure.

Policy-prioritizing procedure   The biennial procedure used in 1979 and 1981 at the NASW's Delegate Assembly to develop, review, and adopt the organization's program and policy goals. The assembly is the chief policymaking body of the national organization.

ELAN   The Education Legislative Action Network of the NASW. It is designed to inform and mobilize the entire membership of the association on social policy legislation matters.

PACE   Political Action for Candidate Election is an independent part of the membership of the NASW. Its major purpose is to support the election of public officials who will pursue the NASW's social policy goals.

BIBLIOGRAPHY

Brager, G. and S. Holloway. *Changing Human Service Organizations.* New York: Free Press, 1978.
Jansson, Bruce S. and Samuel H. Taylor. Search activity in social agencies: Institutional factors that influence policy analysis. *Social Service Review,* 52(2):189–201, 1978.

Lee, Laura J. The social worker in the political environment of a school system. *Social Work*, 28(4):302–307, 1983.

Lipsky, Michael. *Street-Level Bureaucracy.* New York: Russell Sage Foundation, 1980.

Mahaffey, Maryann and John W. Hanks (eds.). *Practical Politics: Social Work and Political Responsibility.* Silver Spring, Md.: National Association of Social Workers, 1982.

Miringoff, Marc L. *Management in Human Service Organizations.* New York: Macmillan, 1980.

National Association of Social Workers. *ELAN Handbook.* Washington, D.C.: National Association of Social Workers, no date. (Mimeo.)

National Association of Social Workers. *Program Priority-Setting Process.* Washington, D.C.: National Association of Social Workers, no date. (Mimeo.)

National Association of Social Workers. *NASW News*, 26(7), July 1981.

National Association of Social Workers. *NASW News*, 27(1), January 1982.

Sheffer, Carol J. *PACE Handbook: A Guide to Political Action.* Washington, D.C.: National Association of Social Workers, 1978.

Weissman, Harold H. *Overcoming Mismanagement in the Human Service Professions.* San Francisco: Jossey-Bass, 1973.

Westchester County Department of Social Services. "Commissioner's memo." White Plains, N.Y., 1980. (Mimeo.)

CHAPTER SEVEN

Setting Social Policy

"In politics as in other things, there is no such thing as getting something for nothing. The payoff may involve compromises of various types that may strike at the ideals and principles one has held dear. . . ."
—ASA PHILIP RANDOLPH (1944)

"To provide for the general welfare by establishing a system of federal old-age benefits, and by enabling the several states to make more adequate provision for aged persons, blind persons, dependent and crippled children, maternal and child welfare, public health, and the administration of their unemployment compensation laws; to establish a Social Security Board, to raise revenue, and for other purposes."
—The Social Security Act

OVERVIEW

In this chapter understanding the policymaking of the legislative branch will be emphasized. The relation of the budget-making of the executive branch to the policymaking of the legislative branch will be covered. In addition a note on the relationship of these two processes to that of judicial policy-making will be offered. How local communities allocate resources and an analysis of line worker input into each process will also be made.

OBJECTIVES

- ☐ Discuss how a bill becomes a law and describe how line workers might make input into the process.
- ☐ Explain how the budget-making of the executive branch relates to the legislative process.
- ☐ Describe how local communities set their social policies.

WITHIN SOCIETY AT LARGE and local communities there are several processes by which decisions are made to allocate major social resources. These include legislating, budgeting, and United Way decision making. An understanding of the legislative process at the national level is also useful for understanding state and local legislative processes. The basic procedures of bill development and sponsorship, interest group input, formal testimony and committee hearings, and decision making based upon compromise are as true for state legislatures and for many municipal or county-wide processes as they are for the federal legislature. The involvement of interest and information-producing groups also takes place at each level. Their activities provide critical input in the development of social legislation.

In addition to the passage of laws, the development of public budgets is a major means for establishing social policy priorities. For society at large, federal, state, and local executives propose budgets, either for response and modification by a legislative body or for implementation by an agency. These proposed budgets represent the policy stances of executives and their advisors. With the power to suggest major resource allocation guidelines in their proposed budgets, executives are able to chart significant policy courses. The budgets of President Kennedy proposed a New Frontier, those of Johnson a War on Poverty, and those of Nixon and Reagan a New Federalism. The first two would have allocated resources at the federal level to the impoverished and oppressed; the latter two would have focused resource allocation decision making at the state and local levels.

State governors also present to their legislatures and constituents budgets in which they outline key policy proposals, such as crime prevention or urban revitalization. At the local level, urban or county executives are charged with developing plans to allocate resources in appropriate and politically acceptable ways. An overview of how the national budget is produced by executive and legislative action is useful for understanding other levels of budgeting in the public sector.

Somewhat akin to such budgetary policy setting mechanisms are the ways local communities decide how to allocate funds raised by so-called voluntary donations to support local social service programs. In some ways, the typical approach to budgeting and policymaking for the allocation of these resources combines the processes of executive budget making with the public hearings of a legislative process. Although the participants are not as directly representative of the community as publicly elected legislators are, the level of interest group participation is as keen, and strong efforts are made to assure community input.

LEGISLATIVE PROCESSES

This process consists of more actors and procedures than only the legislators who debate and vote on bills. Bills must be researched and written, committee hearings held, and floor debates undertaken. Persons other than legislators, including lobbyists and congressional staff members, work to develop legislation. Interest groups not only exert pressure to produce or modify a bill, but provide formal testimony as well. Committee work and committee staffs are also of critical importance in a bill's movement from a draft into a law.

In each branch of Congress, a bill follows a similar path on its way to becoming law. Bills are written, introduced, assigned to a committee and subcommittee, examined in hearings, modified, reported out of committee, scheduled and debated by the full membership, voted upon, and (depending on the vote and whether the other house is considering a similar bill) sent to the other house of Congress for approval or to a conference; it finally is sent to the President. At each stage the bill can die, be modified, or remain unchanged. Each stage will be elaborated on and analyzed to provide details on how and where social workers might intervene (see Figure 11 for an overview of how social legislation is made).

The first step in the development of social policy legislation is the initial drafting of a bill. During this stage of a bill's development, a member of Congress and that member's staff may propose legislation which they believe represents the interests of their constituents or which would implement a major political position of the congressperson. Social policy initiatives may also come from a particular interest group. Such groups seek congressional sponsors for the legislation they propose, or attempt to influence the legislation being written by legislators. The National Education Association, for example, long proposed and supported legislation that would establish a Department of Education. The anti-abortion lobby was responsible for creating the language that prohibited government Medicaid funding for most abortions. Women's groups helped develop legislation that extended the dead-

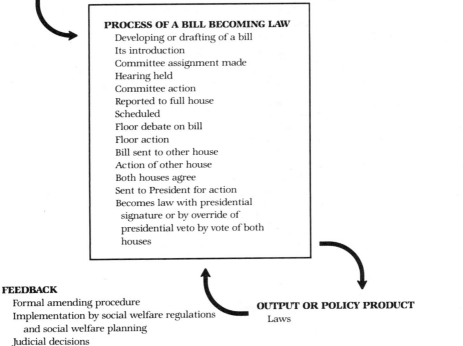

POLICY-RELATED INPUT (which can be made at any of several points in the legislative process)
    Lobbying of pressure groups
    Staff research
    Legislator's analysis
    Political party platforms
    Executive proposals

PROCESS OF A BILL BECOMING LAW
    Developing or drafting of a bill
    Its introduction
    Committee assignment made
    Hearing held
    Committee action
    Reported to full house
    Scheduled
    Floor debate on bill
    Floor action
    Bill sent to other house
    Action of other house
    Both houses agree
    Sent to President for action
    Becomes law with presidential
        signature or by override of
        presidential veto by vote of both
        houses

FEEDBACK
    Formal amending procedure
    Implementation by social welfare regulations
        and social welfare planning
    Judicial decisions

OUTPUT OR POLICY PRODUCT
    Laws

FIGURE 11. **Social policy setting: legislation.**

line for the ratification of the Equal Rights Amendment (*Congress and the Nation*, 1981).

Appropriate sponsorship is critical to the successful transformation of a bill into law. Moreover, a member of Congress may sponsor a measure proposed by the President. Such policy initiatives usually represent the party interests of the executive and of the sponsoring congressperson. Regardless of whether it is prepared by a member of Congress, an interest or professional group, or the executive, advice is frequently sought from other interested parties, such as the NASW.

Frequently, a similar bill or piece of legislation is introduced into both houses of Congress at the same time. Whether introduced at the same or at different times, the bills follow a somewhat similar developmental course in either house. At the time of its introduction, the bill is given a number and is assigned to an appropriate committee. It is sent to the Government Printing Office where copies are made for distribution in the House and Senate document rooms. Congressional members and the public obtain copies of bills from these document rooms. Committee assignment is critical. For most bills, their fate is determined by the response of committees (Dear and Patti, 1981). If the committee takes no action, the bill dies at this point and must be reintroduced in the same or an altered form. Committees in turn assign bills to their subcommittees for action (see Table 17 for a listing of congressional committees involved in social legislation).

If the committee and subcommittee decide to act, hearings are usually held in the subcommittee. From these hearings the committee develops the

TABLE 17
Congressional Committees Relevant to Social Work in the 95th and 96th Congresses

SENATE
  Agriculture, Nutrition, and Forestry
    (human nutrition)
  Appropriations
    (government revenues for welfare, among others)
  Banking, Housing, and Urban Affairs
    (urban affairs and public housing)
  Judiciary
    (civil rights)
  Labor and Human Resources
    (aging, alcoholism, children, poverty, the handicapped)
  Select Indian Affairs
    (services to native Americans)
  Special Aging
    (problems of the aging)

HOUSE OF REPRESENTATIVES
  Agriculture
    (nutrition)
  Appropriations
    (government revenues for urban development and welfare, among others)
  Banking, Finance and Urban Affairs
    (urban development and housing)
  Education and Labor
    (employment and human services)
  Judiciary
    (civil rights and criminal justice)
  Select Aging
    (problems of the aging)

substance and prepares the technical language of the bill. The process of the hearings involves obtaining documentation and hearing witnesses. The staff of the committee provides information requested by the chair and committee members. A committee's staff is a critical contact for anyone seeking to influence legislation. The staff receives information from interested persons, assists in scheduling the testimony, and conducts research (*ELAN Handbook*).

At the hearing, testimony of interested persons follows a somewhat predictable format. Actual testimony or a written statement of it is presented to the committee. Committee hearings are designed to gather information and obtain public opinion. Usually, bill sponsors, governmental bureaucracy representatives, committee staff, and others testify. Those who testify must be familiar with both the issue at hand and the rules or procedures of the committee. Research on the issue would seek background information on any statutes the bill would replace or change and how the proposed law would aid or hamper current laws dealing with it, provide evidence to refute or support the bill's main points, outline what the bill would cost, and summarize the positions of other interest groups. The witness also must be completely familiar with the legislative history and prospects of the bill, including its sponsors, any floor action on it, its opponents, and mechanics of the committee considering it.

In addition, knowledge of individual committee members is important. With a thorough knowledge of the policy issue, the bill, and the committee that is hearing it, witnesses develop either a policy position paper or prepare oral testimony. A position paper is a short statement that addresses bills designed to implement policy and helps assess how the bill relates to an organization's position on the issue. Oral testimony, even if based on a written statement, not only presents a position but objectively states both sides and comments on specific sections of the bill.

The testimony itself includes the speaker's self-introduction, a description of the organization the witness represents, a general position and specific comments on the issue and bill, and an expression of appreciation for being allowed to testify. Questions are usually asked of the witness. Witnesses often use role playing to prepare for questioning and cross examination. The preparation and presentation of expert testimony or the development of a position paper for an agency or professional association is a skill line workers can apply, especially at the state and local levels (Kleinhauf, 1981). After the hearings are held, the bill is considered by the full committee.

Members of the full committee may offer amendments proposing changes in the original bill. The bill may be rewritten entirely or presented with committee amendments. The committee prepares the bill for presentation to the full house. In reporting out the bill for floor action, the committee's report may be favorable or unfavorable. A dissenting minority report may

PATH FROM BILL TO LAW
(introduced separately or in both houses simultaneously)

PATH IF BILL FAILS TO BECOME LAW

DRAFTED
by congressperson, executive, or interest group
SPONSORSHIP

INTRODUCED, GIVEN A NUMBER, PRINTED
and placed in documents room

ASSIGNED
to a committee and placed on its calendar

SUBCOMMITTEE HEARINGS, TESTIMONY, FULL COMMITTEE
redraft or mark up, possible changes

FULL COMMITTEE ACTION REPORTED OUT
favorably or unfavorably, with majority and possible
minority report

NO
ACTION

DEFEAT
NOT
REPORTED

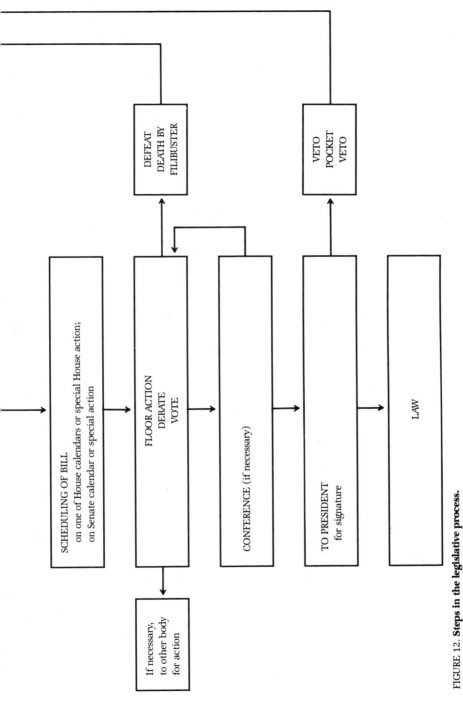

FIGURE 12. **Steps in the legislative process.**

accompany a favorable report. Usually the bill is reported out along with a statement of committee reasoning.

Next, the bill is scheduled for floor action. A bill is placed on a given congressional body's calendar or receives some form of special scheduling action. The House has five calendars, the Senate one. In the House, a bill may be considered out of its scheduled order, that is, it may receive special action. Such special action requires a resolution of the Rules Committee to bring the bill to debate. In the Senate, a bill also usually awaits its turn, but may be considered out of its scheduled order if requested. Senators also may "filibuster," use their right to unlimited debate. They would debate the motion to consider the bill, trying to prevent its reaching the floor of the House. In both houses the bill and any amendments or riders are debated and voted upon by all members of that legislative body. During these debates and up to the point of voting, pressure groups try to persuade members of Congress to vote in line with their special interests. Input from these lobbying efforts, whether by the President, an influential individual, or a paid lobbyist, remains critical at this stage in the development of social policy legislation.

When the bill has passed both houses, sometimes the two versions differ in important ways. If this is the case, a conference committee, composed of members of the respective committees that developed the legislation, meets to work out a compromise bill. The compromise proposal is returned to both houses for a vote. If the bill passes both houses, it is then sent to the President for action. The President may sign it into law, veto it, or take no action. If the President takes no action and Congress is in session, it becomes law without the President's signature within 10 days. If it is not signed, but Congress adjourns prior to the end of 10 days, the bill does not become law but is the victim of a so-called pocket veto. If the President vetoes the bill outright, it is returned to both houses of Congress along with the reasons for its veto. Such a presidential veto might be overridden by a two-thirds vote of both houses. In efforts to override a presidential veto, the actions of lobbyists again may become a major element in the process. If it is overridden, it becomes law without the President's signature (see Figure 12 for a review of the steps involved).

LINE WORKER INPUT INTO LEGISLATIVE PROCESSES

As was indicated in the description of legislative processes, there are several points where input from social workers is possible. The first occurs during the initial stage of drafting and obtaining sponsorship of the bill. If developed by powerful pressure groups or sponsored by important members of Congress, the bill has a significantly greater chance of being accepted by a committee. Professional membership and active participation in a professional group's policy influencing procedures best assure line worker input.

Throughout the process, lobbying tactics can be applied in other ways. Critical points for its use would be prior to any votes in a subcommittee or full committee, on the floor of either house, or in a conference committee. Such tactics could be carried on with committee and member staffs. Another place for input is by giving expert testimony. Written and/or verbal opportunities to give testimony may come from an invitation or it may be solicited by the witness. At the federal level, testimony would more likely be handled by representatives of professional social work associations. In state or local legislative processes, line workers who are expert in a given area have a real opportunity to provide their input.

Of equal importance as a means of input and applicable at many stages in a bill's movement toward becoming a law would be letter writing. Letters would be sent to the worker's senators or the congressperson from the appropriate congressional district. Letters can be a significant means of providing input in the legislative process. The proper time for this form of input would be durng committee or floor debates. As will be developed more in chapter eleven, workers can be directly involved by making policy as an elected official and by shaping the platform of a political party.

A less direct means of input, but an important one, would be voting. The NASW, as noted earlier, has developed a structure to promote the election of candidates of its choice. The line social worker could also collect information about voting records of incumbents and about the kinds of legislation the candidates have sponsored or propose to sponsor. This information could be used by line workers to determine their own voting preferences, as well as to influence the voting of others.

Worker input should be informed input. Line workers can keep abreast of social policy developments by researching federal social policy legislation and related social welfare policy regulations. (For a list and description of sources on legislation see Table 18.) Such information includes details of congressional voting records, schedules of committees and hearings, congressional calendars, committee work, bill introductions, and floor actions. In addition, workers must become knowledgeable about the activities of allied and/or opposed interest groups through familiarity with the publications of such groups. Information from the state or local level also must be sought out and studied.

FORMAL PROCEDURES FOR FEEDBACK

For social policy legislation, feedback or policy modification occurs as it is implemented by the regulatory procedures of the institution of social welfare. That process will be covered in the next chapter. Another feedbacklike process occurs during the enactment of amendments to existing legislation. After legislation has been passed and implemented, those closest to it and

TABLE 18
Sources of Knowledge about Federal Legislation and Regulations

1. *The Advocate for Human Services*
   A publication of NASW, this monthly publication aims to inform subscribers about legislation of concern to social workers. It provides details of efforts by NASW to influence legislation along with details of important social legislation.
2. *Congressional Record and Congressional Record Abstracts*
   Provides a daily account of floor action, bill introductions, hearings, and schedules while Congress is in session. Published by Capitol Services, Inc., it provides a useful record of congressional actions, events, and materials.
3. *Federal Register*
   A publication of the General Services Administration, it presents all federal agency regulations and legal notices of public interest. The Register, appearing on a weekday basis, also prints presidential proclamations and executive orders.
4. *Congressional Quarterly*
   This nongovernmental publication provides a weekly examination of legislative activity, including the role of committees and special interest groups. Voting records and the status of bills are reported.
5. *Copies of Bills*
   Write to the appropriate document room, U.S. House, Washington 20515 or Senate, Washington 20510, requesting a copy of a given bill by including an address label. A similar request could be made of the appropriate Senator or Congressperson.
6. *Pressure Group and Professional Association Newsletters or Other Informational Material*
   These are useful in identifying and understanding the position of allies and opponents. They range from educational and medical association newspapers to the more irregular productions of single issue interest groups. Examples would be the League of Women Voters, Common Cause, and NASW policy-related publications.
7. *Washington Social Legislation Bulletin*
   Published by the Social Legislation Information Service, a division of the Child Welfare League of America, the Bulletin impartially reports on legislation and federal agency activities. It is published twice a month and contains articles on legislation, regulations, and related publications.

most familiar with its operation may suggest changes in, additions to, or deletions from the original legislation. They do so by attempting to get amendments to it passed. Amending legislation follows the same general procedures as the passage of a bill.

The Social Security Act of 1935 has been amended several times. In 1957, a new program covering disabled persons was added. In 1965, there was the addition of two health programs: Medicaid and Medicare. In 1974, the program for the disabled, along with two original programs covering the blind and the aged, were combined into the Supplemental Security Income Program. In addition to such new or altered programs, eligibility has changed over the years. For example, originally workers were eligible for old age retirement benefits at 65; the age of 62 has been added as an option. Size of benefits and size of contributions also have changed with time.

POLICY IN EXECUTIVE BUDGETS

The development of the federal budget is a second primary source of national social policy. The budget grows out of the response of the legislative branch and its policymaking process to the policy initiatives contained in the annual budget proposals of the executive branch. The process of developing the federal budget has increased in complexity as the size and detail of federal spending has increased. The President submits the administration's budgetary proposals to Congress in late January. The annual budget requests set forth basic policy directions through proposals for cuts and/or increases in the entire range of social welfare and non-social-welfare programs.

The process of developing the budget starts about 18 months before the October 31 beginning of the fiscal year. This means that during the spring preceding the President's January presentation of the budget, the administration begins to develop its proposals. The President, officials of departments, and members of the Office of Management and Budget review programs and issue policy directions for agencies to use in preparing their requests for the upcoming fiscal year. These requests are brought in line with presidential policy and with administration projections for tax revenues. The budget proposed by the President consists of explaining how the outlays that are requested would be covered by the projected tax receipts. Presently, the budget covers all agency outlays, including so-called entitlements, under which persons who meet the eligibility requirements of a given program qualify for funding. Many social welfare programs, such as Medicare, involve such entitlements.

Congress uses its legislative process to respond to the budget proposed by the executive. During the last few years, the legislative procedure used to deal with the budget has been modified. The ostensible reason for these changes was to obtain somewhat better control over proposed congressional expenditures.

Prior to the revision enacted in 1974, Congress considered presidential budget requests in a piecemeal fashion, with the House and Senate budget committees first considering spending needs in each of 19 functional categories, and then arriving at an overall total. Under the revised procedures, the first budget resolution, reported by April 15, must set the initial overall total goals for spending and taxing. These goals serve as guides for the appropriations subcommittees as they develop legislation for federal agencies. By May 15 (the deadline for adoption of the first budget resolution), all committees report their authorization bills. Then the regular appropriations process continues on these bills until the middle of September, at which time action on the second budget resolution must be completed. If the second set of spending amounts differs from the first, then the resolution would ask the appropriate committees to reconcile the difference in spending or taxing. By

September 25, action on this reconciliation bill or resolution must be completed (see Table 19 for the timetable of developing the national budget). The new procedure is referred to as a reconciliation process.

The 1981 reconciliation process represented one that somewhat truncated the legislative process. Reconciliation, as used by the executive branch and its congressional allies, was used to bypass much of the budget-making process of Congress. In the past, although Congress reacted to the President's annual budget request, serious departures from or new spending and policy initiatives were often made by the legislative branch. Under the 1981 use of reconciliation, the budget goals of the President were used by congressional leaders to pare down previously proposed outlays. This was achieved by using a single reconciliation bill to keep spending in line with presidential proposals. Detailed reconciliation instructions were issued to the appropriation committees by the congressional budget committees to make cuts and bring spending in line with goals. In setting a budget, the Senate moved quickly, the House more slowly. Both, after adopting the overall cuts and developing committee proposals, issued a final conference committee budget report that was based on 58 subconference reports.

The Senate (and even the House) acted with such dispatch and held only brief hearings, so input from the public and from interest groups was largely excluded. The budget committees gained power at the expense of the appropriations committees. The budget committees issued overall budget goals and developed detailed reconciliation instructions for the other committees to follow. Their actions replaced much of the conventional work of the other committees in shaping the proposed budget in relation to existing and pro-

TABLE 19
The Budget: Timetable and Terms

Late January
    President submits BUDGET to Congress. The budget covers a FISCAL YEAR, October 1 to the following September 30. Budget describes REVENUES (funds raised by taxes) and OUTLAYS (amounts paid out).
April 15
    Committees report FIRST BUDGET RESOLUTION, setting overall goals for revenues and outlays.
May 15
    Committees report AUTHORIZATION BILLS, defining the scope of programs and stating the ceiling federal agencies are permitted to spend, obligate, or lend on such programs. Congress completes action on the first budget resolution.
September 15
    Action on SECOND BUDGET RESOLUTION completed, setting final fiscal goals.
September 25
    Action on RECONCILIATION BILL completed, bringing, as necessary, the proposals of the second budget resolution in line with the spending targets of the first.

posed programs. In this way, the legislative process was truncated. Subconference and conference committee deliberations were far more extensive than usual. Many contend that the entire budgetary process had been altered. (See Congressional Quarterly, *Budgeting for America*, for a discussion of the implications of the new procedures.)

What began as an effort on the part of Congress to reform its process for receiving and reacting to presidential budgetary proposals, became instead a tool to ensure the adoption of the overall presidential budget, with its far-ranging cuts and alterations in previously enacted social programs. The implications of this process are of critical importance for social workers. Access to Congress and ultimately to the shaping of basic social policy, as it is reflected in the budget, may become much more limited if current trends continue.

LOCAL COMMUNITY FUNDING PROCESSES AND SOCIAL POLICY

Most metropolitan areas, and many smaller cities, utilize some form of organized fund raising to collect and distribute local monies for the support of social and human service agencies and programs in their area. The fund-raising segment of these two activities is referred to variously as united appeals, united funds, and united ways. The planning bodies are known as planning councils, community chests, or community planning boards. Often the two activities are not separated in operation or in organizational titles. The first activity is to collect funds from all members of the community; the second is to allocate these funds. The two tasks roughly correspond to the tax-raising and social-legislating activities of government. In that sense, the monies collected and the decisions made regarding their distribution correspond to social policymaking.

Often, a given local community, whether its geographical boundaries are urban or suburban, will have a United Way organization. The structure of these organizations varies. A local board of directors and professional staff oversee the planning, collecting, and allocating activities. Many of these activities involve volunteers. There are more than 2,100 United Way organizations in the United States. Nearly 40 percent have at least one full-time year-round staff member. They grew out of the late nineteenth and early twentieth century Charity Organization Society Movement in this country. From the 1920s through the 1940s, United Ways developed into efficient charitable fund-raising campaigns, especially in the workplace through the use of payroll deductions. The utilization of a citizen review process came to guarantee the input of a broad range of community members (United Way *Fact Sheet*).

In planning for community services, needs are identified and prioritized. United Ways are sensitive to community input. The extensive utilization of the citizen review process ensures accountability to the community. In establishing priorities, necessary service delivery changes are developed, either by decreasing the funding of existing agencies or by increasing that of new programs. These recommendations for cutbacks and increases account for significant shifts in the social policy of local communities. Feedback to existing policy comes from reapplication and worker implementation.

Many of the larger United Ways have divisions geared toward planning, budgeting, allocations, and collections. In all local communities, volunteers are used to study emerging community needs, to decide how these needs could be met through the development of services and programs, and to determine the cost of meeting these needs. The volunteers involved in such a citizen review and allocation process represent different community groups and constituencies. Their work guarantees input and feedback from those seeking to establish new programs and services. Furthermore, new services and agencies benefit from special financial and management assistance as well as direct consultation services that help in getting them developed and established. Such activities of the United Way support new policy directions (see Figure 13 for an overview of United Way decision making).

For the United Way itself, past policy issues have included the relationship between funding levels for agencies serving girls and those serving boys, the representation of women and minorities in decision making and in the kinds of services funded, the charge of coercion in corporate and workplace campaigns, and the role of charitable deductions in income taxes. Charges have been levied against community funding bodies, asserting that they become

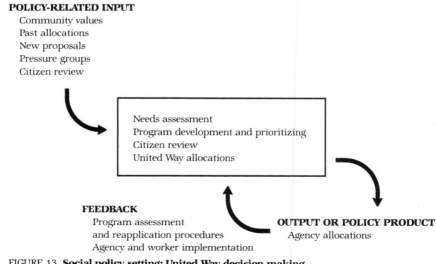

POLICY-RELATED INPUT
  Community values
  Past allocations
  New proposals
  Pressure groups
  Citizen review

Needs assessment
Program development and prioritizing
Citizen review
United Way allocations

FEEDBACK
  Program assessment
  and reapplication procedures   **OUTPUT OR POLICY PRODUCT**
  Agency and worker implementation   Agency allocations

FIGURE 13. **Social policy setting: United Way decision making.**

bureaucracies, funding the same services without change. Such criticism of insensitivity to changing service needs implies lack of public input. It also infers a coercive workplace collection process that excludes the giver from meaningful participation in planning for the distribution of funds. United Way groups have not been insensitive to these charges. Their national board of directors has adopted a policy statement reaffirming voluntary giving, going as far as to discourage the practice of seeking 100 percent participation (United Way *Fact Sheet*).

Line workers, of course, can go well beyond giving. They can become active participants in a local community's United Way planning and related decision making that develops the policies of concern to social workers. The involvement of social workers in policymaking at this level is critical. Voluntary agencies, which once developed services for the working poor or the middle class, two groups less served by the federal government, now work closely not only to complement governmentally funded social services but to cooperate with them in the delivery of services through purchase and contract agreements. Moreover, as the federal role is being redefined, policy decisions will need to be made in the local community to provide services that were once more exclusively funded by the federal government. The importance of line worker input in local community social policymaking at this time is self-evident. The existing accountability structure contained in the citizen review process provides a ready-made point for line worker input.

JUDICIAL DECISIONS

Another basic policymaking approach at the level of society-at-large is that of judicial decision making. Laws and the budgets they enact comprise the bulk of social policy, especially policy that allocates material resources or proposes new opportunities or services. Judicial decisions interpret legislation, clarify or define legal intent, and protect against violations of the Constitution. In its interpretation of law, the judiciary makes policy. Their procedures and jurisdictional boundaries are such that the range of their policymaking and the extent of external input into it are more restricted than in many legislative processes. The three processes of budgeting, legislating, and judicial review are interrelated. Executives propose budgets. Laws are passed that ignore, modify, or incorporate such budget proposals. Courts interpret the legislation that is passed. Interest groups try to bring pressure on all three processes. The social policy produced in turn is implemented or rejected by other of the eight resource systems, including the agency and the social welfare institution.

The next chapter will focus on the major ways used in the institution of social welfare to implement social policy legislation and translate it into social welfare regulations. The bureaucracies (and agencies or workers) charged with policy implementation also carry out judicial decisions. In other words, policymaking in the institution of social welfare focuses less on the policy format issues of "who" and "what" that are emphasized in social legislation, and more on the issue of "how." In this way it provides feedback to social policy legislation.

FOR FURTHER STUDY

1. Collect information about your local United Way. How does it conduct fund-raising and allocating activities? How active are community members in determining the amount of funds agencies receive? What in their allocations raises issues about policies of concern to social workers?
2. Select a bill with a completed history in your state legislature that contains a policy of concern to social workers. Identify its sponsors, committee assignment, hearings, floor actions, and outcome. What factors and actors were the most crucial in its fate?
3. Much has been written about the budgets of the Reagan Administration. Identify how one budget initiative on the part of that administration was translated into social legislation. What role did Congress play? What other groups were important in shaping the outcome?

GLOSSARY

Bill   Refers to a particular piece of legislation as it moves from draft form through hearings and floor action until it either becomes a law or is defeated.

Introduction of bill   When the sponsor of a bill begins its movement through the legislative process by getting it numbered and on the "agenda."

Sponsorship   The person or persons in Congress who, by either drafting a bill or agreeing to support a bill drafted by others, lend their name and backing to it as it moves through the legislative process.

Committee assignment   When a bill is introduced it is sent, after printing, to a legislative committee and one of its subcommittees for basic development and reworking.

Hearings   A committee holds open discussions on a bill to gain invited and solicited information from witnesses about the issue or concern and the proposals contained in the bill.

Testimony   The form used by witnesses to provide information at congressional hearings. Written testimony, verbal testimony, and cross-examination are all used to collect information for committee deliberation.

Reporting out   A range of actions taken by a committee, after holding hearings on and accepting or modifying a bill's language, that moves it to the full legislative body for action.

Floor action   The process, including scheduling, debating, and voting on a bill by which all members of the legislature approve or reject a bill.

Executive budget   The major social policy proposal made by the President about how the federal government will raise and allocate monies for the fiscal year. The budget, in its final form as negotiated by Congress, provides the basic social policy courses for the nation.

Reconciliation   A procedure adopted by Congress to avoid situations in which the final development of programs and their funding proposals exceed the initial amounts targeted for a given area of social spending.

United Way   The chief organization, at the national and local levels, that collects and allocates so-called private, voluntary social welfare donations. The allocations made by the local United Way provide basic social policy directions for that community.

Citizen review   A process used by the United Way to guarantee citizen input into the decision making regarding the allocation of local, private social agency funds. Citizen review is an accountability mechanism.

Judicial policymaking   In the judicial review process, judges and others who participate refine the policy proposed in congressional legislation.

BIBLIOGRAPHY

Baum, Lawrence. *The Supreme Court*. Washington, D.C.: Congressional Quarterly, Inc., 1981.

Congressional Quarterly. *Budgeting for America*. Washington, D.C.: Congressional Quarterly, Inc., 1982.

Congressional Quarterly. *Congress and the Nation*, Vol. II. Washington, D.C.: Congressional Quarterly, Inc., 1981.

Congressional Quarterly. *The Supreme Court and Its Work*. Washington, D.C.: Congressional Quarterly, Inc., 1981.

Dear, Ronald B. and Rino J. Patti. Legislative advocacy: Seven effective tactics. *Social Work*, 26(4): 289–296, 1981.

Kleinhauf, Cecilia. A guide to giving legislative testimony. *Social Work*, 26(4): 297–303, 1981.

Mahaffey, Maryann and John W. Hanks (eds.). *Practical Politics: Social Work and Political Responsibility*. Silver Spring, Md.: National Association of Social Workers, 1982.

National Association of Social Workers. *ELAN Handbook*. Washington, D.C.: National Association of Social Workers, no date.

Randolf, Asa Philip. Why I can't run for Congress on the Old Party ticket. *The Call*, April 28, 1944.

United Way. *Fact Sheet*. United Way of Westchester County, N.Y., undated. (Mimeo.)

CHAPTER EIGHT

Policymaking in the Social Welfare Institution

*". . . in order to reduce the burdens of
existing and future regulations, increase
agency accountability for regulatory
actions, provide for presidential oversight
of the regulatory process, minimize
duplication and conflict of regulations,
and insure well-reasoned regulations, it
is hereby ordered . . . "*

—RONALD REAGAN
Executive Order 12291,
February 17, 1981

OVERVIEW

Social welfare contains many of the resources needed by social work clients. It is a rich source of policies and programs that allocate and contain such resources. In many instances the policies that are produced in this institution are directly related to social policies that have been developed within society at large. This chapter will provide a theoretical look at how social welfare policy and social policy are connected. This knowledge will be used to identify and investigate the major policy formulation processes used in the institution of social welfare. These processes in turn will be examined for the part that line workers might play in them.

OBJECTIVES

☐ Explain the connection between policy contained in social legislation and the policy made in the institution of social welfare.
☐ Discuss how regulations are used to formulate social welfare policy.
☐ Comment on how the development of regulations by bureaucratic agencies influences the direction of policy.
☐ Describe the steps used in the process of social welfare planning.
☐ Discuss how workers might have input into the development of social welfare policy.

THE INSTITUTION OF SOCIAL WELFARE, discussed in an earlier chapter, is a major source of policy for social workers. Briefly, it may be thought of as performing a mutual support function in American society, a function carried out by a range of helping professionals who aid people in meeting their economic, health, legal, family, and personal or social needs. In so doing, these professionals provide services under the auspices of social agencies, special programs, and other settings. They also assist in the identification of needed changes in and new approaches within this service delivery structure. In defining resource systems, it was noted that agencies, colleagues, and social workers are categorized as resource systems, but that they may also be recognized as parts of the institution of social welfare. It was also noted that social welfare has close connections with the society-at-large resource system.

IMPLEMENTATION BY REGULATION AND PLANNING

One way to understand the separate identities as well as the connection of social policy and social welfare policy is to view one as a major input into the policy formulation process of the other. Social policy is made in society at large by legislative, budgeting, and judicial decision making and in local communities by the process that allocates privately collected welfare funds. These policies identify basic needs of people, define eligibility, outline the resources to meet the needs of recipients, and assign these resources to one or more agencies or systems for their delivery to recipients.

After social policy has been developed, social welfare bureaucracies then are frequently assigned the task of designing additional policy to guide the implementation of the social policy allocations. Bureaucracies do so by issuing regulations to carry out the policy contained in social legislation. These bureaucracies exist at the federal, state, and local levels of government. Moreover, other social welfare agencies engage in a form of social welfare planning to implement the social legislation and further refine policy. Thus, social policy itself becomes an input into the policy formulation processes of the social welfare institution whenever its implementation requires the development of bureaucratic regulations of the use of social welfare planning. The issuance of regulations, because they refine the social legislation, may be understood as a feedback mechanism of sorts.

One example of the connection of social policy and social welfare policy is found in the Social Security Act. Under that act, passed by Congress and signed by the President in 1935, initially three of its so-called grant programs for the blind, dependent children, and aged involved complex federal–state funding and administrative arrangements. The original legislation, and later amendments, established basic eligibility guidelines and regulatory responsibility. Federal regulatory guidelines tried to assure some uniformity, but states could set eligibility requirements and benefit levels. By 1980, the average monthly payment for the dependent children program (after 1974 the sole remaining grant program) ranged from a low of less than $90 per month to a high of nearly $400. Hence, the federal–state regulatory arrangement led to great differences in benefit levels for a program based in national social legislation (Federico, 1984).

An alternate way of seeing how social and social welfare policy are connected is to understand each as detailing different aspects of the same overall policy statement. Social policy allocations are carried out by bureaucratic guidelines or by social welfare planning. In understanding implementation, with its emphasis on program details, we can use the simple policy format introduced earlier in this book. That format defines a policy statement as consisting of

☐ Client or beneficiary (the who)
☐ Benefit or resource (the what)
☐ Service delivery approach (the how)

In discussing the format of a policy statement, we also noted that different resource systems emphasize different parts of the policy statement. Social policy often sketches each part rather broadly, with more emphasis on the who and the what. Less attention is paid to details of service delivery, to how the client and benefit are to be connected. The bureaucratic regulations of social welfare provide greater detail about the how. In its detail of the how, policymaking in the social welfare institution has been seen as focusing more on program, less on pure policy (see Figure 14 for an overview of the connections between social policy and social welfare policy).

Implementing social policy, however, does result in the development of new policy departures, especially in the area of policy to guide the effective and humane operation of the systems that deliver services and resources.

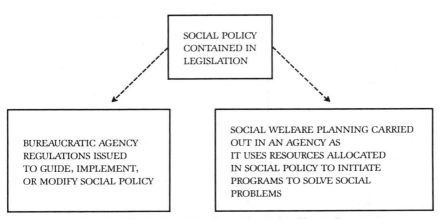

FIGURE 14. **Connections between social policy and social welfare policy.**

This chapter will illustrate ways in which the social welfare institution makes such basic policy. One way is issuing regulations that introduce a new policy course regarding client or benefit. Changes in regulations covering services to children will be examined. The other way, involving service delivery approaches, is to change the level at which regulations are issued, thereby producing a departure in policymaking within social welfare. The so-called New Federalism is a case in point.

The implementation of social legislation or local community funding plans and the creation of policy and service delivery programs are carried out by members of several groups. These include

☐ Welfare bureaucrats
☐ Administrators of agencies
☐ Social welfare planners
☐ Grant writers

They utilize planning skills in their implementation activities. Although each is part of the institution of social welfare, in the scheme of resource systems employed in this text, the discussion will focus more on the activities of bureaucrats and planners. Grant writers and agency administrators would be part of the agency resource system. They, of course, are also actively involved as implementors of social policy. Keep in mind that the same planning approach used in policy development applies to all of these policymakers.

BUREAUCRATIC REGULATIONS

The social welfare institution in the United States consists of a large complex of public and private agencies and programs. The public programs are offered to clients at and by several governmental levels. In the resource system of society at large, as discussed in the previous chapter, the bulk of public social policy is set through legislating and budgeting. Social policy is in turn refined by a range of social welfare agencies, from federal bureaucracies to local community service agencies. At the federal public level, one of the major means for the translation of social policy into social welfare policy is achieved by the development of bureaucratic regulations. The need for implementation arises because social policy legislation is frequently cast in vague terms, with statutory clauses containing the phrases "such as" or "not limited to." Although overall policy goals, funding appropriations, and the designation of service delivery approaches are contained in social policy, the testing of the assumptions about program goals and the design of service delivery systems await bureaucratic implementation (Miringoff, 1980).

A somewhat narrow definition of such bureaucratic regulation would focus on control over economic conditions. At the broadest scope, it would include most of the federal level bureaucratic activity. Nearly every federal agency indicates the procedures to be followed by applicants, such as found in Social Security or grant program regulations. Most authors agree that regulations include (1) greater public control over private sector economic actions; (2) sanctions to discourage undesired behavior or conduct (Congressional Quarterly, *Regulations: Process and Politics*). In either sense, regulations constitute a specific form of policy.

The importance of regulations issued by bureaucracies extends beyond their use in the institution of social welfare. Their utilization and importance in other parts of the federal bureaucracy underscore their vital role in social welfare policymaking. Regulations, for example, are in wide use in controlling the activities of companies operating in the private economy, in setting health and safety standards, and in regulating auto emissions (Stone, 1982). These regulations set policy for and strongly affect the activities of a wide range of businesses and citizens. Not only is the adherence of those who are controlled by these regulations important, but the adherence to the correct procedures by those who establish them is equally important. For example, a federal judge in California dismissed a case against a man who did not register for the draft. One reason given by the judge was that the President began the draft registration program only 21, not 30, days after the regulations implementing the law appeared in the *Federal Register* ("Too Selective," *Time*, 1982).

Social welfare agencies develop regulations in a fashion similar to the one used in public social agencies. At the federal level, the agency charged with implementing social legislation develops any regulations necessary to carry out the law. These regulations are intended to make more specific the policy goals established in the social legislation. Regulations sharpen definitions of eligibility and of services offered, clarify the responsibilities and duties of any service providers, and detail application and accountability rules and procedures.

The regulations are drafted by the staff of the bureaucratic agency. The regulations reflect the values and knowledge of the staff as well as their experience in this policy area. Moreover, any policy issues the administration may be pursuing will also be considered. The proposed regulations as well as all final regulations are published in the *Federal Register*. Although input from the public may have been sought by the agency staff during their development of the proposed regulations, after their publication in the *Register* public input is mandatory.

Public input is sought during regular hearings held by the agency and from written comments made by interested persons directed to the staff of the agency. The public hearings are scheduled by the agency, and, if the proposed regulations are extensive or national in significance, these hearings are held throughout the country. Those directly affected by the regulations and those who would be involved in delivering the services offer expert testimony and critical comments. During the public comment period, letters are also sent to the appropriate staff member by concerned individuals, groups, and organizations (see Figure 15 for a summary of bureaucratic regulation making).

The agency refines or adjusts its proposed regulations in light of the public

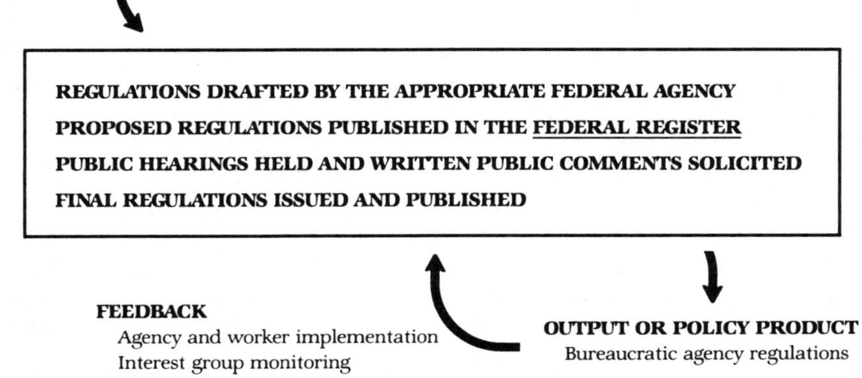

POLICY-RELATED INPUT
Social policy legislation
Planner values
Bureaucratic history
Administrative or executive policy
Interest group ideas

REGULATIONS DRAFTED BY THE APPROPRIATE FEDERAL AGENCY

PROPOSED REGULATIONS PUBLISHED IN THE FEDERAL REGISTER

PUBLIC HEARINGS HELD AND WRITTEN PUBLIC COMMENTS SOLICITED

FINAL REGULATIONS ISSUED AND PUBLISHED

FEEDBACK
Agency and worker implementation
Interest group monitoring

OUTPUT OR POLICY PRODUCT
Bureaucratic agency regulations

FIGURE 15. **Social welfare policy: bureaucratic regulations.**

commentary it receives. The substance of such public comments and their political significance are weighed by the agency prior to issuing the final regulations. These final regulations represent the beginning steps in the implementation of a given social policy and also may contain a basic new policy initiative. In 1982, the Department of Health and Human Services (HHS) proposed a reduction in public commentary and the notices required during its regulation making (Congressional Quarterly, *Regulations: Process and Politics*). If this proposal is carried out, it will greatly reduce public input into this method of social welfare policymaking. One need only reflect on the quotation from President Reagan that introduced this chapter to fathom why HHS might consider such a change in its procedures. The thrust of agency administrators recently has been to reduce all aspects of federal regulatory activity. The next section further illustrates this new direction at the federal level.

REGULATIONS AS POLICY INITIATIVES

The development of bureaucratic regulations involves more than just carrying through on a predetermined course in the implementation of social policy. If bureaucratic policy were so limited, it would not constitute policy per se, because it would be nothing more than a subset of social policy. As we have seen, inherent in bureaucratic regulations are elements of policy: the power to guide the behavior of others as well as the opportunity to make decisions about basic allocations of resources. These policy elements, however, remain dependent to a degree on social policy. On the other hand, the development of welfare regulations can represent new policy departures, independent of social policy initiatives and goals.

One illustration of how regulations affect policy is found in the extent to which their revisions might alter or depart from the original goals contained in the social policy they were intended to implement. Consider the example of a social policy intended to guarantee handicapped children access to public education and the efforts to change it by the issuance of social welfare regulations. In 1975, Congress passed legislation entitled The Education for All Handicapped Children Act, Public Law 94-142. By the beginning of the 1980s, about 4 million children had been identified for and served by special education and related services. In 1981, the Reagan administration failed to get Congress to repeal the law. Based in proposals made by its Department of Education, the administration published in the August 4, 1982 *Federal Register* proposed new regulations for serving the handicapped child, which were intended to reduce the scope of Public Law 94-142—without legislative action. Changes in definitions covering program eligibility and related services and in how education services were to be offered would alter the social policy in significant ways (see Table 20 for an example of how regulations change social policy). A Senate subcommittee on the handicapped held hearings, and a "sense of Congress" resolution demanded that the proposed regulations be withdrawn. Congress could still veto the final regulations if it were in session within 45 days of their issuance date (*Washington Social Legislation Bulletin*, 1982). Significant for an understanding of social welfare policy is the extent to which these proposed regulations—given the safeguards that surround how they are developed, refined, and issued—constitute major policy initiatives. Certainly in the case cited, although it represents a use of the regulatory procedure to negate existing policy, the issuance of a social welfare policy regulation could alter the intent and redirect the goals of social policy.

A second implementation issue grows out of the so-called New Federalism. The debate on this issue is a critical one to social workers because it focuses on the professional purpose of making service delivery systems effective and humane. The debate involves the governmental level at which bureaucratic policy guidelines will be developed and reflects the emphasis in social welfare policymaking on the "how" of policy, on issues of service delivery. It was pointed out in the discussion on the implementation of public social policy that its translation into social welfare policy usually starts at the federal level. Although policy regulations produced at the federal level might be modified at another level, the federal level provides basic directions; regulations formulated at the federal level are important shapers of policy for the institution of social welfare. The New Federalism would change these procedures.

The federal government, through its taxing authority, has dominated other levels of government in the creation of social policy. Few questioned the assumption that the federal government, which collected the revenues, also should be the level at which major public and social welfare policy would be set. The New Federalism represents an approach that challenges this assumption. The federal government would raise revenues and pass major social legislation guidelines. However, the legislation might become less specific than it is now, covering a general allocative area of need in which the money so appropriated could be spent. Much greater responsibility would be given to state and local governments for social welfare policy, for decisions regarding who should receive the benefit, why they should receive it, and how it should be delivered. Thus the New Federalism would shift social welfare policy decision making away from the central to local levels of government (Congressional Quarterly, *Regulations: Process and Politics*).

A number of approaches have been proposed for delivering the New Federalism. Under the Nixon administration, for example, the federal level funded grants to the state and local levels to develop their own programs and services. These "block" grants carried few of the traditional federal "strings" that had necessitated elaborate application or reporting procedures. The

TABLE 20
Bureaucratic Regulations: An Example of Policy Change[a]

SUMMARY OF PROPOSED REVISIONS

Definitions:

1. "Socially maladjusted" is omitted from the definition of "seriously emotionally disturbed."

2. The definition of "related services" would delete school health services, social work services in schools and parent counseling and training. Under the proposed new regulations "medical services" would be defined as "services relating to the practice of medicine." In addition, the proposed regulations would add a guideline which suggests that public agencies may wish to look to the standards, opinions and other determinations of State medical licensing authorities in determining if certain services are medical services within the nature of these regulations. Although the narrative states that the Secretary of Education does not intend to categorically preclude the provision of clean intermittent catheterization (CIC) or particular mental health services, the fact that these determinations are to be made on an individual basis, with the State having the freedom to look to medical authorities for help in defining the services which may be medical in nature, mean that it is conceivable that these particular services could be excluded for some handicapped children. In addition, those children who require medication during the day, such as an epileptic or a diabetic, could be denied the needed education and accompanying related services.

   Related services could also be denied or curtailed due to the fact that the proposed regulations would allow the public agencies to establish reasonable limitations on the provision of related services in the development of a child's individualized education program. The limitations which would be permitted to be placed on the services would include: level, frequency, location, duration, qualifications of service providers, and services required in light of least restrictive environment. The consequences of this regulatory provision could be enormous, since it would, in effect, allow the remaining related services to be "token" in nature, limited in their value to the support for an education, provided by unqualified individuals, and a hardship to parents if provided at some distance from the child's home or school.

3. Special education would be modified in the definition section to include only those types of special education specifically listed in the statute. Therefore, "physical education" would be deleted. In addition, the proposed regulations use the "guideline" (meaning it does not have the force of regulation) to allow the inclusion of special education as a related service if it consists of specifically designed program of instruction.

Individualized Education Program (IEP): The proposed regulations allow for an interval between the identification and evaluation of a child, as do the current regulations. The change in the timelines comes in the elimination of the current 30 day timeline for the IEP meeting after a child has been found to be eligible. The proposed regulations also allow for the actual writing and typing of the IEP to be done after the IEP meeting has taken place, thereby allowing for possible misunderstandings between parents and those officials involved in the meeting.

The nature of the IEP meeting is changed by the proposed regulations in that persons familiar with the child's evaluation, or someone experienced in the evaluation procedures would no longer be required to be present at the IEP meeting. Notice to the parents of the IEP meeting would still be required to be fair and timely, however, the content of the notice is not specified. Finally, detailed procedures for developing and reviewing and revising IEPs for handicapped children in private schools are no longer specified in regulation. Parental consent is also no longer required before a preplacement evaluation is conducted or an initial placement is made.

Free Appropriate Public Education: The public agency has financial responsibility for a child's education when the agency refers or places a child in a school or facility inside or

TABLE 20
Bureaucratic Regulations: An Example of Policy Change (continued)

outside the State. The proposed regulations, however, relieve the local education authority (LEA) of financial responsibility when the child is unilaterally placed in a school or facility by another agency. In this case, the placing agency would bear the financial responsibility unless State law or policy provides otherwise. This provision could have serious implications for children placed in residential facilities by a State department of social services. These children now benefit from P.L. 94-142 monies which finance a portion of their educational costs.

The proposed regulations, in an apparent attempt to shift the financial burden in any way possible, also have added provisions which emphasize the permissibility of using a variety of sources to pay for the education costs of handicapped child. The proposed regulations do, however, prohibit a public agency from requiring the parents to use insurance if this use would pose a realistic threat of financial loss to the parents. Under current regulations, parents may not be charged for the cost of a residential program if the child is referred or placed in a private or public residential program. The proposed regulations would prohibit charges only for room and board and for

special education and related services provided which are in accordance with the child's individualized education program. Since the special education and related services may be reevaluated under the proposed regulations, it is quite possible that parents might have to shoulder a great expense for necessary services in residential placements.

As a final indication of the Department of Education's concern with cost cutting, a guideline has been added to make clear that the regulations do not preclude a public agency from seeking reimbursement for residential costs that it is not required to bear by statute or regulations.

Least Restrictive Environment

Perhaps the most substantial and discriminatory change in the new proposed regulations is the proposal that the public agency be permitted to consider the substantial disruption of educational services to other children in the classroom when a placement decision is made for a handicapped child. While a guideline stresses that this is to be used in limited circumstances, the effect is to undercut the "mainstreaming" of handicapped children on the grounds that they might disturb non-handicapped children in the classroom.

[a]Excerpted from *Washington Social Legislation Bulletin*. Vol. 27 (Issue 42), September 27, 1982, pp. 165–167.

proposals of the Reagan administration also focused on a transfer of programs to the states. These transfers would have shifted administrative responsibility and allocative decision making away from the federal level. In both instances, the use of New Federalism would reduce the role of federal regulations in social welfare policymaking and at the same time expand the use of social welfare planning at state and local levels.

Supposedly, the New Federalism, in permitting local levels greater authority in policymaking, better meets human need because these governments are closer and more responsive to people. Important to social welfare is the issue of closeness to whom. At the local level, there is little evidence of a commitment to social services or to the people served by social welfare. As the New Federalism withdraws the commitment of the federal level, then the most vulnerable populations may be further ignored at the local level and even less well served (Federico, 1984).

SOCIAL WELFARE PLANNING

Understanding policymaking processes in social welfare bureaucracies also requires knowledge of the activities of social welfare planners. These policy-makers, whether they are welfare bureaucrats or agency administrators, grant writers, or some other type of welfare planner, use similar planning approaches. As was introduced earlier in this text, their planning approach adapts problem solving to meet the requirements of policy development. Ideas presented here will be expanded in chapter ten to develop a framework for policy analysis. They use the processes and techniques of problem solving in developing policy proposals, designing programs to refine regulations further, or to establish the new services called for in legislation. These planners also may be found outside the federal bureaucracies, such as at state and local levels and in private agencies. Planning may be necessitated by social legislation that needs more than just regulatory guidelines to implement it.

Gilbert and Specht (1977) and Prigmore and Atherton (1979) identify planning as a policy activity conducted by professionals in a wide range of public and publicly sanctioned voluntary agencies. Planners are hired to solve problems by investigating alternative approaches and by helping interested groups select and pursue a given course of action. In other words, they help determine how to reach policy goals. Social welfare planning represents only a small segment of all planning. Social welfare planning traditionally included deciding how to allocate funds among private social welfare agencies. Such activities were outlined in the discussion of United Fund decision making in the chapter on organizational policymaking. With the new federalism's proposed shift in the level of decision making from the federal to state and local levels of government, social welfare planning may increase in importance for developing social welfare policy and implementing social policy legislation.

One variation of the steps used in policy development or social problem solving was introduced earlier. Perlman and Gurin (1972) identify the following steps:

☐ Defining the problem
☐ Building structures, relationships, and communication networks
☐ Exploring alternative solutions and policies and formulating one approach to solve the problem
☐ Carrying out the plan
☐ Revising the plan from evaluations made and feedback received

Problem definition refines and redefines what might be the needs or concerns of a given population, as they are addressed by a given piece of social policy legislation. Planners also might use such information as input into the making of the social legislation itself. Westhues (1980) refers to the implementation or programming stage of social planning as consisting of three parts:

program design, program implementation, and program operation. These correspond in some ways to the last three phases proposed by Perlman and Gurin. Westhues defines implementation as occurring after policy has been formulated and after problem definition, but prior to evaluation. In other words, it takes place after the problem is defined, and after structures and networks are initiated, but before evaluation and revision occur. Implementation begins just after or with the specification of eligibility requirements and service delivery approaches.

In the program design stage, a model is developed which reflects the social policy goals and follows the agreed-upon policy issues of eligibility and service delivery. This stage involves the following issues:

☐ Target population
☐ Admissions and intake criteria
☐ Eligibility criteria
☐ Nature of the benefit
☐ Staffing issues
☐ Physical plant design and costs
☐ Services distribution, access, and locations
☐ Relationship to existing programs
☐ Necessary administrative and report forms
☐ Budgetary plans and funding mechanisms

In setting up their model for policy implementation, planners undertake research on new services in appropriate literature, conduct an operational review of existing programs, and carry out a thorough study of related legislation and regulations. Service gaps, delivery issues, and additional concerns can be identified, refined, or resolved (see Figure 16 for the steps used in social welfare planning).

Complementing Westhues's discussion of program design and the outline of a basic policy statement format is the discussion by Gilbert and Specht (1974) of issues related to eligibility, benefits, and service delivery. They offer essential detail required for a general understanding of the many decisions made by planners who develop and implement social welfare policy.

Eligibility involves such issues as how universal (all-inclusive) or selective (limited to certain persons) in coverage a policy will be. Eligibility may be attributed to the entire population or to a sizeable subset of it. Eligibility may be based on the principle of compensation for those who have made a contribution to society (such as veterans), those who will make one (such as farmers), and for those who have been abused by societal functioning or prejudicial treatment (such as minorities of color and women). Others are eligible because a professional diagnosis determines that they are part of a group covered in a policy. A final form of eligibility is based on one's inability to pay; that is, it depends on completing a means test.

The benefits that people are allocated include concrete services (such as

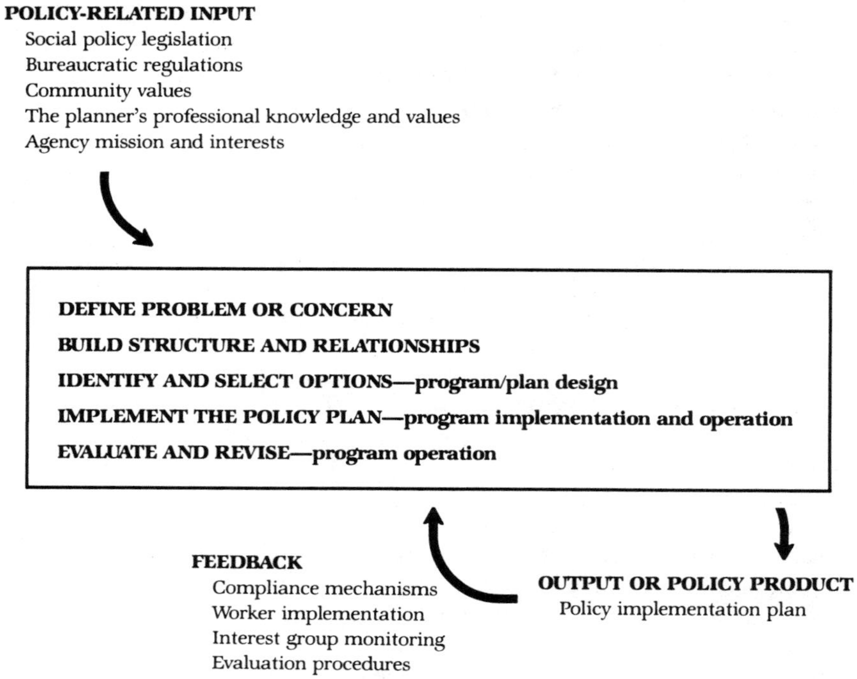

POLICY-RELATED INPUT
Social policy legislation
Bureaucratic regulations
Community values
The planner's professional knowledge and values
Agency mission and interests

DEFINE PROBLEM OR CONCERN

BUILD STRUCTURE AND RELATIONSHIPS

IDENTIFY AND SELECT OPTIONS—program/plan design

IMPLEMENT THE POLICY PLAN—program implementation and operation

EVALUATE AND REVISE—program operation

FEEDBACK
Compliance mechanisms
Worker implementation
Interest group monitoring
Evaluation procedures

OUTPUT OR POLICY PRODUCT
Policy implementation plan

FIGURE 16. **Social welfare policy: social welfare planning.**

transportation or cash), life opportunities, and personal social services (such as counseling). Opportunities are given to people which, if pursued, will result in a situational or behavioral change and might, in turn, lead to other benefits. Personal social services include counseling, therapy, training, and related approaches designed to effect change in individual behavior. Goods or in-kind provisions include resources such as actual housing, clothing, and food. Credits or vouchers are issued and can only be exchanged for a designated resource; for example, Food Stamps can only be exchanged for certain foodstuffs.

Issues of service delivery, or a means of linking the eligibles with their benefits, raise questions of costs, staffing, effectiveness, and the location of services. Services may be fragmented, duplicative, or inaccessible. Planners attempt to coordinate their approaches to ensure that a given delivery network is as comprehensive as possible, without unnecessary repetition of services, and as readily available as possible to all potential beneficiaries.

In her study, Westhues identifies program implementation as involving two components: assigning tasks to actors, identifying what resources are to be used in program implementation; and developing an operational system for the program's staffing, plant, and funding needs. This latter step involves interactional skills in hiring and training of staff and in locating appropriate facilities. Often the planner becomes an advisor to the program at this point, making certain that the implementation plan is carried out.

After this stage of setting up the program and taking steps to put it into operation has been achieved, then actual program operation begins. The major task of this stage is administrative, including data management and the maintenance of policy and program compliance. Issues of feedback develop at this stage. Policy implementation issues involving public policy development and guideline compliance were covered in an earlier chapter. In these situations the part of the planner is one of monitoring (Westhues, 1980; Prigmore and Atherton, 1979) (see Table 21 for an outline of the programming stage of social planning).

POLICY AND THE LINE WORKER

One prominent idea that emerges from the preceding discussion of social welfare planning and bureaucratic regulation is the need for close monitoring of these policymaking processes. Although they provide for public input, such input is not as well publicized nor as actively sought out as it is in the making of social policy legislation. It is evident that social welfare policy, both in scope and in significance, is critical to social work practice. That it needs close monitoring is just as evident. Monitoring of bureaucratic regulations and planning leads to feedback and changes in social welfare policy.

Many authors point out that social policy establishes the goal that will be

TABLE 21
Programming Stage of Social Planning

I. PROGRAM DESIGN, including
    —*Eligibility* by attribution, compensation, diagnosis, or means test
    —*Nature of the benefit*, such as services, opportunities, vouchers, cash, in-kind goods, transfer payments
    —*Service delivery strategies* addressing problems of accessibility, accountability, staffing, service coordination, agency relationships
II. PROGRAM IMPLEMENTATION, involving:
    —*Task assignment and resource utilization*
    —*Development of an operational system*
III. PROGRAM OPERATION, focusing on:
    —*Administration*
    —*Program compliance*

---

pursued in social welfare's implementation process. These goals, however, are sometimes not achieved, or the goal that is reached does not appear to be the one contained in the initial policy statement. Goals may be modified during the stages in the planning process. Poor planning or design and alterations in the policy objectives during implementation can alter the overall direction of the social policy. Goals can also be altered in the issuance of regulations, as discussed earlier in this chapter. In this sense, social welfare policy provides feedback to and modifies some policy.

For the line worker, the stated goals may be used as a point of reference for monitoring the regulations of a bureaucracy or the policy of a social welfare planner. If the social policy goal is in line with the personal policy of the worker or the interests of the social work profession, then regulations and social welfare plans that implement it must be monitored to assure that they have a reasonable probability of attaining that goal. Conversely, tactics to develop a divergent goal in social welfare policy implementation must be pursued if the goals of the social policy differ from those of the worker.

An example of monitoring is found in the experiences of the NASW in Florida. That state's legislature passed a Community Care for the Elderly Bill in 1973. The law, calling for a demonstration project, was passed without an appropriation. A key social worker in the Division of Aging within the state's Department of Health and Rehabilitative Services argued that the division was not responsible for implementation since the bill was passed without funding. At that time, a member of the Florida NASW functioned as a volunteer monitor of the social services bureaucracy. The social work monitor argued that the director should seek outside funding in order to implement the policy. The monitor kept the issue alive, and along with the NASW lobbying activities, gained a funding appropriation in 1979 (Mahaffey and Hanks, 1982).

Monitoring, of course, is not the only policy-related activity that emerges from the discussion of policy formulation processes in this section. A means to examine all policy-related role expectations in relation to practice must be developed. Such a means will be developed in the next section and will translate policy formulation into line worker activities.

FOR FURTHER STUDY

1. Explain the relationship between social policy and social welfare policy. In what ways are they independent and in what ways are they interdependent? Discuss how social welfare policy might be used to alter the goals contained in social policy.
2. Discuss the history of the major bureaucratic regulations issued to imple-

ment a piece of social legislation from the time of its passage to the present. In what ways did it closely follow or diverge from the goals of the social policy legislation itself?

3. Find out if social welfare planning has been used in your practice setting to develop social welfare policy. Who did the planning? In what ways did their approach follow the one you read about in this text?

4. In an earlier chapter, you learned about the process of personal problem solving. Compare the steps used in personal problem solving to those used in social welfare policy planning, as they were discussed in this chapter.

5. Using the ideas and techniques associated with program design, try to create an ideal program to implement a major social allocative policy of interest to you. For which of the steps would you need to do additional research?

GLOSSARY

Implementation   In the social welfare institution, a range of activities that formulate policies designed to carry out or put into operation the goal contained in a given social policy.

Regulations   Detailed guidelines issued by bureaucratic agencies to implement social policy legislation passed by Congress. Regulations may significantly alter social policy goals.

Federal Register   The federal publication in which all regulations are published. It is the source for interested persons to use in familiarizing themselves with new regulations and proposed alterations in existing regulations.

Public commentary   A specified period of time set aside for public input on a proposed regulation, extending from the time of the regulation's initial publication until it has been finalized. Commentary provides for major input from concerned parties.

"New Federalism"   A policy decision-making approach with critical meaning for the development of social welfare policy. It would shift policy decision making from the federal to the state and local levels of government. It would deemphasize the issuance of federal bureaucratic regulations and planning at the federal level as the chief means to develop social welfare policy guidelines. New Federalism would heighten the importance of social welfare planning at the state and local levels.

Social welfare planning   A major means by which social policy is implemented in, refined by, and translated into policy within the institution of social welfare.

Social planning stages   The implementation stage of social planning includes program design, program implementation, and program operation.

Program design   This involves determining who will be eligible for program benefits, deciding on the details of the benefit, and what form it will take, and detailing how it will be delivered. Issues of eligibility, provisions, and service delivery are all involved in the programming stage of social planning.

Monitoring   A key activity that must be used by anyone interested in keeping in touch with policy development in the social welfare institution. The bureaucracies that issue regulations, as well as the agencies that utilize social welfare planning, must be monitored.

BIBLIOGRAPHY

Congressional Quarterly. *Regulations: Process and Politics.* Washington, D.C.: Congressional Quarterly, Inc. 1982.

Ecklein, Joan Levin and Armand Lauffer. *Community Organizers and Social Planners.* New York: John Wiley & Sons and The Council on Social Work Education, 1972.

Education Department proposes reductions in programs for handicapped children. *Washington Social Legislation Bulletin*, 27(42):165–167, 1982.

Federico, Ronald C. *The Social Welfare Institution: An Introduction.* 4th ed. Lexington, Mass.: D.C. Heath, 1984.

Gilbert, Neil and Harry Specht. *Dimensions of Social Welfare Policy.* Englewood Cliffs, N.J.: Prentice-Hall, 1974.

Gilbert, Neil and Harry Specht. *Planning for Social Welfare: Issues, Models, and Tasks.* Englewood Cliffs, N.J.: Prentice-Hall, 1977.

Kahn, Alfred. *Theory and Practice of Social Planning.* New York: Russell Sage Foundation, 1969.

Mahaffey, Maryann and John W. Hanks (eds.). *Practical Politics: Social Work and Political Responsibility.* Silver Spring, Md.: National Association of Social Workers, 1982.

Miringoff, Marc L. *Management in Human Service Organizations.* New York: Macmillan, 1980.

Perlman, Robert and Arnold Gurin. *Community Organization and Social Planning.* New York: John Wiley & Sons and the Council on Social Work Education, 1972.

Prigmore, Charles S. and Charles R. Atherton. *Social Welfare Policy: Analysis and Formulation.* Lexington, Mass.: D.C. Heath, 1979.

Stone, Alan. *Regulation and Its Alternatives.* Washington, D.C.: Congressional Quarterly, Inc. 1982.

"Too selective." *Time.* p. 27, November 29, 1982.

Westhues, Anne. Stages in social planning. *Social Service Review*, 54(3):332–343, 1980.

Williams, Walter. *The Implementation Perspective.* Berkeley: University of California Press, 1980.

PART THREE

USING POLICY
IN PRACTICE

The goal of this text is to create stronger connections between practice and policy. It has been stressed throughout that professional purpose calls for the use of policy in practice. In analyzing and rethinking the linkage between practice and policy, this book has already developed a definition of policies of concern, ideas about where a worker might locate details of each system's policy products, and knowledge of how the policy-formulation process works in each resource system. The purposes of this section are to offer a framework for policy analysis and guidelines for policy action.

This will be achieved by translating an understanding of policies of concern and knowledge of policy-formulation processes into policy-related analysis and action. Chapter nine will discuss the idea of role expectations and various conceptions of practice tasks and "roles." This discussion will be used in chapters ten and eleven to identify the role expectations associated with policy analysis and policy action. Some of these, of course, will be widely practiced by social workers and will be quite familiar to many. Some will be less familiar and less widely used in practice. Illustrations of policy analysis and action will be offered in chapter twelve. These examples demonstrate how a policy issue might be translated into a policy of concern during a worker's assessment of a situation, and how policy-related role expectations might be carried out in getting the desired policy adopted by the appropriate resource system. (Figure 17 presents an overview of how role expectations explain the use of policy in practice.)

Earlier in this text, a policy definition, a format for stating a policy, and steps in social welfare planning and program design were introduced. The

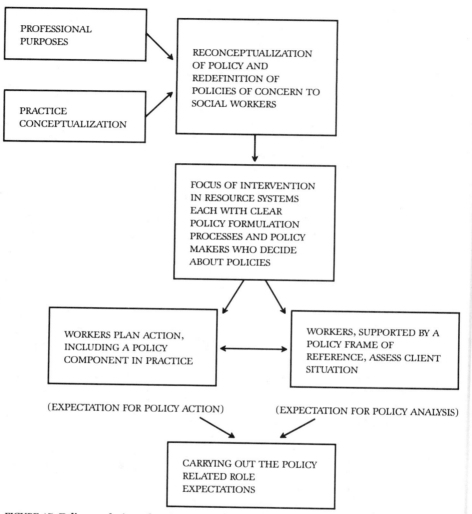

FIGURE 17. **Policy analysis and action tasks.**

*work of the authors used in discussing these ideas, including Gil (1976), Prig-
more and Atherton (1979), Gilbert and Specht (1974, 1977), and Huttman
(1981) will be used to develop a framework for policy analysis and development. The framework in this section builds on and goes beyond existing frameworks. Typically, frameworks for policy analysis are geared toward social
policy or social welfare policy. They focus on understanding a policy or developing an ideal one. In many of these frameworks, how to connect a policy to
the processes by which policy is made is often only briefly described. For line*

workers, policy analysis and policy development are inadequate in their conception if they remain unrelated to action or apply only to making social policy. The preceding discussions in this text have carefully linked each area of policy with potentials for input from practitioners. This section will introduce a framework for policy analysis for workers to use in moving from "case" to "cause." Policy-related assessment, planning, and implementation will be discussed. Workers will be enabled to analyze and develop a policy of concern, decide where to go to seek its adoption, and develop a plan designed to get it adopted. How to determine where to focus a policy-related intervention will be covered as well as how to employ policy-related role expectations to guide the implementation of a plan.

CHAPTER NINE

Identifying Policy-Related Role Expectations

> *"Students are expected to develop skills in the . . . analysis and development of . . . policy. . . ."*
> —Council on Social Work Education
> (1982)

OVERVIEW

The discussion in this chapter will help students understand how societal and professional expectations are placed on the role of the generalist social worker. Issues involved and an approach to extract the major policy-related role expectations from among the total generalist social work role will be offered.

OBJECTIVES

☐ Define social role and role expectations and illustrate them with the social work role.

☐ Define and illustrate practice roles as used in the social work literature.

☐ Discuss how to translate the terminology of practice roles into that of policy-related role expectations.

ROLE EXPECTATIONS

Sociologists conceive of the many tasks and social behaviors that need to be carried out in a society as following a structure of rules that are determined by the dominant culture and that are patterned and predictable. There are numerous such patterns, including social institutions, positions, and roles. Social institutions (such as social welfare, the family, and religion) are organized around basic social functions whereby people are categorized according to the performance of given tasks. Positions are these groupings of people who do the same thing in carrying out the function of a given social institution, such as the position of social worker in the institution of social welfare. Norms, the most basic of social rules, are associated with positions and determine and reinforce what are appropriate behaviors by people in particular social positions. Roles, then, are clusters of expected behaviors (norms) that a society's dominant culture places on categories of people. People may have a variety of roles derived from different social positions. Key ideas in a sociological approach are *role expectations* and the *association of roles with categories of actors* in a given social grouping or pattern.

For example, consider the two roles of a person who is a social worker and a parent. In addition to the person's position in the institution of social welfare, the individual also occupies a position in the social institution of the family. Expectations associated with the role cluster of the social worker position might include linking family members with needed material resources, working with troubled children in school systems, and enhancing the ability of a juvenile delinquent to differentiate between socially appropriate and inappropriate behaviors. In the position of a parent within the family, the person would nurture and provision children, help children with school, and guide their moral development. The obvious parallels in these roles, as well as differences in their emphasis, could produce conflicts as the person tries to be a successful parent and also tries to help children who have not had effective parenting.

The emergence of policy-related expectations for the line worker reflects how flexible and changeable a role is. The person in the social work position also seems to face role ambiguity, because a clear societal definition has not emerged, sometimes leaving unclear expectations for the social work role. For example, many members of American society believe that social workers deal exclusively with poor people and expect line workers to control and punish those poor people. They expect social workers to force the poor to be successful and to make them rely upon other social institutions, such as the family and the economy, for help. Others think that social workers should handle a broad range of human concerns that develop out of people's interaction with (and within) social institutions. They expect the social work role to support a mutual assistance function. Social workers faced with such differences in expectations frequently need to defend and define their role.

In spite of some areas of role ambiguity, many of the role expectations coming from the profession are clear for the position of generalist social worker in the social welfare institution and in other social organizations where workers carry out tasks. Part of the expectation deals with policy-related practice behaviors. Evidence drawn from the profession itself, as used earlier in this text, implies that an expectation for policy activities does exist for the social worker's role. That such evidence need be marshaled, however, does indicate some professional ambivalence in identifying the policy aspects of its role. That policy-related role expectations are not being met, or that agreement on it is not definitive, does not detract from its being an expected part of the generalist social worker position.

As generalist social workers have policy-related practice expectations placed on them in their position within the social welfare institution, similar expectations for their behavior could be identified within the other systems they use in their practice. Some of these expected behaviors, of course, could be shared with other positions in a given system. This is true of policy tasks in the resource systems of society-at-large, the local community, colleagues, and in an agency. For example, other professionals, who are members of professional associations, would be expected to be politically active in promoting their organization's policy interests within society and within their local communities. Moreover, social work colleagues would be expected to develop networks within an agency to affect its policymaking and to influence the policymaking efforts of other resource systems. In other words, there would be role expectations made by society, by the institution of social welfare, and by other social groupings such as professional associations and social agencies (see Figure 18 for an overview of the relationship of the generalist role and its policy role expectations).

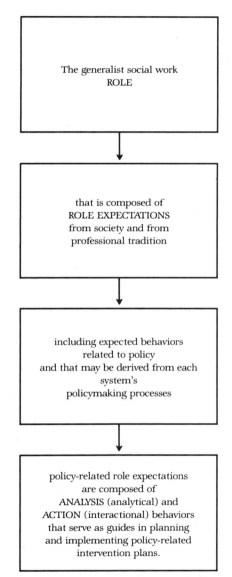

FIGURE 18. **Relationship of the generalist role and its policy-related role expectations.**

SOCIAL WORK PRACTICE TASKS AND ROLES

Studt (1968), Siporin (1975), Compton and Galaway (1975), and Baer (1979) have developed basic practitioner roles and identified them as guiding a series of tasks necessary to the successful achievement of an intervention plan's objectives. The tasks and "roles" are often linked to processes in problem solving. In this way, the establishment and implementation of a plan can be guided by a series of specific practice tasks and so-called roles.

A practice role implements an intervention and in so doing blends analytical and interactional tasks. The blend created serves holistic practice, because the so-called practice role consists of *analysis* and *action*. Analytical tasks are related to the cognitive aspects of assessment, intervention, and evaluation. Interactional tasks are linked to the procedural or relational activities of assessing, planning, intervening, and evaluating. A practice role grows out of both sets of tasks or activities. In blending the analytical and the interactional in a given practice role, equal proportions of the two are not necessarily required. Some roles are clearly skewed more in either an analytical (analysis) or an interactional (action) direction. The same roles, of course, apply to more than one resource system, as well as to more than the policy-related aspects of a practice situation. In other words, a practice situation may call for policy in different systems but use a similar role in each system.

Examples of analytical tasks might include the collection and analysis of information about an agency's board members and their positions on a given policy issue. Analytical tasks might be researching the history of a congressional bill and finding out about the positions of various interest groups regarding it. Or, analytical tasks could be identifying and weighing the effectiveness of potential policy stances that might be taken by a professional association. Interactional tasks could be talking to and trying to influence agency board members, based on the analysis of their positions. It could be the actual give and take of testimony during a legislative hearing. And, interactional tasks might include leading the discussion of a committee composed of professional colleagues as they decide on a policy course for their association.

A review of the social work literature produces a number of practice role examples, some similar and some different. There are two sources of such practice roles in the literature: those from writings that deal with general practice and those that cover the specialized area of policy analysis and planning. The first of these provides a basic elaboration of generalist practice roles. The second focuses on a definition of analytical and interactional problem-solving tasks in a policy context.

Teare and McPheeters (1970) developed a list of 12 roles that helping professionals engage in as they develop and implement a problem-solving plan. These grew out of their work in defining major social welfare needs or problem areas. They identified obstacles that create people's difficulties in each area, and categorized major functions to help meet people's needs in these areas. This resulted in the development of 12 practice goals and their associated roles (McPheeters, 1971):

(Detection) Outreach worker—In reaching out into the community, the worker identifies people who are in difficulty or at risk and identifies conditions causing these difficulties.

(Linkage) Broker—In helping people use and negotiate the existing system, the worker serves as the intermediary between specialists and people who need direction, assistance, support, or additional knowledge in contacting a helper or resource.

(Advocacy) Advocate—Fights to ensure that underserved groups obtain services and that services are expanded to meet their needs, including case (the client) and class (all such clients) advocacy.

(Evaluation) Evaluator—Evaluates and monitors the effect of programs, and growing out of such activities, develops new ways to meet needs.

(Instructional) Teacher—Teaches people new knowledge about their environment or insights about their behavior as well as trains people in specific new skills and approaches.

(Behavior change) Behavior changer—Changes specific parts of people's behavior, habits, or perceptions.

(Mobilization) Mobilizer—In energizing people to expand existing services, the helper works to develop new resources and to make their utilization more effective.

(Consultation) Consultant—Works with professionals or agencies to upgrade their efficiency and skills in service delivery.

(Community planning) Community planner—Works with groups, agencies, and community governments as they develop programs and services.

(Information processing) Data manager—Worker carries out the range of data collection, processing, and data analysis skills used in decision making.

(Administration) Administrator—Manages, directs, or implements a service or program.

(Continuing care) Caregiver—Provides ongoing support for people who require constant care and who are not able to meet their needs or resolve problems on their own.

Although Perlman and Gurin (1972) describe problem-solving tasks in a policy context, their discussion of the analytical and interactional nature of the activities involved in each stage offers a more general formulation of social work practice. The policy-related problem-solving steps include

☐ defining the problem
☐ building structure

☐ formulating policy
☐ implementing plans
☐ monitoring

In defining the problem, the analytical tasks involve studying the problem, conceptualizing the problem as a system, and assessing opportunities and limits. Interactional tasks include dealing with those affected by the issue as well as with experts in eliciting and receiving information.

The analytical tasks involved in building structure include determining relationships, deciding on structures to be developed, and selecting people to carry out various parts of the plan. The interactional tasks would be the establishment of communication and the recruitment of people.

To formulate policy entails the analytical tasks of assessing previous efforts, developing alternative goals and strategies, and selecting a policy. Its interactional side involves the communication of strategies to various actors as well as helping them express their preferences and assisting them in their decision making.

Policy implementation utilizes the analytical activities of specifying tasks, people, and time frames. Obtaining commitments, overcoming resistance, and marshaling resources are some interactional tasks.

Monitoring involves the analytical tasks of designing a feedback system and analyzing data generated by it. The interactional tasks of communication with and obtaining information from various participants are utilized in this stage.

Other roles of a more policy-related practice nature emerge from the writings of authors who focus even more exclusively on policy analysis and planning. Baer (1979) serves as a bridge between discussions of generalist practice roles and policy-related roles. She identifies important helping roles as those of enabler and supporter; caregiver, teacher, and counselor; mediator; and broker and mobilizer. She specifically excludes advocate, maintaining that it is a part of all interventive roles. She departs further from the conventional listing of practice roles by introducing one associated with policy, the cooperative/collaborative role. She sees this role as critical in carrying out tasks that aim to impact on policy.

Other authors have focused more exclusively on policy-related tasks and roles. For example, Specht (1968) identifies the tasks that accompany stages of policy formulation and relates professional roles to these. These stages were developed with the creation of social policy in mind as well as with the assumption that persons other than line workers carry out many of these major policy roles. The eight stages are

☐ identifying the problem
☐ analyzing the problem
☐ informing the public

☐ developing policy goals
☐ building public support
☐ developing legislation
☐ implementing policy
☐ evaluating the effectiveness of policy

The problem is identified through using cases and recordings to discover gaps in service. This is the role of the *practitioner*. In problem analysis, data collection and analysis are the role of a *researcher*. The role of *community organizer* is used to inform the public through a variety of public communications media and through the use of public relations techniques. A community organizer or *planner* role is employed to develop policy goals by creating strategy and analyzing programs. Public support is generated in the role of *lobbyist* or community organizer by developing leadership and achieving consensus for the policy plan. The role of planner or *legislative analyst* is used to draft legislation in the legislative policy stage. The *administrator* or practitioner is involved in carrying out the tasks of program organization and administration during the implementation stage. Evaluation is conducted by the practitioner through the tasks of case finding and data collection.

Perlman and Gurin (1972) define practitioner roles as the prescriptions for how workers should conduct themselves in the pursuit of their tasks. They listed the following in their review of organizing and planning literature:

Enabler or catalyst—Workers skilled in developing relationships and thereby increasing people's problem-solving effectiveness through the process of working with them. Such workers create the climate for or belief in change.

Planner, expert, guide, or interpreter—As a skilled problem solver and with an expert command of the problem or issue, the worker proposes policy for others and guides or assists in their decision making on policy.

Advocate—Nonneutral experts in the techniques of organized action through which the goals of the cause they support are reached.

Broker—Workers who put people in touch with resources.

Activist—Those who reject a neutral or passive stance, being committed to one side in a conflict situation.

Implementor—One who builds power structures and new programs.

Researcher—They contribute to the knowledge and skills base of the profession.

Administrator—One who deals with the functions of management and guidance of agencies in relation to policy activities.

Additional activities, tasks, roles, or subroles identified more recently include search activities involved in policy analysis, influencer/persuader, implementor, expert in networking, lobbyist, expert witness in testifying, and monitor. Jansson and Taylor (1978) stress the importance of search activities regarding policy analysis. It emerges as a role that emphasizes keeping informed through the constant search for and studying of descriptions of policy and programs. Simons (1982) describes influencing as a role by discussing how various aspects of it support the client in carrying out a range of tasks. Two authors elaborate and reinforce the importance of the implementor role. Williams (1980) discusses what he terms an implementation perspective, which focuses policy on service delivery. Westhues (1980), in covering implementation as operationalizing what goal has been decided upon, implies the worker role of implementor, with its associated tasks. The collaborative role, proposed by Baer (1979), encompasses the tasks to be achieved in networking and the series of activities that bring together long- or short-term coalitions. Sarason and Lorentz (1979), in their discussion of networking, point out the important role of the ombudsperson. Lobbying, defined as a series of tasks, is covered by Dear and Patti (1981). Kleinhauf (1981) offers an elaboration

TABLE 22
Examples of Generalist Practice Roles

Enabler or catalyst or enabler and supporter
Planner, expert, guide, or interpreter
Activist
Implementor
Researcher
Policy search activities
Influencer/persuader
Networking or cooperator/collaborator
Ombudsperson
Lobbyist
Expert witness
Monitor
Outreach worker
Broker
Evaluator
Teacher
Behavior changer
Mobilizer
Consultant
Community planner
Care giver
Data manager
Mediator
Advocate
Administrator
Practitioner
Community organizer
Legislative analyst

of the tasks involved in testifying. Cates and Lohmann (1980) identify monitoring as a subfield of policy analysis. Their ideas, along with those found in Mahaffey and Hanks (1982), stress its importance as a policy role (see Table 22 for examples of generalist practice roles). From the work of these and of earlier writers, we can see that the role of the generalist social worker is a complex one that includes wide-ranging tasks, including a number in the area of policy.

TRANSLATING SOCIAL WORKER ROLES INTO POLICY-RELATED ROLE EXPECTATIONS

The terminology used by these authors, however, could prove to be confusing. Many levels of roles are presented in their discussions:

☐ The role of practitioner
☐ Role as part of what a practitioner does, such as community organizing
☐ Role as a subpart of the practitioner role, such as a broker

In attempting to make sense of and draw as much as possible from their descriptions of practice roles, a return to the sociological use of role is useful. Here the *role* would be that of the generalist social worker. The *role cluster* of the generalist social worker would be established through the societal expectations and professional traditions that define the expected behavior of the role. These expectations indicate how the social worker role *should* be carried out. What many social work authors refer to as "practice roles" are the professional and societal expectations for the generalist role. A practice role is in fact one of the behavioral *expectations* for that role cluster. Put more simply, practice roles often identify what the worker should do. Flowing out of these role expectations are the practice activities the worker carries out. These activities have analytical and interactional components. In using this sense of role expectation, we can focus our discussion on the policy-related expectations and practice activities for the generalist social worker role.

This text's approach to policy-related practice activities will use the sociological concept of role expectations to translate the more pragmatic listings of social work practice roles into policy-related expectations. In this fashion, it will focus attention on the policy expectations of the line worker role. The question of what the analytical policy expectations are for line workers will be taken up in the next chapter, the action expectations in chapter eleven.

A serious limitation in identifying expectations for policy activities does exist. Caution must be taken in translating examples of practice roles into policy-related expectations. The language used by authors sometimes applies more to the first purpose of social work (enhancing people) or to the second (linking people with resources) than to the third (making resource delivery systems more effective). Even when focused on all three, practice roles are frequently cast in language that dichotomizes them, with some workers limited to client concerns and other workers restricted to service delivery issues. Because practice roles are conceived of in this way, any role expectations based upon them would prevent workers from viewing policy and practice as intimately connected. The language used also frequently covers client interaction only, and usually only individual clients. Such language is inherently limiting when used to translate practice roles and activities into policy-related role expectations appropriate to the range of systems in which the line worker practices.

For example, what describes expected interventions with clients does not necessarily apply to a colleague, a council leader, or a committee chairperson. Being an enabler or a teacher assumes a patient and open-minded client that might not apply to the ideologically oriented colleague or the administrator oriented toward budget cutting. In the literature devoted to policy-related activities, implementation is assigned exclusively to the administrator. In many cases, however, this is done by line workers, who thereby alter the outcomes envisioned by those who formulated the policy.

Regardless of these limitations, policy-related expectations can be identified and described. The next two chapters will continue our discussion of the policy-related role expectations that can be derived from the policy-formulation processes covered in Part Two. The policy-related role expectations that contribute to the generalist social worker role are derived from activities critical to the processes in those systems that formulate policies of concern. In some instances, in the translation of the practice role language, the policy-related role expectations and activities will be retitled to ensure that they support the development and maintenance of a policy frame of reference and that they apply to the broadest of practice systems.

Certain role expectations are used to guide the development of a policy-related intervention plan. Policy issue identification; research about clients, their needs, and system resources; and policy-related intervention planning are necessary to fulfill the expectation for policy analysis. The next chapter will help students develop skills in the analysis of a policy issue and in the development of a policy of concern.

FOR FURTHER STUDY

1. What positions do you occupy and how would you characterize their role clusters? How would you describe the role cluster of the position of social worker?
2. With which of the so-called social work practice roles are you most

familiar and least familiar? Which have you either carried out in another position or seen performed by someone in another position?

3. Talk to a social worker to find out what practice roles they perform. Compare the roles they designate with those identified in the social work literature. Do they stress any roles of a policy-related nature?

GLOSSARY

Role expectations   The cluster of normative behaviors associated with a position, such as the social worker position in the institution of social welfare. Societal expectations are indicated by the nature of a position's role cluster and related social tasks.

Social work practice tasks and roles   Used by social work authors to identify and describe the overall nature of interventions needed to carry out specific tasks in a given practice situation. Roles guide the interventions. Social work roles are a blend of interactional tasks and analytical tasks.

Interactional tasks   The nature of these tasks is procedural or relational, focusing on interactions with others.

Analytical tasks   The nature of these tasks is cognitive or analytical, focusing on thinking and planning.

Policy-related practice "roles"   Those practice roles most likely to be used in guiding policy-related interventions. Some examples include:

1. Activists who move assertively within the political processes of society to bring about policies they support or those supported by their client or profession.
2. Those who engage in policy activities constantly seek out and utilize knowledge of policy from sources describing the products of the resource systems.
3. Influencers attempt to persuade members of other systems either to change their personal policy or to adopt a more favorable allocative policy in their system.
4. Lobbyists work through informal and formal channels of decision makers to propose those policies favored by the lobbyists or to modify existing policy in line with the lobbyists' interests.
5. Cooperators/collaborators build coalitions of and work cooperatively with members of their own and of other systems to affect policy decision making.
6. Implementors are those charged with putting into place the policy made by others. In so doing, they develop policy by modifying and adapting the original policy.
7. Expert witnesses make presentations based on their knowledge base before some formally convened group, such as an agency board, legislative committee, or regulatory commission.
8. Policy analysts are those who examine policy issues and propose ways to deal with them.

Policy-related role expectation   The expectation that the generalist worker engage in a variety of analytical and interactional policy-related practice activities.

BIBLIOGRAPHY

Baer, Betty L. "A Conceptual Model for the Organization of Content for the Educational Preparation for the Entry Level Social Worker." Unpublished doctoral dissertation, University of Pittsburgh, 1979.

Baer, Betty L. and Ronald C. Federico (eds.). *Educating the Baccalaureate Social Worker: A Curriculum Development Resource Guide.* Cambridge, Mass.: Ballinger, 1979.

Berger, Robert L. and Ronald C. Federico. *Human Behavior: A Social Work Perspective.* New York: Longman, 1982.

Cates, Jerry R. and Nancy Lohmann. Education for social policy analysis. *Journal of Education for Social Work,* 16(1): 5–12, 1980.

Compton, Beulah and Burt Galaway. *Social Work Processes.* Homewood, Ill.: The Dorsey Press, 1975.

Council on Social Work Education. Curriculum Policy Statement, 1982.

Dear, Ronald B. and Rino J. Patti. Legislative advocacy: Seven effective tactics. *Social Work,* 26(4): 289–296, 1981.

Federico, Ronald C. *The Social Welfare Institution: An Introduction.* 3rd ed. Lexington, Mass.: D. C. Heath, 1980.

Jansson Bruce S. and Samuel H. Taylor. Search activity in social agencies: Institutional factors that influence policy analysis. *Social Service Review,* 52(2): 189–201, 1978.

Kleinhauf, Cecilia. A guide to giving legislative testimony. *Social Work,* 26(4): 297–303, 1981.

Mahaffey, Maryann and John W. Hanks (eds.). *Practical Policies: Social Work and Political Responsibility.* Silver Spring, Md.: National Association of Social Workers, 1982.

McPheeters, Harold L. and Robert M. Ryan. *A Core of Competence for Baccalaureate Social Welfare and Curricular Implications.* Atlanta: Southern Regional Education Board, 1971.

Perlman, Robert and Arnold Gurin. *Community Organization and Social Planning.* New York: John Wiley & Sons, 1972.

Pincus, Allen and Anne Minahan. *Social Work Practice: Model and Method.* Itasca, Ill.: F. E. Peacock, 1973.

Sarason, Seymour B. and Elizabeth Lorentz. *The Challenge of the Resource Exchange Network.* San Francisco: Jossey-Bass, 1979.

Simons, Ronald L. Strategies for exercising influence. *Social Work,* 27(3):268–274, 1982.

Siporin, Max. *Introduction to Social Work Practice.* New York: Macmillan, 1975.

Specht, Harry. Casework practice and social policy formulation. *Social Work,* 13(1):42–51, 1968.

Studt, Elliott. Social work theory and implication for the practice of methods. *Social Work Education Reporter,* 18(2):13–16, 1968.

Teare, Robert and Harold McPheeters. *Manpower Utilization in Social Welfare.* Atlanta: Southern Regional Education Board, 1970.

Westhues, Anne. Stages in social planning. *Social Service Review,* 54(3):332–342, 1980.

Williams, Walter. *The Implementation Perspective.* Berkeley: University of California Press, 1980.

CHAPTER TEN

Policy Analysis and Action: Part I—A Framework for Analysis

> " . . . *The movement from case to cause is essential.*"
> —FLORENCE HOLLIS (1980)

> "*Intelligence is quickness to apprehend as distinct from ability, which is capacity to act wisely on the thing apprehended.*"
> —ALFRED NORTH WHITEHEAD.
> Dialogues, December 15, 1939.

OVERVIEW

The goal of this chapter is to develop policy analysis skills and understand how analysis relates to action. This goal will be reached by presenting a framework for policy analysis. The concept that role expectations guide analysis and action and the idea that there are identifiable behaviors expected of those who seek input into policy formulation processes were introduced in the preceding chapter. This chapter will expand upon that introduction by covering the expectation that workers be able to analyze policy. Skills in policy analysis and action will be linked to the needs assessment, intervention planning, and implementation stages of the social work problem-solving process. To reach this goal material already covered in the text, including the format for describing a policy of concern, will be reviewed and extended in this chapter.

OBJECTIVES

- ☐ Define the framework for policy analysis.
- ☐ Explain the relationship between a specific client system situation and identifying a policy of concern.
- ☐ List the four elements usually covered in the statement of a policy of concern.
- ☐ Identify the steps used in the analysis of a policy issue and the development of a policy of concern.
- ☐ Describe the steps used in planning the policy action.

A FRAMEWORK FOR POLICY ANALYSIS will be developed for use in identifying and developing policies of concern as well as planning policy-related interventions. The framework accomplishes the following:

☐ Ties analysis to a policy of concern developed from client need
☐ Utilizes a general format to state a policy of concern
☐ Identifies systems that could produce the policy and provide needed resources
☐ Sets priorities and develops a policy-related action plan

Policy analysis and action are connected through the problem-solving process of assessing needs and planning and implementing interventions. Assessing and planning are two of the interrelated helping stages used by professional social workers in their problem solving and helping. Growing out of their holistic assessments of specific client situations, workers can examine policy implications and issues. Such an examination enables workers to begin their movement from "case to cause" by understanding the policy issues contained in the situation and by developing a policy of concern to deal with them. This movement is brought to fruition by making use of existing policies, as well as by planning and implementing an intervention plan designed to get the desired policy of concern produced in the appropriate policy formulation process.

There are related and parallel policy-related activities for the line worker which ought to accompany the steps in the problem-solving process. The parallel steps to address the client situation begin with holistic assessment and continue through setting goals, formulating plans, carrying them out, and evaluating results. In a similar fashion, the policy aspect of the situation is shaped into a policy of concern and a plan is formulated to get any needed policy adopted. The policy side of these parallel processes include:

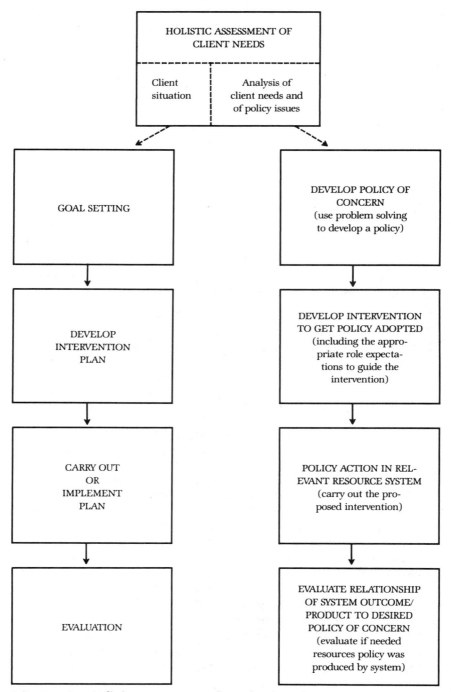

FIGURE 19. **From Holistic Assessment to Policy-Related Interventions.**

☐ Analyzing needs and developing a policy of concern
☐ Planning a policy action
☐ Carrying out the policy-related intervention plan

In a practice situation, of course, the "parallel steps" would not be carried out in isolation from each other. Each of these steps will be fully covered in this and the next chapter (see Figure 19 for an overview of holistic assessment and policy).

DEVELOPING A POLICY OF CONCERN

The worker can develop sound policy analysis and policy development skills by building upon knowledge about the format of a policy statement and the process employed in general problem solving. In chapter five it was suggested that the steps used in personal policymaking and those relied upon in professional problem solving could be translated into skills for use in the identification of need, the analysis of policy issues, and in the development of policy. The format of a policy statement, as introduced in chapter four and as further applied in chapter eight, includes the identification and specification of

☐ Who the recipient will be, with the related questions of eligibility and client need
☐ What resource the recipient is entitled to receive, involving issues of the nature of the benefit or the form the resource will take
☐ How the resource will be delivered to the recipient
☐ What resource system can supply needed resources

This latter area of policy analysis and development covered by some authors (see Gilbert and Specht, 1974, for an example) involves the financing or funding of policy. Funding extends not only to paying for the benefit, but also for the costs associated with its service delivery. In the sense of policy used in this text, these issues relate to getting a specific resource system, during its policy formulation process, to commit all the resources called for by a policy of concern. The resources needed would cover both the benefit and the cost of delivering it to all who are eligible.

The broad areas of beneficiary or client, benefit or resource, and service delivery are researched, refined, and developed by workers in their analysis of the policy issue identified in their practice. The analysis and development of a policy of concern, organized into the format of a policy statement, corresponds to the goal-setting and planning stages of the client-based problem-solving process. Developing such a policy relies on the use of general problem-solving steps including collecting data, conducting research, and refining and developing the policy of concern (see Table 23 for the steps used in the analysis of a policy issue and the development of a policy of concern).

Preceding the development of a policy of concern would be the translation of "case" into "cause." The policy of concern, of course, usually develops out of needs and issues regarding a worker's given clientele. Client need is analyzed in the context of professional purposes. In working with their clients, social workers define the need for new resources, identify the existence of limited resources or partially met client needs, and come across the occurrence of service delivery problems and gaps. Each of these translates into a policy-related issue; that is, they form the basis for the "cause" which the worker will address during the development of a policy of concern and the plan to get it adopted. Such causes are based on the worker's assessment of the need for a policy in relation to the purposes of social work. The cause that underlies the development of a policy stems from the needs of clients and the purposes of the profession of social work. When client needs are aggregated into a policy issue, the worker has moved from case to cause in assessment.

It is important to emphasize that line workers are the most knowledgeable of anyone about the realities of people's lives. They come to know what people already have and what they might need or want. The information they obtain about the lives of groups of similar people is up-to-date and constantly changing. This information can be aggregated to determine need. As a result of their daily practice, workers have real, usable skills for under-

TABLE 23

Steps in the Analysis of a Policy Issue and the Development of a Policy of Concern

---

☐ Identifying and defining a resource allocation issue, problem, or concern
    ABOUT A SET OF CLIENTS

☐ Collecting and analyzing evidence
    ABOUT CLIENTS AND THEIR NEEDS

☐ Researching and thinking about policy goals, options, and plans
    ABOUT BENEFITS AND SERVICE DELIVERY

☐ Using knowledge, assumptions, and values to decide on a policy of concern
    ABOUT THE DELIVERY OF RESOURCES TO CLIENTS
    TO MEET THEIR NEEDS

☐ Identifying the system(s) that could potentially produce the policy of concern, provide resources called for by the policy, and shape the policy action
    ABOUT THE POLICY OF CONCERN

---

standing policy issues or causes. The research process, similar to problem solving, can be used by workers to gain any additional information they might need about the policy aspects of their clients' lives.

Workers also should keep in mind the holistic nature of assessment. It is critical that needs assessment result in the development of policies that recognize the complexity and diversity of human behavior and the inter-relatedness of professional purpose. For example, income support may meet only part of people's needs. Their needs might also include feelings about not having enough money and about having to ask for help. These needs relate to the purposes of enchancing people and resource linkage. Another example would be how affirmative action programs do not get implemented equally among all groups, leading to the development of other compensatory pro-grams, which in turn create their own problems. The professional purpose of ensuring effective and humane service delivery provides the context for this policy issue.

The issues of income support and affirmative action would be approached during the worker's ongoing examination of similar cases in order to identify the policy issues they contain. Holistic assessment would enable the worker to focus on all aspects of the client system and its needs, including those that are directly related to policy.

In order to specify the policy issue more completely, once the concern itself has been identified and described and data has been collected and analyzed about the clientele and its needs, workers undertake similar re-search about policy goals and options. The primary focus of this research will be on benefits and service delivery. Such research deals more with ideas about resources and notions about how to deliver them to recipients and less about client need.

In conducting research about possible policy and program options, exist-ing and proposed approaches that address issues should be investigated. Literature reviews, as well as interviews with persons familiar with the options, would provide information. All proposals and existing options need to be assessed in relation to client need and the identified policy issue. The two interrelated research·efforts encompass the practice-based policy issue or client need and resources and resource delivery. Sometimes the worker will be quite familiar with the clientele and its needs or with existing policy options. Although this may be the case, workers can begin establishing con-tacts with others during their analysis of the policy issue and their develop-ment of a policy of concern.

The next and related step is for workers to use the knowledge gained in their data collection and analysis, along with their personal and professional values, to decide on and formulate the policy of concern they will seek to get adopted. It is at this point in their problem solving that the actual policy is formulated.

In their analysis of the policy issue and client need, and in their development of a policy of concern, social workers will have identified the systems that hold the resources and that could develop policy to allocate them. The appropriate resource system may already possess a policy that must be changed; it could hold the resources called for in the policy of concern developed by the worker, or its service delivery approach could be affected by the proposed policy. The correct identification of the system(s) indicates in what form the policy statement might be delivered. The policy of concern could be expressed in the form of a memo to colleagues, a proposal to an agency, written testimony, lobbying stances, an invitation to others to join in a policy initiative, or a suggestion to a professional organization to take action.

The proposed policy action as contained in the intervention plan provides for appropriate input into the policy formulation process that delivers the policy of concern and the resources called for by the policy. Knowing where to go to get the policy produced emerges from the worker's careful analysis of the policy-related issue and from the identification of needed resources. With the policy of concern in mind, planning how to get it adopted becomes the focus of attention for the worker.

PLANNING POLICY ACTIONS

In conducting research to develop the policy of concern, workers will have gained some familiarity with a given system's products, with its policies, and with the resources they entail. Workers should become as familiar as possible with the system involved. Such familiarity includes learning about any related policy a system has already developed. To obtain such information, workers will utilize sources of knowledge about a system's policy products. These sources were introduced in Part Two. Every worker needs to maintain an up-to-date knowledge base about such relevant policies of concern.

It is also critical for the worker to become as informed as possible about how a system's policy formulation process works. Most line workers will already have a general knowledge about agency, professional, United Way, local or state government, national legislative, and bureaucratic policymaking. This knowledge should be reviewed and updated as necessary. Workers should deepen their general knowledge about a system's formulation process to include specific information about critical decision-making actions and time schedules. This would include such information as the dates of upcoming committee meetings and hearings, timetables for public input into regulatory hearings, agendas in professional organizations relating to policy development, times of appropriate staff meetings or sessions, scheduled supervisory discussions, arrangements for formal or informal meetings of colleagues, and announcements of local community meetings. Such current knowledge about the operation of a system's policy formulation process will help workers schedule activities and allocate tasks in their intervention plan.

As workers research and review a system's policy formulation process they will also gain greater knowledge about its decision makers and about others who have input into its policymaking process. The formal and informal relations each decision maker has in a system should be understood. Knowing how a colleague decides is as important as understanding how decisions are made by the chair of a committee, the head of a United Way, or the director of an agency. Who influences whom and who provides information to others help shape the plan of action. For example, some colleagues turn to others for assistance and advice, a Congressperson might rely on a particular staff member, or an agency director seeks out one or more workers to sound out new ideas.

These informal relationships need to be understood as well as the formal part each actor plays in the process. Such understanding must extend also to any outsiders who attempt input into a given system. Clues for testimony before a legislature can be derived from the input of representatives of other organizations who have testified successfully. Approaches to influence colleagues or agency directors can be culled from interviews with those who have undertaken such input.

Detailed knowledge of a system's workings, its policy products, its resources, its decision makers, and those who have input into its process will be analyzed to determine the best plan to follow in getting the system to adopt the policy of concern (see Table 24 for an outline of the steps used in developing a policy-related action plan). The feasibility of getting what the worker seeks can be tested against past output of the system. For example, it is improbable that a system that unwillingly relinquishes its resources would be generous in dealing with the worker's policy proposal if that proposal calls for substantial outlays. Decision makers that do not listen to outsiders may be more amenable to an insider who would be willing to present the worker's policy of concern. A colleague or client who needs time to think over a

TABLE 24
Steps in the Development of a Policy-Related Intervention Plan

- ☐ Identify and become more familiar with the appropriate system's policy products and the resources it controls
- ☐ Research and/or review the policy formulation process of that system
- ☐ Develop knowledge about the system's decision makers and about others who have input into its policymaking process
- ☐ Develop a plan, based on knowledge of the system, about how to gain input into that system
- ☐ Think about and select from role expectations the one(s) that would appropriately guide the intervention plan's implementation

decision may need to be approached at a later time before giving a commitment or agreeing to a policy change. Who has greatest input in a system and how they have such input will guide the worker's allocation of tasks in carrying out the intervention plan. A United Way planner with exclusive decision-making power, for example, would be the focus of a worker's input.

The plan itself will be put into action and will be guided by the role expectations appropriate for policymaking in that system. The role expectations that workers utilize include ongoing analysis, which pervades the worker's action expectations. Some of the role expectations for action are self-evident, such as being an expert witness in a legislative hearing or delivering public commentary on a bureaucratic regulation. Others, dependent on the urgency of a situation or based in other considerations, may lead the worker to follow less frequently used role expectations. A reluctant colleague may need more pressure to change than that which is exerted in a simple conversation. A professional organization may respond better to the input of a coalition rather than to that of an individual worker. The plan itself must consider what behavior or action will be expected of the worker and of others in carrying it out. A few of these role expectations will be examined in greater detail in the next chapter.

FOR FURTHER STUDY

1. How is analysis, as a role expectation, defined by the author? List as many ways as you can how analysis and action are linked. In what ways, if any, are they ever used in total separation from one another?
2. Review the steps used in the analysis of a policy issue and the development of a policy of concern. Which are you best, which least, prepared to perform?
3. Which parts of the social work curriculum have contributed most to your development of analytical abilities? What experiences have you had outside formal education that have developed your ability to analyze?

GLOSSARY

Expectations for analyzing   The expectation that the profession has for workers to develop skills in the analysis of policy issues and the development of policies of concern.

Steps in developing a policy of concern
- ☐ Identifying an issue
- ☐ Collecting evidence about clients, their needs, and about policy options
- ☐ Deciding on a policy of concern

☐ Identifying an appropriate system for input/intervention
☐ Drawing up the policy of concern in an appropriate form

Forms in which policy of concern is presented

☐ Self-assessment
☐ Memos
☐ Proposals
☐ Written testimony
☐ Position papers or lobbying stances
☐ Committee documents

Policy-related intervention plan   Workers familiarize themselves with a given system's resources, products, policymakers, and policy formulation process. They develop a plan that will affect the system's input and select behaviors expected by that system for such input in order to get their policy of concern adopted.

BIBLIOGRAPHY

Baer, Betty L. and Ronald C. Federico. *Educating the Baccalaureate Social Worker: A Curriculum Development Resource Guide.* Cambridge, Mass.: Ballinger Publishing Co., 1979.

Baer, Betty, L. and Ronald C. Federico. *Educating the Baccalaureate Social Worker: Report of the Undergraduate Social Work Curriculum Development Project.* Cambridge, Mass.: Ballinger Publishing Co., 1978.

Cates, Jerry R. and Nancy Lohmann. Education for social policy analysis. *Journal of Education for Social Work. 16*(1):5–12, 1980.

Gilbert, Neil and Harry Specht. *Dimensions of Social Welfare Policy.* Englewood Cliffs, N.J.: Prentice-Hall, 1974.

Hollis, Florence. *Casework: A Psychosocial Therapy,* 2nd ed. New York: Random House, 1980.

Jansson, Bruce S. and Samuel H. Taylor. Search activities in social agencies: Institutional factors that influence policy analysis. *Social Service Review, 52*(2):189–201, 1978.

Mahaffey, Maryann and John W. Hanks (eds.). *Practical Politics: Social Work and Political Responsibility.* Silver Spring, Md.: National Association of Social Workers, 1982.

Prigmore, Charles S. and Charles R. Atherton. *Social Welfare Policy: Analysis and Formulation.* Lexington, Mass., D.C. Heath & Co., 1979.

CHAPTER ELEVEN

Policy Analysis and Action: Part II—Expectations for Action

"An act has no ethical quality whatever unless it be chosen out of several all equally possible."
—WILLIAM JAMES (1890)

"Nothing is more terrible, than ignorance in action."
—JOHANN WOLFGANG VON GOETHE

OVERVIEW

Chapter nine explored how role expectations could be used to conceptualize policy analysis and action, that is, how a policy of concern could be formulated and translated into policy-related practice activities. Skills underlying the expectation that workers analyze policy issues and develop a policy of concern were presented in chapter ten. This chapter will develop some of the expectations for policy action that are used when operating within the policymaking processes. In exploring expectations for action, it should be noted that these expectations may apply in more than one system and that they contain an analytical component. In this chapter's discussion, a summary of the behaviors associated with the expectation for ongoing policy analysis will be followed by a discussion of several key behaviors to influence the policymaking of others and to shape policy across a number of systems. Finally, the expectation that line workers participate directly in making a given system's policy will be covered.

OBJECTIVES

☐ Comment on how policy analysis is an ongoing part of action.
☐ List the role expectations that are used in influencing others to shape policy and describe three of these more fully.
☐ Explain two ways workers may be directly involved in making policy.
☐ Discuss how the competencies of the West Virginia Project reflect role expectations for policy related action.

ANALYZING AND EVALUATING POLICY is made up of research, problem detection, data management, and evaluation activities. It bears a special relationship to assessment, but in some ways is also a component of all action expectations. Influencing others and shaping policy is composed of ways to interpret, influence, cooperate with, testify before, lobby with, change the policy positions of a range of actors in a number of systems, and redirect organizations and their policymaking. Active, direct policymaking takes place as workers conduct policy self-assessments, implement policy, and act as official policymakers in the policy-formulation process of a given system. A brief definition and discussion of each of these behaviors will be offered along with a statement of how they apply in one or more policymaking processes. (See Table 25 for an overview of the relationship of policymaking processes and the behaviors workers might be expected to use. See Table 26 for illustrations of expected behaviors within policy-related role expectations.)

ANALYZING AND EVALUATING POLICY

Included in this role expectation are such behaviors as analyzing, researching, detecting problems, managing data, conducting searches to increase policy-related knowledge, and evaluating policy outcomes. Specific skills in issue analysis and policy development were discussed earlier. In addition to these activities, line workers would be expected to build their knowledge about policy and program options. Policy analysis, for example, is an expected behavior of legislative analysts and social agency administrators; they are expected to study and know about policy. Social workers also must keep informed about resource systems and their policies by being knowledgeable about the sources describing the products of a system. This role expectation includes not only researching policy, but also evaluating it.

TABLE 25
Relationship of Policy-Making Processes and the Behaviors Workers Might Be Expected to Use

Policymaking Process	Related Role Expectations (analysis is a concurrent expectation for these action expectations)
Personal policymaking using PROBLEM SOLVING by	
social workers	Policy-related self-assessment
colleagues	Influencing or persuading
individual client	Interpreting or guiding
Group policymaking using PROBLEM SOLVING in:	
small formed groups,	Influencing or persuading
families, or local	Interpreting or guiding
community groups	Cooperating
Organizational policymaking of Professional association—	
PRIORITIZATION	Influencing, participating, lobbying
ELAN	Participating
PACE	Participating
Private social agency—	Participating, testifying,
BOARD OF DIRECTORS	implementing, cooperating,
Public social agency—	advocating organizational shaping
POLICY REVIEW	Cooperating, implementing organizational shaping
Setting social policy in local community by United Way through—	
CITIZEN INPUT	Participating, advocating, lobbying, cooperating
society at large—	
LEGISLATION	Testifying, lobbying, cooperating
BUDGETING	
Making policy in the institution of social welfare via:	
REGULATIONS	Monitoring, testifying
SOCIAL WELFARE PLANNING	Advocating, cooperating organizational shaping

Analyzing policy and keeping abreast of it are expectations that exist apart from its use in developing a specific policy. Jansson and Taylor (1970), for example, conclude that policy "search activities" should be an ongoing activity of agency administrators. These authors view the scrutiny of important policies as critical to the effective running of an organization. Similarly, it

TABLE 26

Illustrations of Expected Behaviors Within Policy-Related Role Expectations

Role Expectations for:	Illustrative Behaviors within the Policy Formulating Process
ANALYZING POLICY	☐ Analyzing, researching, searching for information about policies, detecting policy issues, managing data and information about problems and concerns, evaluating system outcomes
INFLUENCING OTHERS AND POLICY SHAPING	
☐ Interpreting or guiding	☐ Teaching, enabling, supporting decisions, providing expert knowledge, instructing, consulting with groups or agencies, helping others decide
☐ Influencing or persuading	☐ Changing policy of others, presenting issues, using coersion, providing information
☐ Cooperating	☐ Networking, coalition building, maintaining contacts with decision makers
☐ Testifying	☐ Preparing testimony, public speaking, responding to questions, preparing and delivering critiques of regulations
☐ Lobbying	☐ Contacting decision makers, presenting policy proposals, seeking support
☐ Advocating (class)	☐ Assertively presenting the cause of a class of clients for consideration
☐ Monitoring	☐ Keeping up to date on bureaucratic regulations, responding to calls for public input
☐ Organizational shaping	☐ Changing policy of organizations within and ouside channels
DIRECT POLICYMAKING	
☐ Policy-related self-assessment	☐ Examining practice in relation to policy issues, changing ones own policy
☐ Implementing	☐ Putting policy into operation, making changes as feasible
☐ Participating directly	☐ Holding political office, participating on committees, being a political activist, serving on boards, holding office in associations, leading other policy-related intersest groups

may be concluded that the continuing analysis of policy and of related issues by the line worker constitutes important preconditions for her or his analysis of a policy-related issue and for the development of a policy of concern. Analyzing policy, then, is a critical, ongoing activity. It is an important one not only in the analysis and development of policy, but also in the reinforcement of a policy frame of reference. Analysis, of course, is part of the evaluation procedure used during the plan's implementation. Moreover, the worker is expected to use analysis and evaluation to determine if, or to what extent, the desired policy has been produced by a given system.

INFLUENCING OTHERS AND SHAPING POLICY

Several role expectations are connected with influencing others and with policy shaping. These include:

☐ interpreting or guiding
☐ influencing or persuading
☐ cooperating
☐ testifying
☐ lobbying
☐ advocating (class)
☐ monitoring
☐ organizational shaping

These expectations range from helping others decide and changing the policy decisions of others to changing a system's policy. In addition to such behaviors that would affect the policy decisions of others, workers are expected to shape a system's policy by testifying, lobbying, advocating, or monitoring.

Interpreting or Guiding

Line workers are expected to interpret policy options to others and to guide them in their development of a policy. Workers who engage in such behavior utilize their own skills as an expert problem solver or use the depth of knowledge they possess about a policy-related issue. They propose policy to or guide others in their decisions regarding policy. Interpreting a policy or guiding the decision making of others would be used in carrying out a policy intervention plan that is designed to help an individual client system or a group of clients decide about a personal or group policy. Incorporated in this expectation would be the related behaviors of instructing others about policy options, enabling them to make decisions, and supporting their policy decisions. In guiding the policy decisions of people, especially clients, workers would be expected to act in a capacity similar to a policy consultant with an agency or large group. The expected behavior would be that of a supportive, helpful expert who assists others in understanding issues and developing a policy to deal with them.

Influencing or Persuading

Influencing or persuading also may take place in more than one system. Influencing involves attempting to persuade decision makers within a system to adopt an allocative policy more in line with one favored by the worker. In systems such as legislatures and bureaucracies, such means of influence or persuasion have been formalized into presenting testimony or lobbying. Simons (1982) defines influence as involving persuasion (giving new information), inducements (offering rewards or incentives), or constraints (using punishment). With colleagues, local community groups, funders, or members of social agencies, and in other systems where the method for influencing decision makers has not been formalized, Simons suggests important ways to increase the probability that the worker's policy of concern will be accepted.

One approach is to present both sides of the policy issue, especially when the listener is not favorably inclined, and to present the worker's viewpoint last. Because people are more likely to adopt the viewpoint of someone they like, Simons suggests using skills in warmth and unconditional acceptance in order to be liked. He also proposes using as a spokesperson someone who is well liked by the listener. Finally, the author suggests using role reversal. This entails getting decision makers to assume, via role play, the place of those whose needs would be addressed by the policy. In so doing, opinions of the decision makers would be changed as they are forced to approach the policy issue from a different point of view.

Cooperating

Networking, coalition building, and cooperating with others in efforts to affect policymaking take place in a number of systems. Cooperating could involve working with colleagues, members of agency boards, interested lay people, representatives of professional groups, or elected officials. Cooperating or collaborating with others involves building coalitions of and working collaboratively with others to affect policy decision making. All social workers in their practice should develop networks of colleagues and allied professionals. Workers in a particular agency or setting should maintain contacts with that setting's decision makers and with those who influence such decision makers. In public agencies, this would mean contacts with those who are involved in any policy review and development process.

As a role expectation to guide policy input, social workers need to be proficient in the skills of developing coalitions of interested others. In instances where power is needed to affect policymaking, coalitions help to guarantee or maximize any input into a system's policymaking. For example, a presentation before a board might be enhanced by the appearance of a group of agency workers. Testimony before a committee made in conjunction with others could heighten the appeal of the policy position being presented. Cooperating with others in lobbying efforts and in monitoring bureaucracies significantly reinforces such efforts.

Testifying

Expert testifying is usually associated with the policymaking process of legislatures. This behavior, however, could be used by line workers in other systems as well. Boards, professional associations, local community groups, and bureaucratic hearings may also seek the opinions and ideas of experts. Thus, the line worker is provided with an opportunity for input into the system as it formulates policy. Input, based upon issue analysis and policy development, is given because of the worker's status as an expert in a particular policy area. As discussed earlier, the expert witness who testifies before a legislature thoroughly researches the history of and the issues surrounding the policy, the procedures used by the legislature, and the nature of the legislative committees and their membership. The witness prepares and delivers testimony, answers any questions raised at the time of the testimony, and follows the legislative action on the bill until its final disposition (Kleinhauf, 1981). This role expectation would guide the worker's input whenever formal presentations from outsiders are part of the system's means to critique and shape its policy. Although its format may vary slightly, testifying could be used in agencies, local communities, and the institution of social welfare.

Lobbying

Lobbying, of course, is connected to testifying in that it also takes place in legislative policymaking. It also is a part played by an outsider. The lobbyist works within the formal and informal processes of a given system to cause its decision makers either to support or propose a policy in line with the interests of the lobbyist. Lobbying can be used effectively by line workers as input into a system's policymaking. Lobbyinglike activities can also be used to persuade representatives of other policy formulation bodies to support or adopt a policy. Its techniques are like those for influencing and persuading.

Lobbying might be used selectively with other social workers in the NASW's policy-prioritizing process and with the decision-making structure of local United Ways. It could be used along with influencing or persuading in such a context. Lobbying also would be used along with cooperative behaviors in a local community and in society at large. Lobbying is used most frequently by workers who represent an organization or interest group.

Advocating (Class)

As part of their generalist role, line social workers are expected to advocate for their clients. In the context of a policy intervention, the emphasis would be on class advocacy. Class, as opposed to case advocating, involves assertively working for policy that would meet the needs of all members of a client group. It is related to lobbying in some ways but is based in different assumptions about what a system might deliver.

Whereas lobbying assumes that there is a reasonable chance to be heard by a sympathetic, or at least a courteous, audience, advocating assumes that greater pressure or stronger arguments must be used with a much more skeptical assembly. Advocating for policy would sometimes guide input with social welfare planners, local funders, legislators, and social agencies. It would be used along with cooperating with others. Dear and Patti (1981), in their discussion of advocating for social policy legislation, suggest a number of behaviors that enhance success. Some of these can be applied to advocating in other systems. They are much like the role expectation for cooperating. Such behaviors include getting on the agenda early, gaining broadly based support within the system, getting the backing of interested others who would also have significant input into the system, and cooperating with others when speaking in support of the policy.

Used together, advocating, testifying, and cooperating with others are often the best behaviors for guiding the worker's input. Class advocating not only entails the presentation of a policy of concern to planners or funders, but at times also involves supplying these decision makers with data about the clientele and its needs. In shaping policy by advocating, workers would behave somewhat like political activists. Activists move assertively within the policy processes of society to bring about policies they believe their clients need.

Monitoring

Monitoring refers to the expectation that workers check the development, refinement, and implementation of bureaucratic regulations. In chapter eight, the issuance of bureaucratic regulations was used to exemplify one way in which policy is made in the social welfare institution. Monitoring is used by a group concerned with the functioning of a specific social, legal, or health agency. Members of such groups carefully scrutinize the operations of the monitored agency. Groups other than social workers, of course, engage in the monitoring of public agencies. A good example can be found in the "Jury Box" column of the *New York Native*. A staff member monitors court cases to see how well protected are the rights of gay men and lesbians (Dowing, 1983).

In the Mahaffey and Hanks book (1982) it is argued that the monitoring of bureaucratic activity is a basic policy-related responsibility of all workers. Cates and Lohmann (1980) propose that workers should monitor the extent to which an agency's policy is changed as it is implemented. In Mahaffey and Hanks, monitoring is viewed as watching closely how the agencies charged with the issuance or implementation of regulations follow the intention of the policy guide. In this sense, monitoring corresponds closely to analysis and evaluation. Monitoring includes making certain when a bureaucracy has failed to ensure that the policy is actually implemented. It also includes making certain that proposed changes do not alter the original policy too greatly and that the regulations are as close as possible to the worker's desired policy of concern.

Organizational Shaping

Workers may use cooperation and collaboration within an agency setting to achieve the policy ends they seek. On the other hand, their resistance to or noncompliance with agency standards may be blocked by their supervisors or by the agency administration. In such instances, workers can use the power and connections they have developed within and outside the agency to seek change in organizational policy and to reshape the direction of its policy. Social agencies, regulatory bureaucracies, and even professional associations may at times need to be approached with conflict or confrontation behaviors. In policy change within organizations, the goal usually is to achieve the desired change while remaining within the organization. Class advocating, with its pressure tactics and assumption of conflict, is similar to organizational change but does not assume that the worker is within the organization where the policy change is sought. The key to success in such organizational policy shaping is the worker's power base and professional credibility, as discussed in chapter six.

DIRECT POLICYMAKING

Workers are not only expected to influence policy makers and shape the policy under consideration in a system but they are also expected to make policy in a more direct way. Workers make policy directly by conducting policy-related self-assessments, implementing policy, and participating directly in a system's policy formulation process.

Self-Assessment

Workers should be able to carry out self-assessments of their personal policy. Such self-assessments should be as deliberate as the self-assessment of other aspects of their practice. The steps in an individual's assessment process were discussed in chapter five. Briefly, they include the identification and specification of an allocative issue involving resources the worker controls, the exploration of alternative policies, and the adoption and implementation of the new policy. As a guide to implementing new personal policies, workers need to build in feedback about how consistent and/or effective the new policy has been. For example, a worker's self-assessment may be that he or she consistently excludes working with nonprofessionals, and prefers instead teamwork with members of the social work and allied professions. The worker concludes that this allocation of resources is a detriment to clients. Having changed the personal policy, the worker's continued self-assessment is important to check out its effectiveness and to determine the extent to which it has been put into operation. Hence, self-assessment becomes both a guide for analysis and for action, that is, both for assessment and for implementation.

Implementing Policy

Implementing includes behaviors associated with putting into operation the policy made within other systems. Implementing policy includes the modification and adaptation of the original policy. Some aspects of implementation have already been discussed in chapter eight's exploration of how social policy is utilized in the development of social welfare policy. Implementation also is an expectation for line workers.

Workers are expected to implement the policy that comes from within or outside their agencies. Those in authority expect workers to adhere to the policy as stated, clients expect workers to modify the policy to meet their needs better. Cates and Lohmann (1980), in covering policy analysis and monitoring, suggest that implementation provides workers with great discretion, that is, with the opportunity to make policy. Williams (1980) emphasizes the power that implementation, at the point of service delivery, has in guiding policy. This point is too often taken for granted. A worker's implementation may not transform an inadequate program into an adequate one. A worker can, however, reallocate and combine resources in critical ways. On the other hand, a worker might further reinforce proposed cuts by being more stringent than the official guidelines. Implementation in many ways is linked to a worker's perception of what constitutes the feasibility for changing a policy.

Implementation, of course, would be closely connected to policy analysis and to monitoring bureaucracies. In implementing a policy, evidence is constantly collected regarding gaps, unmet needs, and client perceptions. Monitoring yields additional evidence about bureaucratic activity. In implementing, policy workers should always use such evidence to create feasible alterations in the policy they implement. In turn, all these activities lead to the development of new policies of concern and help to identify additional policy-related intervention plans.

Direct Participation in Policy Formulation

In addition to many of the previously discussed expectations, which assume that the worker will operate from outside a given system, line workers should also be direct participants in a system's policymaking. As such, the line worker would be expected to become and then behave as any other decision maker in that system. Such participation could take place in a number of ways. The worker could serve on the board of a social agency and thereby participate in its decision-making process. In a professional association such as the NASW, the worker could assume policy leadership by holding an office that helps shape policy, including active involvement in organizations such as PACE and ELAN.

In addition to participating on and leading committees, the worker could also represent a chapter as a national delegate and directly affect policy in the NASW's prioritizing process. Both the local community and society at large offer opportunities for active, direct participation in policymaking. Line workers could run for elected political office, especially in nonpartisan elections such as school boards. In this capacity, they would be able to develop social policy directly and in line with the policies of concern they have developed in their practice. Moreover, they could shape the platforms of political parties. Similarly, they could play a leadership part in a local United Way. Such participation, and some of the others exemplified, could occur in addition to the social worker's daily practice activities.

ROLE EXPECTATIONS AS ACTION GUIDES

The role expectations outlined above are usually not isolated from one another. It has been emphasized that analysis always accompanies action. In addition, some of the expected actions are used together. Lobbying and testifying are one example. Similarly, cooperating with others is used along with other actions, such as advocating for a class of clients. Participating in a system's policymaking does not preclude using other actions, including influencing or persuading. In the most general sense, workers create policy by attempting to change the policy positions held by others, shaping the policy product as it moves through a system's process, and participating directly in policy formulation processes. As discussed above, the means for changing the opinions of others may be informal or they may be highly structured. Participation ranges from self-assessment to holding elected political office (see Figure 20 for an overview of expectations associated with various policy-making approaches).

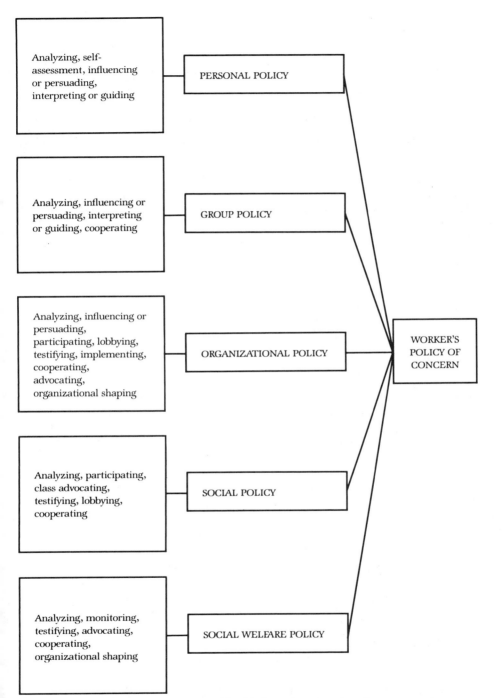

FIGURE 20. **Role expectations that could guide input in categories of resource system policymaking.**

A policy-related intervention plan is one that basically provides an approach for input into a given system's policy formulation process. Its objective is for the system to produce the policy of concern that the worker desires. The input of the intervention plan is guided by one or more of the role expectations for participation in that system. These role expectations are appropriate guides for the worker's input and actions, which are based in the kinds of input used in the system's process.

For example, a colleague's values may be the most significant input into her or his personal policymaking. A worker wishes to change the policy of that colleague. The role expectation of persuasion appropriately guides the worker's intervention. The values of the colleague, the critical system input, become the emphasis in addressing the colleague. Similarly, testifying would guide intervention within a legislative context. The worker would emphasize whatever input that was identified as being critical. For a given legislative committee, statistical data and a careful presentation of it might be such critical input for that system.

POLICY-RELATED PRACTICE EXPECTATIONS
AND ENTRY-LEVEL COMPETENCIES

The West Virginia Project's practice competencies developed by Baer and Federico (1978) are useful in summarizing policy-related practice activities. As used earlier in the text, the knowledge of policy required by the competencies was used to support the contention that policy is a basic part of generalist practice. An alternate way of thinking about these competencies is to view them as statements of role expectations.

The competencies, with their emphasis on data collection and analysis, planning, and evaluation, require *policy analysis.* For example, in assessing the relationship between people and social institutions, analytical skills are called for in identifying social problems, collecting data about institutional functioning and unmet community and social needs, and in relating such problems to existing or needed services. Policy analysis is also a skill needed to promote the effective and humane operation of systems. Similarly, such data collection and policy analysis skills would be used in understanding the unmet needs of vulnerable and discriminated-against populations and in creating new services.

Skill in the general area of influencing others and in shaping policy is needed as part of enhancing people, especially by *guiding* their decision making. In promoting the effective operation of systems, workers would be expected to use their personal power to *influence* others by means of bargaining and by using confrontation within organizations. *Cooperating* with colleagues is an expectation while assessing the relationship between people and institutions, making efforts to improve service delivery, attempting to promote the effective operation of systems, and while creating new services, resources, or opportunities. Cooperating with citizen groups, community groups and indigenous networks is called for when making special efforts on behalf of discriminated-against groups or when creating new services. *Testifying* or *lobbying* is required in presenting data to improve service delivery and in using legislative and agency processes to create new services. *Class advocating* is a skill used within policy contacts designed to make special efforts on behalf of oppressed groups. In linking people with resources, *monitoring* service delivery, and *organizational shaping* are necessary skills.

Skills in direct policymaking also contribute to the competencies. *Implementing policy* by facilitating organizational functioning is part of linking people with resources. *Participating* is called for in professional associations to improve service delivery in decision making by using personal power to promote the more efficient operation of systems, and in planning and policy-making to create new services.

FOR FURTHER STUDY

1. Discuss what part expectations for action play in getting a policy adopted. Select one role expectation and develop a detailed explanation of what skills are needed in its utilization.
2. Interview social workers in your practice setting to determine if they participate directly in the formulation of policy. Which action expectations do they see themselves usually carrying out in their practice?
3. From the number of action expectations discussed in this chapter, select two and discuss the ways you have used them. If you have not acted on them, what skills would you need to develop in order to do so?

GLOSSARY

Expectations for action   Behaviors expected of those who wish to have input into the policy formulation process of a given system. These role expectations guide workers in carrying out an intervention plan and having appropriate input in a system; it is designed to get their policy of concern adopted.
Interpreting or guiding   Workers interpret policy issues to others, especially clients, and guide them in their development of a personal policy.
Influencing or persuading   Using information, rewards, incentives, or punish-

ment to cause others to adopt a policy favored by the worker. Workers would be expected to behave this way with colleagues, members of agencies, funders, and others whose authority is equal to that of the worker.

Cooperating   The worker would be expected to use this behavior in a situation or in a system where the worker's authority could be expanded by connecting with others of similar interests and thereby increasing the likelihood of getting the policy of concern adopted.

Testifying   A formal means used frequently by legislative committees and other systems to obtain information about a policy issue. Workers utilize these opportunities to influence and persuade.

Lobbying   Used in legislative policymaking for input of ideas and policies from interested parties who are not actual decision makers.

Advocating (class)   Workers are expected to be assertive in presenting the policy issues of a group of clients. Advocating is more forceful than testifying or lobbying and could be used in conjunction with cooperating or collaborating.

Monitoring   Regarding services of the social welfare institution, workers are expected to check (or monitor) the issuance and refinement of regulations as well as to analyze their application and implementation within the agency.

Organizational shaping   Changing agency–organization policy by working within and outside channels.

Self-assessment   One way in which workers are expected to make policy directly. This should be a conscious action on the part of workers to analyze and change their personal policy.

Implementing policy   Another way that workers are expected to make policy. In this case, they modify and adapt policy produced by others, or other systems, but carried out by them in their practice.

Participating   Workers are expected to participate directly as policy makers in many systems, including professional associations, local communities, agencies, and society at large.

BIBLIOGRAPHY

Baer, Betty L. and Ronald C. Federico. *Educating the Baccalaureate Social Worker: A Curriculum Development Resource Guide.* Cambridge, Mass.: Ballinger Publishing Co., 1979.

Baer, Betty L. and Ronald C. Federico. *Educating the Baccalaureate Social Worker: Report of the Undergraduate Social Work Curriculum Development Project.* Cambridge, Mass.: Ballinger Publishing Co., 1978.

Cates, Jerry R. and Nancy Lohmann. Education for social policy analysis. *Journal of Education for Social Work,* 16(1):5–12, 1980.

Dear, Ronald B. and Rino J. Patti. Legislative advocacy: Seven effective tactics. *Social Work,* 26(4):289–296, 1981.

Dowing, Bob. The jury box. *New York Native,* 3(5):56, January 31–February 13, 1983.

Gilbert, Neil and Harry Specht. *Dimensions of Social Welfare Policy.* Englewood Cliffs, N.J.: Prentice-Hall, 1974.

James, William. *Principles of Psychology.* Cambridge, Mass.: Harvard University Press, 1890.

Jansson, Bruce S. and Samuel H. Taylor. Search activity in social agencies: Institutional factors that influence policy analysis. *Social Service Review,* 52(2):189–201, 1978.

Kleinhauf, Cecilia. A Guide to giving legislative testimony. *Social Work*, 26(4):297–303, 1981.

Mahaffey, Maryann and John W. Hanks (eds.). *Practical Politics: Social Work and Political Responsibility.* Silver Spring, Md.: National Association of Social Workers, 1982.

Prigmore, Charles S. and Charles R. Atherton. *Social Welfare Policy: Analysis and Formulation.* Lexington, Mass., D.C. Heath, 1979.

Simons, Ronald L. Strategies for exercising influence. *Social Work*, 27(3):268–274, 1982.

Williams, Walter. *The Implementation Perspective.* Berkeley: University of California Press, 1980.

CHAPTER TWELVE

Policy in Practice: Applications

"Knowledge must come through action . . ."
—SOPHOCLES
Trachiniae, 1. 592.

THE SUGGESTION BY SOPHOCLES that action leads to knowledge is especially true for professional social workers and for the way in which they are educated. In professional education, knowledge is further developed through its application in practicelike situations. Knowledge and its application are similarly connected in professional practice itself. In social work one experiences, applies, or tests ideas in practice. The connection not only means that practice produces knowledge, but also indicates that formal knowledge is better understood, further refined, and continually strengthened in its practice applications. Although it might not be possible at this point in their education for students to test out the policy approach developed in this book, practice-based illustrations of how it all fits together should be a useful substitute for their personal application. The illustrations that follow outline the application efforts of others.

Each illustration contains a description of the practice setting and its services, an introduction to the worker and the worker's major practice focus, an outline of the agency's policies and their sources, and a discussion of the policy analysis and action undertaken by the worker. I would like to thank the people who shared their practice experience with me and engaged in examining the part that policy played in it:

☐ BILL AUSTIN
BSW student
The College of New Rochelle, New Rochelle, New York, and The Westchester Social Work Education Consortium

☐ VALERI FEKETE
At the time of this experience, director of a northern Arizona social services agency

☐ GRACIELA M. CASTEX
Assistant Professor
Mercy College, Dobbs Ferry, New York, and The Westchester Social Work Education Consortium

☐ BERNICE W. LIDDIE
Assistant Professor
Marymount College, Tarrytown, New York, and The Westchester Social Work Education Consortium

Each of these people practice in a setting that provides opportunities for the generalist line worker to carry out policy-related analysis and action. No situation, of course, is ideal or typical in its "fit" with generalist practice or in the opportunity it provides for becoming involved in policy activities. Hopefully, the following illustrations will also point out how a policy frame of reference guides workers as they analyze and act on policies of concern.

ADVOCACY WORK WITH THE ELDERLY

The Setting and Its Services

This agency operates a long-term ombuds (advocacy) program under funding from the Older Americans Act. The program is supervised by a county mental health association. The agency sends out trained volunteers to long-term care facilities located throughout the county, which is a suburban, residential area, with an expanding elderly population. The facilities where the volunteers work include health-related, skilled nursing, and adult homes. The volunteer, known as an ombudsperson, carries out multiple roles such as advocate, mediator, and teacher.

The Worker

The worker was a student in the second semester of his senior year field placement. In addition to his classroom work, he underwent extensive training in the agency covering the following areas:

☐ Knowledge of policy rules and regulations encountered in long-term care facilities
☐ Skills in interacting with the entire system of an agency's clientele, staff, and administration
☐ Understanding the delicate nature of the process and the complex purposes involved in a community's monitoring of agency practices

The student–worker investigated such concerns as violation of patient rights, quality of care, and financial and legal issues. Generally speaking, he made frequent contact with residents to discuss their concerns and, in an unbiased fashion, operated as a mediator with agency administrations. The position required sensitive linking between the interests of the community and the services of the facilities. The student–worker had an extensive background as a volunteer, both in working with the elderly and in advocacy and outreach roles within his own community.

Agency Policies and Their Sources

Since the program received funds from the Older Americans Act and since these funds were administered and supervised by the county mental health administration, federal regulations and county association policies applied. In addition, regulations from the program's advisory board, as well as the personal policies of administrators of the long-term care facilities, were important to the worker. A range of county, state, and federal level policies dealing with Medicare-Medicaid were also part of the worker's practice. All together the policies included

1. personal policies of the program coordinator, its supervisors, long-term care facility administrators, and other staff members
2. policies of the program's advisory board, consisting of the executive director of the mental health association and staff members selected from the program's constituent agencies
3. county mental health association guidelines in its capacity as the administrator of the funding
4. state regulations for long-term care facilities
5. state and federal regulations for Medicare and Medicaid
6. federal regulations derived from the Older Americans Act

Worker Policy Analysis and Action

One policy situation grew out of the student's work in an adult home. The administrator faced the problem, especially on weekends, of acting out behavior among patients. In his client contacts in this agency, the student–worker determined that alcoholism existed as an unmet need. The worker documented such behavior. He suggested to the director that the real issue was alcoholism and collaborated with this administrator in establishing an agency policy to find resources for and develop an alcoholism program. To implement this policy, two interventions were planned and carried out: (1) to establish a cooperative program within an agency located close to the adult home; (2) to bring an Alcoholics Anonymous program into contact with the facility.

In another center, the student–worker also encountered a policy issue involving recreational facilities. The need for male-centered recreational activities was identified. The worker conducted a formal survey to determine what the recreational interests of the male residents had been before they entered the facility. He discovered that the majority had been interested in golf. In researching how the agency had developed any previous recreation policy, the worker discovered an unimplemented policy. The agency had decided to utilize video games, because of their usefulness in maintaining muscle tone and coordination, as recreation. Funds had been allocated for this purpose, however, the items had not been acquired by the purchasing agent. The worker found out that this official did not see these items as a priority. The worker approached the agency's administrator about implementing that policy, as well as about establishing a new policy covering golf. The worker had decided that miniature golf would be a feasible approach and had conducted a "trial run" with residents. They liked it and the worker proposed it as a new recreational program. The policy was accepted and put into operation.

In both of these instances, the worker was able to identify unmet needs or service gaps. To meet these needs, he formulated a policy of concern based on the agency's resources. In seeking to get the policy adopted, he carefully investigated how policy was made in each setting and who could make or set it. This information grew out of and was augmented by his routine contacts with facility administrators.

POLICY WITH LESBIANS AND GAY MALES

The Setting and Its Services

The agency had been recently established to provide general social services, including information, referral, and client advocacy programs. As a newly established agency, part of its mission called for developing needed social services for women in the communities it served. It is located in a rural area of northern Arizona. The area served by the agency is made up of eight towns, with populations ranging from 400 to 9000. These towns are located within 10 to 20 miles of each other and are about 110 miles from the Phoenix metropolitan area. The communities are predominately conservative, traditional, and fundamentalist in outlook. At the time of its establishment, the agency had no special services for lesbians or gay men. One of the new services it initiated, a 24-hour telephone crisis line, did bring the agency in contact with a few lesbian and gay clients. This development was not a major or a planned objective of the agency. Services to these populations, however, became a concern of the worker.

The Worker

The worker functioned as the executive director of the agency, but also provided direct services to its clients. In addition, the worker developed a broad base of contacts, professional and personal, within the eight communities. The network so developed was a direct outgrowth of the worker's practice. The worker was as new to the area as was the agency. To members of the rural communities they served, both the worker and the agency also represented unfamiliar approaches to helping and to service delivery. The worker had recently headed a rape crisis center in Phoenix. Her interest in, experience with, and advocacy for services to women marked her as different. The focus of the agency on information, referral, and program development for women also made it somewhat different from other agencies in these communities. These differences in emphasis between worker (and agency) and the rural communities were basic factors in shaping the policy approaches of the worker.

Agency Policies and Their Sources

The policies of the agency were developed by its board of directors during the development and implementation of the programs called for under the guidelines of its newly acquired funding. Some of the agency's board members were also service providers of other social service agencies within the local communities. The worker–director also brought a number of policy priorities to the agency. Because the agency was new and not encumbered with the constraints of well-developed policy guidelines, in one sense the time was opportune for the development or creation of policy initiatives. The existing agency policy was basically contained in

1. personal policies of the worker–director
2. agency policies from its board of directors
3. guidelines supplied by CSA (Community Service Administration), its funding source

Worker Policy Analysis and Action

The worker–director identified several unmet needs among the lesbian and gay communities. As agency director and as service provider, as well as from the perspective developed in her initial assessment of the communities themselves, the worker identified a lack of meaningful support systems among lesbians or gay men who lived in the area. The lesbians and gay males who resided in these small communities, in most cases, lived in isolation from people of their own sexual orientation. They lived in fear of discovery and the consequent exposure that they believed would lead to loss of their employment. Several lesbians and gay men had negative experiences with other workers or employers around the issue of their sexual orientation and had shared these with the worker. In these rural communities, everyone knew everyone; the employees of agencies knew and talked about their neighbors or clients who were among those their agency served. Hence, anyone with a lesbian or gay identity tended to keep quiet about it and about their needs.

The lack of gay counseling services and social activities further prevented members of these communities from getting together. Their existence was one of hiding or passing as straight. No role models, other than the popular, negative ones, existed for them. In other words, neither lesbians nor gay males had any group to turn to for help or for helping others.

The worker also identified the need for the larger community to think of lesbians and gay men in a more positive way. The public needed to be reeducated in their attitudes and behaviors. Moreover, the worker–director detected the lack of legal assistance as a major drawback. No attorney in any of the eight communities displayed sympathy for or interest in working with the legal concerns of such clients. The worker became aware of job loss, police harassment, and other suspect police actions, all of which called for legal services for which there were no interested lawyers. The single referral source, the state's Civil Liberties Union, required rigorous proof of harassment, a procedure that frequently prevented a client from becoming involved with this organization. As one might guess, legal issues were fought individually, without group support, or they were not dealt with at all.

In sum, the worker identified the following interrelated needs or concerns:

☐ Support networks to strengthen a sense of identity
☐ Development within the general community of a better image of lesbians and gay men
☐ Legal assistance
☐ Outreach and services to lesbians and gays, especially counseling and health

The worker decided to begin the arduous task of developing support groups for lesbians and gays and to get an agency to establish a policy allocating resources for this purpose. Given the nature of the area and its values, this objective was, at best, a long range one. The worker–director decided to pursue it at several levels and in several systems that seemingly had the needed resources or could best develop them. First, a local mental health clinic was approached about initiating support groups for lesbians and gay men. The clinic had the resources, but not the policy, for dealing with lesbians and gay men. The worker discovered that the priorities, or policy goals, for the next five years did not include services for lesbians or gays. Staff of the agency also expressed concern that if they were to allocate resources for these populations, the general community would respond negatively. In the short-term, the worker developed a personal policy of referring clients to needed support services outside their own communities. Lesbians were referred to a support group in a nearby college town and gay men were referred to gay organizations in Phoenix, while further work on the long-term policy goal was being planned and implemented.

The major policy intervention of the worker–director, however, was aimed at the second client need that she had identified: developing a better image of lesbians and gay men among lay and professional people. Such a change in attitude was necessary before agencies would participate with these populations. The National Association of Social Workers in the state developed a task force to deal with lesbian and gay issues. The worker–director became involved with this group in implementing and refining the organization's policy that had established the task force. The worker collaborated with other professionals in developing an NASW-sponsored workshop to educate all social workers in the state about lesbians and gay men. The workshop was designed to achieve the policy goals of an enhanced public awareness about the lives and needs of this population.

The critical place that values and attitudes play in shaping policy is evident in the actions taken by this worker. She concluded that the community (and agency) value base, in the form of overriding homophobia, would have to be altered if any significant changes were to be made in the resource allocations of the community and its agencies. Although she met the immediate need of lesbians and gay men by developing a personal policy, she chose to work within her professional association, seeking a more significant policy change for them. The worker continued her work with the NASW after leaving the agency. She provided in-service training to mental health professionals and pursued the goal of public education: her personal policy of how best to allocate her own professional knowledge and skills in the policy arena.

WORK WITH REFUGEE CHILDREN

The Setting and Its Services

The agency is one of four branches of a private, nonprofit children's psychiatric social service agency. This branch is located in Hialeah, part of the greater Miami area. As a community, Hialeah's population is becoming Hispanic, predominantly Cuban. In 1980 in the greater Miami area, Hispanics comprised 37.5% of the population of whom 90% were Cuban. During the "Mariel Boat Lift" of Spring 1980, 116,000 additional Cubans had arrived in Miami. Of these, 23%, or more than 18,000, were children under the age of 17.

The agency in Hialeah provided services to children and their families, basically as programs for individuals, groups, and families. The primary clientele of the agency, however, was children. Most of the clients came from Hialeah or from areas close to it. There were eight MSWs, a psychiatrist, a sociologist, and an educational specialist (in a remedial education program) on staff at the time. All but one were bilingual. All services were offered in Spanish.

The Worker

The worker was employed part time and worked during the agency's evening hours. She had practiced in child welfare, as a supervisor of a student field placement unit, and in a psychiatric hospital setting. She is bilingual. The practice focus, or primary responsibility of the worker in this agency, was developing services for the newly arrived Cuban refugee population. To keep abreast of the rapidly changing issues about and policies regarding refugee children, the worker, an immigrant herself, routinely clipped newspaper, magazine, and journal articles about them. Her experiences, background, and interests permitted her to be effective in this agency and to help it implement an innovative service for a unique population.

Agency Policies and Their Sources

The branch was headed by a director. There was an executive director of the four branches. The directors of each branch reported to the executive director. A single board of directors, with input from the executive director, made policy for the agency as a whole. Each branch, of course, was expected to follow board-developed policy guidelines. The Hialeah branch, because of funding sources of several of its special programs, was also affected by state and federal regulations. Its basic policies were

1. personal policies of the branch director and the executive director
2. agency policy, for all four branches, made by a board of directors
3. state Medicaid regulations
4. federal regulations from specific grants, such as for programs for Haitians (a non-Hispanic population) or for remedial education

Worker Policy Analysis and Action

The agency received a federal grant to develop services for newly arrived refugee children, from infancy to age 19. This special program was part of the coordinated response made by agencies in the Greater Miami area to deal with the anticipated needs of these newly arrived refugees. The federal funding was for a pilot project. Because of the worker's task of implementing grant guidelines as well as delivering services, and because of the short-term nature of the program and the additional needs it uncovered, the worker became involved in an ongoing process of policy analysis and action.

The pilot project was designed to develop a short-term program to help the refugees cope with their new residence. Their traumatic departure from Cuba and subsequent arrival in the United States left a range of needs: personal, cultural, legal, economic, and/or linguistic. Although the thrust of the project was short-term crisis intervention, with a focus on therapy, it nonetheless generated policy activities, especially planning and ongoing analysis.

Such policy activities began with the preservices component of the program. Contacts were made with major community agencies, schools, religious organizations, and local governments to make the program available to the newly arrived refugee children. This led to a further refinement of the program as forms were planned, eligibility procedures developed, data schedules set up, and staff were deployed. The worker, because of her active role in implementing the program, was active in this planning.

A basic part of the program setup was the establishment of data collection schedules that reported how the project was working. Data were collected on who inquired about the program and about whether or not they arranged and completed an intake interview. A careful accounting of who received what services was also made. The reasons for the services received by clients were recorded and tabulated. These sources of data gave the agency a clearer picture of what the refugee children needed on a long-term basis and how best to deliver these services to them.

As noted earlier, the worker kept in close contact with changing policies regarding refugees, especially the newly arrived. With her knowledge of such resources, statistical data about refugee response to the pilot project and their long-term needs, and an understanding of how the agency made policy, she formulated a policy of concern and a plan to get it approved. The findings of the pilot program indicated that a long-term therapeutic program would benefit the children. Group programs operated in the schools would overcome the transportation problems that had reduced participation in the pilot project. It was also recommended that the new services be operated in the evenings. The agency director, of course, had been kept closely informed about the program. Cooperating with the director, the agency board of directors was approached about providing additional resources for the staffing of a new, evening therapy program for those children who needed further services and for the additional children who would come to the agency from its earlier outreach work.

Program design, of course, is itself a basic part of creating policy by implementation; this was so in the case of this worker's practice with refugee children. Moreover, she used planning and additional needs assessment to develop a new policy of concern, one calling for the allocation of new resources by the agency.

WORK IN A DAY CARE–HEAD START SETTING

The Setting and Its Services

The agency is located in a suburban New York county, which is part of the greater New York City Metropolitan area. The county is composed of small to medium-sized cities, many of which provide residences for those who work in and commute to nearby New York City. The county also has manufacturing sites, corporate headquarters, and service and governmental offices. Located in one of the larger cities of the county, the agency provides medical, mental health, educational, cultural, and recreational services.

Its day care program is the largest single such service in the county, serving 250 children, aged 4 months through 12 years. The agency's population of children is 80% black, 10% white, 5% Hispanic, with the remaining 5% Philippino, Japanese, Peruvian, and other European. The majority of the children live in the local community near the agency. Their socioeconomic level ranges from very poor to very wealthy. These children are in need of agency services because their parents have returned to work or they are children in need of protection.

The agency staffing pattern varies according to the age of the child, with infants requiring a lower staff ratio. Every classroom has a certified teacher. Some of the teachers have special education training in order to serve the handicapped population. Total staff numbers about 80 workers.

The programs include a Head Start Program and day care for the entire day as well as for part of the day. Infants (4 to 12 months), toddlers (13 months to 2 years), and 2- to 5-year-olds are in day care. The infants' room serves eight children. They are taken for walks, given toys, and held (but not excessively), in addition to being given basic care. Eight to nine toddlers are served per room by two staff members with the assistance of a foster grandparent. Games, stimulation, and motor development are program goals for these children. Age-appropriate activities and medical services are provided for the 2- to 5-year-olds in groups of 10 to 12.

Head Start services are also offered to some members of this last group. A kindergarten session, attended by 3-, 4-, and 5-year-olds, is scheduled either in the morning or in the afternoon, with their Head Start session following or preceding this class. In addition, day care for those aged 6 to 12 years is provided before or after their regular school hours. Such day care includes tutoring, counseling, and recreational programs.

The Worker

Initially, the worker was hired on a part-time basis to provide social work services in the agency's day care-Head Start program. She was expected to maintain and to increase enrollment in the program and to work directly with the department of public social services. Previously, the worker had been employed in residential treatment facilities for children and their families. In addition, she had worked in other child welfare settings and in health care. Her focus in the agency included recruitment, referral, family outreach, program maintenance, and counseling of children and their families.

Agency Policies and Their Sources

A board of directors was the official policymaker in the agency. The agency was also guided by the personal policies of the director. Its day care and Head Start programs were subject to numerous local, state, and federal regulations. The major policies included:

1. unrecorded personal policies of the director
2. minutes of the board of directors
3. agency policy and procedures manual
4. state and county day care regulations
5. state Medicaid regulations and legislation
6. federal Head Start regulations

Worker Policy Analysis and Action

On several occasions the worker used, analyzed, and created policy. The first instance of policy analysis and action began almost from the day she joined the agency. Other situations followed as she became more familiar with and further analyzed the needs of agency clientele.

When the worker first came to the agency, it had as its stated policy of concern the welfare of families and children. On paper, its policy called for direct counseling and referral to outside services. In addition, state and federal regulations regarding day care mandated that a social worker, located in the facility, should provide services 12 hours per week. This regulation provided the basis for the worker's employment.

In the worker's judgment, the agency needed a social worker on a full-time basis. The worker's personal policy was that the families and children deserved better monitoring and that the agency needed a policy to offer full-time social work services. She collaborated closely with the agency director in assessing need and in developing a rationale that would support the proposal to hire a full-time social worker. The worker already had observed children who were experiencing difficulty in the classroom setting. She had established relationships with the parents of some of these children, to explain her concerns and to offer assistance through direct services or referral. Several such cases had been identified. Their needs could not adequately be met by a part-time worker. The needs represented in these cases served as the basis for the policy proposal.

The worker formulated a plan to have the director present the proposal to the agency's board of directors. Because the director had a personal policy that excluded others from dealing directly with the agency board, the worker collaborated with the director in developing a presentation for the board. This policy of concern asked for additional funding (resource allocation) to pay the salary of a full-time social worker. The board agreed and the policy was put into operation immediately.

A second instance of policy development occurred when the worker tried to implement an existing agency policy that called for outreach to parents. The parenting program contained an outreach component, without further specification. The worker explored, with the director, what the intent of this policy might be. The director left its interpretation and implementation open-ended. By refining this policy during its implementation, the worker actively created a policy.

Although the agency director was unfamiliar with the use and importance of needs assessment and its place in policy development and implementation, the worker decided to collect data from the parents to identify their expressed needs. She used BSW students placed at the agency to conduct the survey. She had discovered that the local Youth Bureau and United Way would give grants to programs that included community outreach. The needs assessment uncovered the perception held by many of the parents that a parenting support and skills development group was needed by minority families.

Combining the agency policy of outreach with the data of the needs assessment, she wrote a policy proposal requesting funding from the Youth Bureau and from the United Way. She used the help of the director in presenting the proposal to these groups. The proposal was funded.

After receiving the money, the worker discovered that the agency, if it continued to operate in its usual fashion, would not be able to meet the implementation guidelines of the funding agencies. She met with decision makers from the two agencies and convinced them to alter their guidelines to accommodate agency procedures. Moreover, in developing and implementing the policy for a parent support group, agency guidelines regarding the role of several support staff were renegotiated. In both instances existing policies, both internal and external to the agency, were modified to implement the new parenting policy better.

SUMMARY

Policies can be defined as decisions, guidelines, rules, regulations, or standards made to allocate resources within a society or one of its systems. Policies are developed at different levels ranging from individual or personal policies to policies of society at large. Each resource system arrives at policy by using a policy formulation process. This process varies within the different resource systems but has the basic elements of input, a policy formulation process, a policy product or output, and feedback about the product. Input includes existing policy, the personal policy of the decision makers, and the values, assumptions, knowledge, and experiences of those who have input into the process. Depending upon the system in which the policymaking occurs, the policy formulation process could be individual decision making, the meetings of a board of directors, or the decision-making process of a United Way.

The illustrations contain a range of policies—personal, social, local community, agency, professional association, or social welfare. Each was developed in a policymaking process by a single person, an agency's board of directors, a United Way's decision-making structure, or by bureaucrats in the issuance of regulations. The examples also reinforce the point made several times in this book about the interrelatedness of policy and how policy is modified. In a sense, policies build on policies. In several instances, social policies at the federal level existed which helped support the development of additional policies. Conversely, policy at one system level was augmented by seeking policy development or change at another. Policy must be understood as being connected and interactional, just as the resource systems make up a network.

These examples did not stress policy of larger systems. Several examples of lobbying and bureaucratic monitoring were discussed in earlier chapters. Such activities, of course, are critical. Indeed, they underscore the interrelatedness of policies at the several levels of resource systems and how implementation acts to modify and provide feedback about policy.

In each of the examples, policy is discussed as a major part of professional practice. It was not an all-consuming task for these workers nor was it ever neglected by them. In some instances, the policy interventions were successful. Not in all situations was the existing policy either effective or their efforts to develop a new policy fully achieved. At other times, although the policy they sought was developed in their own or in another system, the new policy required revision. Their policy actions were always based in an analysis of client need. Sometimes their analysis developed from a carefully thought out, formal act of data collection. As frequently, the analysis grew quite naturally out of on-going work with their clients.

Also readily apparent in the cases is the workers' belief in the importance of policy action in creating effective relationships with client systems. Policy-sensitive workers do not believe they can be close to clients and their needs unless they interpret, challenge, and create policy. They do not just enforce or implement policy. To ignore the policy needs of clients is to ignore significant communications from them or another part of their system.

Furthermore, these cases demonstrate the importance of close working relationships with colleagues. In several instances, cooperation and collaboration was required to get a new policy adopted or put into operation. This indicates that professional autonomy in policy creation depends on the worker's adaptive skills in an organization. Often, in colleague contacts, workers must be assertive and must challenge the policy ideas of others and seek to replace them with their own policies of concern. Such contacts, of course, lead to appropriate "referrals" of policy issues and interventions to their contacts in other systems.

These workers also relied on developing and using personal policy, theirs or others. To them, policy is not a passive role. It is an active, creative one. The idea that line workers passively implement the policy of others is inaccurate. Implementation leads to the refinement of an existing policy or the creation of a new one. Independent of implementation, new policies of concern are developed and their adoption actively pursued.

CHAPTER THIRTEEN

Opportunities and Challenges

"Only in time of fear is government
thrown back to its primitive and sole
function of self-defense and the many
interests of which it is the guardian
become subordinated to that."
—JANE ADDAMS (1915)
Women, War, and
Suffrage. *Survey:*
November 6, 1915.

"The biggest sin is sitting on your ass."
—FLORYNCE R. KENNEDY.
The Verbal Karate
of Florynce R. Kennedy, Esq.
Ms.: March, 1973.

REPOSITIONING SOCIAL WORK WITHIN POLICYMAKING

This text proposes that line workers become as active as possible in all systems that produce policies of concern to them. For those who adopt this point of view, it is important to understand the societal and professional challenges and opportunities they face. The comment made by Jane Addams succinctly characterizes contemporary American society and the sense of policy that guides the decisions of our national leadership. Ms. Kennedy's observation is an unfortunate but accurate assessment of professional social work's response to challenges that question the profession's sense of a just society and the kind of helping structures needed to create socially just relationships and opportunities.

Too many social workers still seem to be sitting down regarding policy; they have not effectively countered the challenge of contemporary political events. This inactivity partially stems from the way in which policy is conceptualized in the professional curriculum. This book has proposed a model that reconceptualizes policy, connecting the substance and the creation of policy to actual practice activities. For the profession to achieve this needed reorientation toward the definition, use, and formulation of policy, it can turn to its line workers.

Social work as a profession and the people who are members of it already possess considerable strengths and useful resources that will prove to be valuable in the policy arena. Social workers need not sell themselves short, or find themselves lacking in ability, as the profession struggles with a policy reorientation. The metaphor of an overcrowded, unsafe, and thereby inoperable elevator describes the position of social work within our society's current scheme of resource allocation and policymaking. For that elevator to operate and carry the limited number that has been deemed safe for it, some of those who are in the elevator must get out. Those who were last to enter the elevator are usually those who are the first to be forced out. Our society, in an era of intensifying need and operating within the constraints of a nationally imposed limit on available resources, is in the midst of deciding who will be forced out. Unfortunately, as in the metaphor of the emptying elevator, societal decision makers assume that our efforts to help people are overextended and that we must cut back. These decision makers are forcing the last in to become the first out.

Social work as a profession, the clientele it represents, as well as the institution of which it is a part, are among this society's "last in." During hard times, such as those we experience today, many of society's last in— women, members of minority groups of color, lesbians and gay men, the poor, the developmentally disabled—clearly become the first out. The associated activities of budget cutting and redefining who should be eligible for social subsidy, support, and protection and who should help people meet their needs are used to exclude them.

Women lost on the Equal Rights Amendment. Minority groups find that the federal government is significantly less active in protecting their civil rights. Lesbians and gay men are excluded from protection in employment and housing. Food stamps are cut for the poor. The developmentally disabled are regulated out of educational programs. Unfortunately, these actions took place *not in spite of* social work efforts; they mostly took place *without* major social work intervention or opposition.

To reach the goal of policy involvement for all social workers, they must come to possess what this text identifies as a policy frame of reference. Once this frame of reference is adopted as a professional goal, then the worker's knowledge, experience, and attitudes contribute to that frame of reference and heighten the worker's level of policy consciousness. The worker's policy frame of reference is put into operation through interaction with other policymakers as well as with clients and colleagues. As the policy frame of reference is used, it will be individualized by client need and by worker knowledge and skill.

For workers to carry out the policy analysis and action that is promised when they adopt a policy frame of reference, a means must be developed to identify, reinforce, and learn from those who already support such an approach. In addition, those who are willing to join in this repositioning must be helped to learn how to achieve it, and those who would waiver in or resist this effort need to be resocialized. This calls for a review of the curriculum that prepares for practice to see if it supports a policy frame of reference. Exploring the resources and strengths already available in the profession for use in policy-related activities is also indicated, as is an examination of the benefits to be derived from the integration of policy and practice.

All segments of social work—students, practitioners, educators, and members of professional associations—can be involved in such a repositioning of the profession and of its line workers in the arenas that make policy. Social workers can reassess their policy commitment and their level of policy consciousness, rethink their approaches to making policy, and reevaluate ways of incorporating policy into their practice. It is important for social work students to begin to think about these issues and the part they might play in any policy repositioning of the profession. The following discussion will focus as much as possible on posing the opportunities and challenges that social work students or new line workers might encounter as they become active users of policy.

THE SOCIAL WORK CURRICULUM

Those who develop the curriculum to educate professional social workers must value the potential of all line workers to create significant changes in the lives of clients and to develop the authority and the connections needed to address and change policy. A social work curriculum need not reinforce the assumption held by some that line workers are helpless and powerless people, reduced to a state in which their only allies are their even less powerful clients. These assumptions are true neither for line workers nor for their clients.

The social work profession has included women, a group frequently denied control over their own lives. More recently, social work has made efforts to recruit and prepare social workers who are members of minority groups, another group to whom our society has tried to deny power. Additionally, the profession has acknowledged the special place of its lesbian and gay members. Historically, social structures have been created in an effort to exclude each of these groups from decision making. During the last two decades, however, they have gained considerable experience as leaders in movements aimed at addressing social inequities. Instead of furthering the erroneous assumption that these groups and others interested in becoming social workers are, and will remain, powerless, the experiences of these groups should be built into the curriculum so that their members can more readily attain a policy frame of reference. As members of such groups, students can explore the relationship of these efforts to policy analysis and action.

The challenge for the curriculum and student lies not only in identifying and addressing such inherent values or experiences that might support or inhibit the development of a policy frame of reference, but it also lies in identifying and utilizing relevant learning opportunities in foundation courses, in professional courses, and in the field education program. These should provide students with a substantial knowledge and skills base which supports valuing policy analysis and policy change in their practice.

One source of relevant knowledge and skill is social research methodology, including skill in issue specification or problem definition, data collection, and data analysis. These abilities, when applied to issue analysis and to policy development, greatly enhance the line worker's facility in dealing with policy formulation. Students should also gain understanding of political processes and organizational functioning. Knowledge of individual decision making and group dynamics might also be acquired in foundation courses.

All professional social work classes can deal with policy. The courses need not cover just the history and details of past and current policies and programs; a curriculum can be conceptualized so that foundation knowledge is incorporated into professional courses. All of these courses could contribute to developing the student's ability to analyze and act on policy as a basic part of their practice. Policy analysis and action can be "mainstreamed" into practice courses. Field education needs to include opportunities for field-based supervisors and instructors to guide students in utilizing policy in their practice, and in participating in activities to make and shape policy.

For example, content on human behavior in the social environment in the professional curriculum can incorporate material from foundation courses on organizational functioning, political processes, and decision making. Any conception of how people behave within, and are affected by their environment must include the place of policy and of related decision making about resource allocation. For social workers and their clients, the processes and products of policymaking are critical factors in the environment of people. They also contribute to the worker's understanding of how and why people behave as they do. As with any knowledge regarding human behavior, knowledge of this material can be connected to the part it would play in holistic assessment. Knowledge of individual, group, and organizational or political decision making would be utilized to assess the behavior of colleagues and policymakers. Knowledge of policy and the responses of people to it would assist the worker in assessing the needs and functioning of client systems.

In practice or methods courses, as might be anticipated from previous discussions in this text, any presentation of problem-solving approaches can cover how they would apply in a policy-related context. Skill in professional self-assessment could also focus on its policy aspect. Communicating and relating could be extended to include such skills as public speaking and establishing cooperative networks. Opportunities to analyze and learn how to operate within policymaking processes can be offered. The ability to persuade and influence, to guide others in their decision and policymaking, and to work assertively in an unfavorable situation could be developed in practice courses.

The curriculum can be rethought to insure that policy is neither undervalued nor overvalued. It can be recognized both as a knowledge source—about resources, policies, programs, and human behavior—and as a basic ingredient in successful practice (in every worker's analysis and in her/his intervention plans). In this way, the curriculum could model and reflect a policy frame of reference.

PROFESSIONAL ASSOCIATIONS

The professional curriculum, of course, is not the only source for developing and reinforcing a policy frame of reference for line workers, and for assisting in the repositioning of social work in policymaking. Learning about policy is furthered by involvement in professional associations. In their ongoing socialization of members, they offer many opportunities and can develop additional ones that support line workers and others in meeting the expectation that all social workers shape and make policy.

The Council on Social Work Education, in its educational standard setting and interpretation activities, can help guide programs away from the unproductive separation of policy and practice. It can redirect programs and help them to develop curricula that integrate policy and practice. The organization can also assist in the development of educators who are able to prepare students for this part of their professional role. The Annual Program Meeting and Council publications are two places in which to further the aims of integrating policy and practice.

The National Association of Social Worker's ELAN and PACE groups are excellent places for involvement, especially in the arena of social policymaking. The lobbying day activities that are conducted by many chapters could be training grounds for new workers and could provide a means of reinforcing practitioners in their decisions to participate in policymaking. Workshops on policymaking at all levels are useful. The NASW, for example, has sponsored symposia on political involvement, and recently adopted the position that knowledge and skills regarding policy and politics be mainstreamed in all professional symposia and conferences. This development indicates that this professional association will continue to bear major responsibility for the socialization of practitioners who are currently in the field and provide support to those who use policy in practice. The support of the NASW will help further the repositioning of social work in policymaking and assist all workers to raise their level of policy consciousness.

CURRENT PRACTICE

Much of the discussion in this text is predicated on two basic assumptions. The first is that the conception of social work used to define and shape the worker's practice should be derived from professional purposes. These purposes call for a broadly based approach to social work practice that aims at helping people develop more satisfactory lives by helping them locate and use the resources they need. This definition of social work and of professional purpose is not entirely new. The expectation that entry-level professionals be generalists who fulfill such purposes is a reemphasis of a professional commitment made years ago that balances helping people, developing resources, and changing delivery systems.

This generalist reemphasis leads to the second major assumption of this work. It is that any conception of professional practice must define policy in a way that focuses on those policies of concern to social workers, and that directly links policy to practice analysis and action. Such a routine application of policy-related practice activities will develop from workers who are educationally prepared for and are professionally supported in these activities. This task is also made easier by the increasing use of practice models that stress analytical tasks, problem solving, system change, and creative thinking. Such practice models are used by workers who are systematic and holistically focused in their analysis of client concerns. These same skills, as we have seen throughout this book, can be used to incorporate policy-related activities into everyday practice.

With the rediscovery of the importance of policy analysis and action for the profession, politics has reentered the agenda of professional workshops and conferences. Such training and emphases serve as a starting point for those currently in practice. They will provide the basis for the worker's entry into other policymaking arenas. These policy aspects of the profession should not be narrowly assigned to the lobbyists of professional organizations or to a few social welfare planners. The profession, of course, needs such persons. Their work in turn needs to be augmented by a solid core of policy-shaping line workers.

Much of line worker practice also calls for skill in the implementation of policy. As has been pointed out in an earlier chapter, implementation is active, not passive. It is a creative activity. Line workers do not passively implement the policy of either legislators or other social workers. The experiences in creating policy that are provided by implementation and by political and professional policy activities, when connected to holistic practice models that emphasize analysis, provide a basis for repositioning line workers.

OPPORTUNITIES FOR ENRICHMENT

There is much to be found within social work education, the activities of professional associations, and current practice trends that new workers can use to promote their repositioning in policymaking and to foster their adoption of a policy frame of reference. Individual practitioners could benefit greatly from this change in professional focus. The adoption of a policy frame of reference and the incorporation of policy-related activities into their practice could help social workers derive more excitement, more sense of accomplishment, and more growth from their work.

Many social workers come to believe, often after a short period of time, that their jobs trap them in unrewarding routines that do not always help their clients. Such feelings of professional uselessness engender a sense of frustration, leading to apathy and to so-called burnout. For line workers, an increase in policy involvement could open up additional ways to help clients and thereby reduce somewhat feelings of professional helplessness that result in frustration and discouragement.

Policymaking activities would also call on a range of skills that workers do not always use in direct client interventions. It would require that workers become involved in resource systems with which they are less familiar. Policy activities could open up a range of relationships with different people within these systems, and these new relationships could move line workers beyond working only with their clients and colleagues. The use of policy skills in unfamiliar settings with different people broadens the line workers' horizons and increases the complexity and depth of their practice.

CHALLENGE AND OPPORTUNITY

The opportunities for the profession are as obvious as the challenges. The profession would greatly benefit from line workers who are capable in their everyday practice of analyzing and shaping policy wherever they might encounter the need to do so. Workers armed with such capability would be able to make the quickest response in many resource systems to the shifting nuances of policy. They would be able to make the most subtle changes in policy within their own practice.

Before workers begin such an approach to practice, all members of the profession must be helped to acknowledge that even the most highly specialized clinician or the most general of line workers can be more involved in policy activities. Without such involvement neither professional purpose nor client need will be fully met. Many social workers recognize the merits of this approach. Professional purposes, the NASW Code of Ethics, the generalist conception of practice, and practice needs lay a supportive groundwork. The political climate lends pressure and an external incentive to this repositioning of the profession.

In repositioning social work within policymaking, every worker must be challenged by this new approach to analyze and act. Workers, in facing the challenge to integrate policy and practice, will in turn challenge the order that currently exists in agencies and in the political world. The political climate may change but its processes are fixed, and workers can and should use them to achieve the purposes of the profession. Line social workers, with much of their practice based in linking people with resources, must gain greater control of, and have more input into, the development of the policies that allocate these resources and that so greatly shape their profession and so deeply affect the lives of their clients.

Practitioners must keep in mind that the needs of their clients will change as the times demand. Their practice, however, will always need policy analysis and action skills. A given time and particular political climate will present specific topics for such policy-related analysis and action. It should not be thought that a *particular time* places the demand on social work to develop line workers who are skilled in policymaking. The ongoing needs of *social work practice* itself make such a demand.

Index